KENNETH BURKE: FROM MYTH TO ECOLOGY

BY AND ABOUT KENNETH BURKE FROM PARLOR PRESS

Equipment for Living: The Literary Reviews of Kenneth Burke
  Kenneth Burke. Edited by Nathaniel A. Rivers and Ryan P. Weber
    (2010)

Humanistic Critique of Education: Teaching and Learning as Symbolic Action
  Edited by Peter M. Smudde (2010)

Kenneth Burke and His Circles
  Edited by Jack Selzer and Robert Wess (2008)

Essays Toward a Symbolic of Motives, 1950-1955
  Kenneth Burke. Edited by William H. Rueckert (2007)

Kenneth Burke on Shakespeare
  Kenneth Burke. Edited by Scott L. Newstok (2007)

Letters from Kenneth Burke to William H. Rueckert, 1959-1987
  Edited by William H. Rueckert (2003)

KENNETH BURKE

From Myth to Ecology

Laurence Coupe

Parlor Press
Anderson, South Carolina
www.parlorpress.com

Parlor Press LLC, Anderson, South Carolina, USA

Kenneth Burke: From Myth to Ecology was published in a first edition by
Taylor & Francis Books (Routledge) in 2005 as *Kenneth Burke on Myth: An
Introduction*.

SAN: 254-8879

Library of Congress Cataloging-in-Publication Data

Coupe, Laurence, 1950-
Kenneth Burke on myth : an introduction I Laurence Coupe
p. cm. - (Theorists of myth)
Includes bibliographical references and index.
ISBN 0-415-93640-3 (alk. paper)
1. Burke, Kenneth, 1897-Contributions in concept of myth. 2. Myth-
History-20th century. I. Title. II. Theorists of myth

BL304.C67 2004
201 '.3'092--dc22

2004050899

ISBN Paperback: 978-1-60235-455-5
ISBN Adobe eBook: 978-1-60235-456-2

1 2 3 4 5

Cover design by David Blakesley.
Cover photograph: "Vernal Falls, Yosemite" by Matthew Blakesley
Production editing by Meagan Blakesley.
Parlor Press QR Code designed by Chelsie Messenger, Elizabeth Blasi, and
    Zachary Zweibon

Parlor Press, LLC is an independent publisher of scholarly and trade titles
in print and multimedia formats. This book is available in paper, cloth and
eBook formats from Parlor Press on the World Wide Web at http://www.
parlorpress.com or through online and brick-and-mortar bookstores. For
submission information or to find out about Parlor Press publications, write
to Parlor Press, 3015 Brackenberry Drive, Anderson, South Carolina, 29621,
or email editor@parlorpress.com.

CONTENTS

ABBREVIATIONS

Books

ATH	*Attitudes Toward History*
CP	*Collected Poems*
CS	*Counter-Statement*
DD	*Dramatism and Development*
GM	*A Grammar of Motives*
LSA	*Language as Symbolic Action*
PC	*Permanence and Change*
PLF	*The Philosophy of Literary Form*
RM	*A Rhetoric of Motives*
RR	*The Rhetoric of Religion*

Articles

AIPEM	"Ahsen's 'Image Psychology and the Empirical Method'"
AIWS	"As I Was Saying"
D	"Dramatism"
DL	"Dramatism and Logology"
DS	"Doing and Saying: Thoughts on Myth, Cult, and Archetypes"
IM	"Ideology and Myth"
OAV	"Order, Action, and Victimage"
PAC	"Poetics and Communication"
PM	"The Poetic Motive"
RSA	"Revolutionary Symbolism in America"
TL	"Theology and Logology"
WS	"Why Satire, with a Plan for Writing One"

ACKNOWLEDGMENTS

I am grateful to Robert Segal, who commissioned the original book, and to David Blakesley, who suggested this paperback version and then made it happen. Thanks are due also to Patrick Curry for his helpful comments on part of the manuscript. I am indebted, as ever, to my wife Margaret.

INTRODUCTION

BURKE'S LIFE AND TIMES

Kenneth Duva Burke was born in Pittsburgh, Pennsylvania, on May 5, 1897. He attended the Peabody High School from 1911 to 1915, where one of his classmates was Malcolm Cowley, who would later be known as a literary critic; they were to remain lifelong friends. In 1916 Burke enrolled briefly at Ohio State University, switching to Columbia University later the same year. However, he found no course of study to his liking, and he dropped out at the beginning of 1918. Persuading his father to provide him with a modest income, he became a full-time writer from then on, living initially in New York City's Greenwich Village, where he befriended many of the leading literary figures of North American modernism.

In 1921 Burke decided to withdraw from urban life, and he bought himself a dilapidated farm in Andover, New Jersey, which he renovated himself. The process of renovation was undertaken slowly, the aim being to keep expenditure to a minimum and live as frugally as possible. Between 1920 and 1925 he began to publish poems, short stories, and reviews (though he had begun writing verse in 1915). In his early years he was known in particular for his experimental fiction: a collection of short stories, *The White Oxen*, appeared in 1924, and a novel, *Towards a Better Life*, in 1932. The poetry was not collected until 1955, when *A Book of Moments* was published; however, Burke's considerable importance as a poet was only recognized with his *Collected Poems 1915–1967*, published in 1968.

Burke became a regular contributor to *The Dial*, an avant-garde literary journal, in 1923, publishing his first exercise in critical theory, "Psychology and Form," two years later. Supporting himself with a variety of jobs throughout the late 1920s and early 1930s, Burke moved politically to the left, briefly becoming a communist "fellow traveler." His first theoretical book, *Counter-Statement*, appeared in 1931. While it owed much to modernist aesthetics, it also indicated his concern for the social function of literature, formulated in terms of a psychology of communication. From the mid-1930s on, Burke began to distance himself from Marxism while still trying to formulate a politically engaged theory. This theory emerged in two highly ambitious and original works: *Permanence and Change* (1935) and *Attitudes Toward History* (1937). The first of these substantial works applied the psychology of communication to human relations in general, seeking out the "permanent" features of social life even while acknowledging that we are always subject to temporal "change." The second sought to demonstrate how communities are built upon "attitudes" of acceptance and rejection—these "attitudes" being best understood in terms of "poetic categories" such as tragedy and comedy, elegy and satire.

By now he had begun to accept part-time teaching positions at various universities, even though he had no academic qualifications of his own. This routine was to set the pattern for the rest of his life: he would write at home in Andover, traveling across the United States for semesters as required. Universities at which he taught include Chicago, Princeton, Indiana, California at Berkeley, and Harvard. In 1943 he began his longest association with one particular institution, Bennington College, which was to last on and off for eighteen years. A collection of writings from the 1930s, together with a lengthy title essay, was published in 1941 as *The Philosophy of Literary Form*. This work proved extremely influential, and not just within literary circles; the ambitious title essay firmly established him as an independent and suggestive thinker with a significant project. This project was to be partially realized with two complementary volumes: *A Grammar of Motives* (1945) and *A Rhetoric of Motives* (1950). These formulated, among other things, his theory of "dramatism." As we see in Chapter 3, this philosophical position best defined the middle period of Burke's thinking. Still, it was in his late period—which, given his impressively long life, lasted for about thirty years—that he developed his most important contribution to the humanities, "logology." This position was articulated in *The Rhetoric of Religion* (1961) and elaborated in several of the essays collected in *Language as Symbolic Action* (1966).

From then on, he continued to review and revise the logological principle in a series of substantial articles, which were still appearing in
the late 1980s.

Burke lived long enough to see his work honored. From 1970 onward he began receiving honorary degrees from various universities.
In 1981 he was awarded the National Medal for Literature for his
"distinguished and continuing contribution to American letters," as
a "truly speculative thinker." In 1984, he had also been present at the
launch of the Kenneth Burke Society, held in Philadelphia at Temple
University, and the next meeting of the Society in 1990 in New Harmony, Indiana. He died on November 19, 1993, at his farm in Andover at the age of ninety-six.

No other North American writer had a career that spanned eight
out of the ten decades of the twentieth century. In that period Burke
sought to engage with the main issues that affected not only his
country but also the world. He was never evasive of difficulties. For
example, in the 1920s and 1930s, he was particularly conscious of
the Great Depression, as manifest in the stock market crash and the
suffering of agricultural laborers in the midwestern states; but he
also responded to the threat posed by the rise of fascism in Europe,
a threat that for him was akin to the continuing influence of the Ku
Klux Klan nearer to home. In this period he felt obliged to come to
terms with the Marxist diagnosis of the ills of capitalism, but soon
found its emphasis on the "means of production" too restrictive. He
decided that any social revolution that did not involve a querying of
the existing attitude to technology was likely to be disastrous. Thus
from early on, Burke tried to make sense of the relation between the
exploitation of people and the exploitation of the planet. His concern
for the natural environment was consistent throughout his career, becoming increasingly urgent in his last years.

BURKE AND MYTH

Burke was variously a literary critic, a theorist of rhetoric, a philosopher, an anthropologist, a sociologist, a theologian, and an ecological
polemicist. But it might be said that the unifying theme in all his work
is the meaning of mythology: one can hardly turn four or five pages
in any of his books without coming across some speculation on the
subject. Whenever he seeks to elucidate his intention, in whatever of
the above capacities he is writing, he invariably refers to a myth. Moreover, in doing so, he moves quite happily among the archaic, ancient,

modern, and contemporary eras, refusing to see mythology as a quaint worldview that has been superseded. Indeed, Burke always insists most vigorously on finding mythic patterns to be very active in the present.

Perhaps that is why Burke has proved so popular with those working in the area of cultural studies. He demonstrates an uncanny knack for uncovering the hidden structures, both narrative and symbolic, that underlie our everyday means of establishing identity, whether individual or communal. However, as I hope to show in this study, if Burke seems to endorse the approach of scholars in cultural studies to these structures, which both he and they would call "mythic," he consistently seeks to go beyond the given culture. Mythology for Burke is at once historical and universal, temporal and transcendent. Indeed, we should take him at his word when, in *Permanence and Change,* he explicitly espouses a "philosophy of being" in preference to a "philosophy of becoming." Thus he reads myth not only as a means of effecting social cohesion but also as a bridging device to relate humanity to the earth and the wider universe—in short, the cosmos. This inclusive mode of thought can make reading Burke an invigorating exercise, demanding our full attention. Often, where he appears to be thoroughly materialist in his thinking, he may well be on the verge of endorsing a kind of mysticism—even if he never quite does so.

Another notable feature of Burke's writing is that, in the process of establishing a context for his insights, he is always producing neologisms (e.g., "dramatism" and "logology") and giving old words new meanings (e.g., "piety" and "congregation by segregation"). This habit is no mere affectation: Burke sees language as "action," so that it really matters what terminology we use to describe the world and our relation to it. However, it should be emphasized that Burke's preoccupation with language cannot be divorced from his preoccupation with mythology. For him, as we shall see in due course, *logos* and *mythos* go hand in hand.

The present study is, as far as I know, the first attempt to read Burke's oeuvre in terms of mythography. While many commentators on his work have acknowledged Burke's recurrent interest in mythic themes, and while there has been much discussion of Burke on the scapegoat ritual and the sacrificial motive, no critical study of his work has made a claim to read him systematically as a myth theorist. Given the ambitious scope of his thinking, and given his habit of wandering from digression to digression, it has proved necessary, in presenting my exposition, to provide the background of his ideas, without which specific pronouncements on mythology would make little sense. Thus it will be necessary within each chapter—particularly in Chapters 3 and 4—to expound a good deal of theory that does not seem directly mythographic in order to make the necessary connection between Burke's broad intellectual framework and his specific characterization of myth.

The first two chapters establish the theoretical territory, so to speak. In Chapter 1, I discuss two important essays that seek to affirm the social function of myth. Burke is seen to be alert, early in his career, to the challenge posed to the very use of the word "myth" in what has been called the age of ideology. In this chapter I emphasize Burke's belief in the unifying power of myth. In Chapter 2, I try to give due weight to the fact that Burke is by reputation a literary critic. Indeed, I concentrate here on two essays that make a case for criticism as a more comprehensive approach to mythology than is provided by the more literal-minded kind of anthropology. I debate what is implied by Burke's "poetics," and I relate it to his interest in the function and form of myth, which for him is about the present even while it speaks of the past.

Chapters 3 through 5 address the key themes of Burke's theory of myth. In Chapter 3, I discuss his notion of the "dramatic" basis of social relations. This theme allows me to address also Burke's concepts of ritual, of magic, of piety, and—above all—of comedy. I contrast his philosophy of "dramatism" to other theories of myth, notably those of J. G. Frazer, Sigmund Freud, and Lord Raglan. In each of these cases we see that Burke is the more methodical, inclusive thinker, who is willing to, in his terms, "discount" rather than "debunk" the views of others.

In Chapter 4, I focus on the hidden principle underlying the drama of human relations, namely, the scapegoat mechanism. I try to show how Burke makes sense of a ritual that has its roots in the distant past by reflecting on the permanent power of human language itself to persuade its users to enforce what he calls "congregation by segregation." That is, to understand words of persecution, we need to have "words about words." This analysis requires an exposition of Burke's "logology." The chapter covers Burke's complex reading of Jewish and Christian myth, which in turn necessitates discussion of his preference for comic over tragic ritual. Here I intend to demonstrate that Burke not only diagnoses "victimage" but also provides a suggestion for a cure. In this connection, I consider his influence on both René Girard and Victor Turner.

In Chapter 5, I move from the topic of victimizing other human beings to that of victimizing nature itself. I suggest that Burke from his first to his last writings, appeals to the findings of ecology as a corrective to human hubris and, specifically, to the "technological psychosis." In his harsh critique of industrial capitalism Burke makes an important case for rediscovering an "ancient collective revelation." I identify this position as broadly Taoist, though without attempting to limit Burke to the espousal of a particular religious faith. What matters, I suggest, is that Burke finds a mythic perspective on modernity that enables him to offer a critique of unbridled "progress." I conclude with a reading of an important late essay in which Burke offers the draft of an apocalyptic myth for an era in which the pollution and degradation of the planet seem inevitable.

In the course of this introduction to Burke as myth theorist, we come across various definitions by Burke of myth, often arising in the course of his theorization of wider issues. These various statements are, I believe, consistent, which is remarkable, given the length of his writing career. However, others who have been inspired by Burke have attempted to produce their own Burkean definitions. For example, Dan Nimmo and James Combs, in their *Subliminal Politics: Myths and Mythmakers in America*, offer this: "A credible, dramatic, socially constructed re-presentation of perceived realities that people accept as permanent, fixed knowledge of reality, while forgetting (if they ever were aware of it) its tentative, imaginative, created, and perhaps fictional qualities."[1] This definition does justice to the Burke favored by those working in sociology, politics, and cultural studies. But to me it aligns him too closely with Roland Barthes, who famously limited the function of myth to persuading people that the culture they inhabit is natural and necessary rather than historical and contingent.[2] Reading Burke has persuaded me that he has a fuller, richer, more affirmative understanding of myth than Nimmo and Combs suggest. Here, then, in an attempt to redress the balance, is my own attempt at a Burkean definition of myth, which may be worth bearing in mind as we proceed: "A narrative that effects identification within the community that takes it seriously, endorsing shared interests and confirming the given notion of order, while at the same time gesturing toward a more comprehensive identification—that among humanity, the earth, and the universe."

1

MYTH AND SOCIETY

Kenneth Burke's interest in myth was constant throughout his extremely long career. However, much of his discussion of myth occurs in the course of writing about something else—for instance, language, culture, or the definition of humanity. In order to understand his main principles as a myth theorist, we will spend the first two chapters concentrating on his four most important statements on the nature of mythology. These statements were made at various stages of his career. For the sake of convenience, I will refer to them throughout as "essays," though in fact the first of them originated in a speech given at a political conference, and the second and fourth were journal articles. It is perhaps indicative of Burke's way of thinking that he did not let the constraints of any format get in the way of his fascination with the idea of an integral vision. Everything he wrote was preparatory for a final word that never came. This may seem a cause of regret; but, as we shall see, Burke was consistent in his very suspicion of the value of finality. If we seek a definitive summation of his ideas in extended form, we will look in vain: it was the nature of Burke's enterprise, like that of his hero, Samuel Taylor Coleridge, to be in a permanent state of what we might call "notes toward."

We will consider the first two of these essays in this chapter, where the focus is on the social function of myth. We will consider the third and fourth essays in Chapter 2, where the focus is on the literary form of myth. In both chapters, we will conclude by demonstrating briefly how the thesis of the essays finds resonance in related statements from the books. While not offering detailed exposition, these concluding sections will perhaps indicate the range and depth of Burke's thought.

That is, while the essays are chosen for their accessibility, it is always important to bear in mind a comment made by William Rueckert, one of the most important authorities on "Burkology," as it is sometimes known. He suggests that "If there is a single overriding lesson to learn from Burke, it is that everything implies everything else, and everything is more complicated than it seems."[1]

The first essay, "Revolutionary Symbolism in America," represents the Burke of the mid-1930s, the communists' fellow traveler, seeking to open up Marxism to new possibilities by encouraging an appreciation of the socially unifying potential of myth. The second essay, "Ideology and Myth," shows us Burke ruminating, after the end of the Second World War and the struggle against Nazism, on how an "ideal myth" for a new age might take shape.

"REVOLUTIONARY SYMBOLISM IN AMERICA" (1935)

Kenneth Burke's first formal definition of myth was made in 1935, in the course of a talk he gave at a conference of politically engaged intellectuals. Burke was not an academic theorist; he developed his ideas about myth during his involvement in wider issues. Yet he realized early on that it was important to clarify what he meant when he used the word "myth," as it was central to his developing philosophy.

In April 1935 the League of American Writers, a Marxist organization dedicated to promoting politically progressive literature, held a congress to which various sympathetic authors were invited to contribute discussion papers. Burke's subject, and the title of his paper, was "Revolutionary Symbolism in America." It proved to be the most controversial contribution of all. Nearly all the other speakers had taken it for granted that the aim of the communist writer should be to promote proletarian literature. Burke, dissenting from this view, chose to speak mainly about the fundamentally mythic form of political thought.

Burke's speech to the American Writers' Congress begins: "When considering how people have cooperated, in either conservative or revolutionary movements of the past, we find that there is always some underlying principle about which their attachments as a group are polarized." Granted that "the communal relationships by which a group is bound" do not possess the "primary reality" of "tools, shelter, productive technique," he nevertheless insists that attachment to a cause is an indicator of "a genuine social motive" (RSA 267). These relationships, and this motive, belong to the sphere of "myth":

"Myths" may be wrong, or they may be used to bad ends, but they cannot be dispensed with. In the last analysis, they are our basic psychological tools for working together. A hammer is a carpenter's tool; a wrench is a mechanic's tool; and a "myth" is the social tool for welding the sense of interrelationship by which the carpenter and the mechanic, though differently occupied, can work together for common social ends. In this sense a myth that works well is as real as food, tools, and shelter are. As compared with the reality of material objects, however, we might say that the myth deals with a *secondary* order of reality. Totem, race, godhead, nationality, class, lodge, guild—all such are the "myths" that have made various ranges and kinds of social cooperation possible. They are not "illusions," since they perform a very real and necessary social function in the organising of the mind. But they may look illusory when they survive as fossils from the situations for which they were adapted into changed situations for which they were not adapted. (RSA 267–268)

One has to bear in mind here that within the orthodox Marxism of the time, the mythical was treated as synonymous with the illusory. That is, both were identified with ideology, and ideology was understood as a falsification of reality, demanded by the capitalist mode of production in order to ensure a compliant labor force. One of the main tasks for Marxists, apart from building the party and encouraging militant activity, was to challenge the ideology fostered by the bourgeoisie: that is, to challenge a misrepresentation of the world that diverted the attention of the proletariat from the economic contradictions of capitalism. Burke's paper, however, proposes that one cannot challenge an ideology unless one has a distinct and positive view of mythology; the two are not the same thing, though they frequently appear to overlap. For Burke, myths usually have an ideological function, embodying as they do cultural assumptions; but as we shall see, he believes that they do much more.

Indeed, the implication of "Revolutionary Symbolism in America" is that Marxism itself may be viewed as a kind of myth. It is a symbolic story designed to encourage a significant part of the population to cohere in order to promote social justice. The question is: If this is a symbolic story, who is the symbolic hero? Burke deliberates about this question. Even if we assume that a revolutionary period is one in which allegiances shift from one symbol to another, we can yet see that the "symbol of bourgeois nationalism is in ... a state of decay to-day," and that it needs replacing: "Hence the attempts of communists to put the symbol of class in its place" (RSA 268). According to Burke, however, there is a danger of an overemphasis on class, and in particular on the proletariat. That is, he argues against making "the worker" into the symbolic hero. He does so quite deliberately from "the *propaganda* aspect of the symbol," considering it "a device for spreading the areas of allegiance": "In the first place," he declares, "I assume that a symbol must embody an *ideal*. The symbol appeals to us as an incentive because it suggests traits which we should like to share. Yet there are few people who really want to work, let us say, as a human cog in an automobile factory, or as a gatherer of vegetables on a big truck farm. Such rigorous ways of life enlist our *sympathies*, but not our *ambitions*. Our ideal is as far as possible to *eliminate* such kinds of work, or to reduce its strenuousness to a minimum" (RSA 269).

Having argued against one symbol, Burke argues for another: "the people" should rank "highest in our hierarchy of symbols," as it offers "more of an ideal incentive" than that of "the worker" (RSA 269). On the one hand, he is commending the symbol of "the people" for strategic reasons, in response to the crisis of capitalism and the immediate opportunities for communist propaganda. To that extent he may be seen as engaging in ideological struggle; he knows that no Marxist, or even "fellow traveler," can escape this requirement. On the other hand, he is also drawing on the residual power of mythology to provide what he previously called, in his first published work of theory, *Counter-Statement* (1931), a "universal pattern" or "psychological universal" (*CS* 47, 149). In doing so, he suggests that we have to recognize that "the worker" is a less comprehensive symbol than is "the people," which encompasses the worker; and we have to acknowledge that the concept of "the people" is more psychologically effective than that of "the worker," for the present conflict implies a vision of future harmony, which stands before us as a stimulus to action:

> The symbol of "the people," as distinct from the proletarian symbol, also has the tactical advantage of pointing more definitely in the direction of unity (which in itself is a sound psychological tendency, for all that it is now misused by nationalists to mask the conditions of disunity). It contains the *ideal*, the ultimate *classless* feature which the revolution would bring about—and for this reason seems richer as a symbol of allegiance. It can borrow the advantages of nationalistic conditioning, and at the same time be used to combat the forces that hide their class prerogatives behind a communal ideology. (RSA 270)

Thus if the ideology of the ruling class perpetuates division and inequality under the guise of shared interests, Marxist mythology should offer a vision of a true community, a harmonious humanity. A myth whose hero is "the people" certainly has an ideological function appropriate to the given historical conditions, but it also has a universal dimension that is transhistorical:

> For we must remember that among the contradictions of capitalism we must also include the contradictions of anti-capitalist propaganda. Marxism is war to the ends of peace, heresy to the ends of unity, organization to the ends of freedom, glorification of toil to the ends of greater leisure, revolution in the interests of conservation, etc. Such a confusion cannot be settled once and for all. It is our particular "burden" at this particular stage of history. In the last analysis, art strains towards *universalization*. It tends to overleap imaginatively the class divisions of the moment and go after modes of thought that would apply to a society freed of class divisions. It seeks to consider the problem of *man*, not of *classes of men*. We are agreed that the current situation militates against this tendency, which is all the more reason for artists to enlist in the work of changing it. For a totally universalized art, if established in America to-day, would simply be the spiritual denial of an underlying economic disunity (the aesthetic of fascism). The strictly proletarian symbol has the useful advantage of emphasizing the temporary antagonism—but it has the disadvantage of not sufficiently embodying within its connotations the *ideal* incentive, the eventual state of unification that is expected to flow from it. (RSA 272)

However, Burke is fully aware of the hypothetical nature of the promise given by a myth centered on the symbolic figure of "the people." A narrative culminating in harmony, and a symbol of integration: these are the elements of the social imagination. At the same time he wishes to invoke a "universal pattern" that precedes and informs—but should not be confused with—ideological claims to consolidate a specific group of people. This is a hard distinction to maintain, given that the proffered ideal is unity. Conscious as he is of the immensity of the historical task, Burke seems to think it worth the effort:

> I believe that the symbol of "the people" makes more naturally for such *propaganda by inclusion* than does the starkly prole-

tarian symbol (which makes naturally for a *propaganda by exclusion*, a tendency to eliminate from one's work all that does not deal specifically with the realities of the workers' oppression and which, by my thesis, cannot for this reason engage even the full allegiance of the workers themselves). And since the symbol of "the people" contains connotations both of oppression and of unity, it seems better than the exclusively proletarian one as a psychological bridge for linking the two conflicting aspects of a transitional, revolutionary era, which is Janus-faced, looking both forward and back. (RSA 272–273)

Despite such attention to the exigencies of history, Burke knew when he delivered his address that he was going against the grain of the congress. He even anticipated in his speech that he would be accused of expressing a "petty-bourgeois" attitude toward social revolution. After all, his very point was that the Marxist vision should be as inclusive as possible, and that middle-class sympathizers should not be excluded in the interests of proletarian solidarity (see RSA 269). This charge was indeed leveled in the subsequent discussion, but the main fire was directed against his choice of the symbol of "the people" rather than "the worker." This choice was interpreted as a betrayal of the proletarian cause, which in turn led to further, related objections, which Burke made a special point of addressing.

First, there was the objection to his use of the word "myth," which was felt to undermine the rigor of the Marxist worldview. Burke's response was as follows: "A poet's myths, I tried to make clear, are *real,* in the sense that they perform a necessary function. They so pattern the mind as to give it a grip upon reality. For the myth embodies a sense of relationships. But relationships cannot be pointed to, in the simple objective way in which you could point to a stone or a house. It is such a sense of *relationships* (I have sometimes called them 'secondary reality') that I had in mind when I used the word 'myth' " (RSA 279).

Second, there was the objection that Burke "made Communism appear like a religion." Burke's response was as follows: "As the Latin *religio* signifies a *binding together,* I take religion and Communism to be alike insofar as both are systems for binding people together—and the main difference at the present time resides for me in the fact that the Communistic vocabulary does the binding job more accurately than the religious vocabulary. Let us compromise by saying that Communism is an ethic, a morality. But whenever you talk about an ethic, you must talk about much the same sort of things as you would if you were talking purely and simply about religion" (RSA 279).

To identify Marxism as a myth and communism as a religion was not a proposal that endeared Burke to other writers on the political left in the mid-1930s. Burke was always insistent, however, that myth and religion are essential modes of human understanding. This viewpoint may surprise those who know only his reputation as a secular, leftist-oriented intellectual and as a thorough materialist. Perhaps the fact that he took the Marxist case against capitalism so seriously has encouraged this view of him. However, as we shall see, Burke from the outset began looking beyond Karl Marx for his understanding of the social imagination. In doing so, he had to articulate in much more detail his intuition that the distinction between myth and ideology should be maintained, despite their obvious affinities.

"IDEOLOGY AND MYTH" (1947)

While the title of this essay may suggest that Burke is about to distinguish these two phenomena once and for all, the essay itself has much to say about what they have in common. Specifically, the essay shows awareness of the sinister turn that the proximity of ideology and myth had taken in the years prior to its composition. "Ideology and Myth" was, after all, written in the wake of the Second World War and the horrors that had led up to it. Hence Burke's readiness to situate his definition historically: "Ideology, like rhetoric, gravitates to the side of ideas (the term originally referred to systems of ideas considered *in themselves* without reference to external factors); and myth, like poetry, gravitates to the side of image. But perhaps Nazi pageantry had something to do with the fact that we so often class political ideas under the heading of 'myth,' since the Nazi showmen were so skilled in using imagery and ritual to reinforce the appeal of their political ideology" (IM 195).

We might pause here to note this seemingly casual conjunction of ideology with rhetoric. For Burke, the classical definition of rhetoric, as the use of speech for the purpose of persuasion, is inadequate. From the beginning, rhetoric is for him a device that fosters "identification" between otherwise disparate people; hence he associates it consistently with ideology. Indeed, he sees it as the very basis of ideology. One of the most important books from the middle of his career, written shortly after this essay, is significantly titled *A Rhetoric of Motives* (1950). Here Burke declares that rhetoric "is rooted in an essential function of language itself, a function that is wholly realistic, and is continually born anew; the use of language as a symbolic means of inducing cooperation in beings that by nature respond to symbols" (*RM* 43). This statement is intended to put an end to the fallacy that rhetoric is a fanciful embellishment of language that has accidentally survived from antiquity. As long as there are societies, there will be division. As long as there is division, there will be the need for unification. Ideology is intrinsic to this process.

"Ideology and Myth" now goes on to consider the complications introduced when we note the way the "ideas" of ideology and the "images" of myth overlap in modern societies, as hinted in the passage quoted. Ideology, in the sense with which Burke is immediately concerned here, may be defined as "the system of ideas that constitute a political or social doctrine and inspire the acts of a government or party" (IM 195). But on one the hand myths may be philosophical, and thus be like ideologies, whereas on the other hand ideologies may function better by identifying themselves with powerful symbols, such as those provided by myths. Thus it is not just a matter of opposing ideas and images and then registering their interaction. Rather, one has to address the tenacity of myth in a world where "ideology" seems to be the more comprehensive and accurate term.

By way of example, Burke refers to philosopher Karl Mannheim's attempt to construct a "sociology of knowledge" that will situate and explain ideology without recourse to the notion of myth. Burke discusses Mannheim's *Ideology and Utopia*, which he begins by praising for its alertness to the "ambiguities ... lurking in terminologies." On the one hand there are "terminologies that would stabilise the *status quo*, thereby giving special comfort to the ruling groups that profited most by these conditions." On the other hand there are "terminologies that would prod men to action by their promissory, futuristic nature." Mannheim calls the first "ideologies" and the second "utopias." But what he ends up demonstrating, despite his initial definition of each term, is that the distinction is hard to maintain. For, as Burke addresses the matter, "a 'utopia' that comes to prevail, by the same token becomes an 'ideology'" (IM 198). So far, so good. But Burke's inference is that the attempt to renegotiate these two kinds of thinking, in such a way that they turn out to be versions of each other, still begs the question of how to transcend them:

Mannheim's notion is that, in the clash of the various ideologies and utopias, their advocates can unmask one another's strategic ambiguities—and from the conflict as a whole there can emerge, as with the development towards truth got by the competing kinds of opinion in a Platonic dialogue, a body of true distinctions and analytic methods which he would call a "sociology of knowledge." But we can easily think of that too being called an "ideology," particularly by someone who wanted, for this basic terminology of human motives, such a resonantly imaginative and poetic synthesis as we find rather in religious or cosmic myths. (IM 198)

However, Burke notes that Mannheim realizes his own central problem when he confesses that if his "sociology of knowledge" were to succeed it would effectively defeat its own noble project. Burke quotes Mannheim's own concern that "the complete elimination of reality-transcending elements from our world would lead to a 'matter-of-factness' which ultimately would mean the decay of the human will." By "playing ideologies against one another," Mannheim "has built up a science that transcends their factionalism. Yet his motives were derived from this same factionalism. Hence, as soon as he thinks of faction as transcended, he can find no further source of motives" (IM 198). In order to get beyond Mannheim's deadlock, we need to move on to another plane entirely, to move from ideology to myth. Burke has already referred to Plato, and it is to him that he now turns for a more complete perspective.

Burke acknowledges that, in the traditional, more neutral sense of the word, Plato's philosophy could be seen as ideology in that it offers a system of ideas. More precisely, he suggests that each of the Platonic dialogues is an "argumentative conversation" that offers a justification of the very idea of "Reason." This does not mean that the presence in Plato's philosophy of narratives that we call myths is to be explained away simply as an illustration of his system of ideas. Drawing on his reading of J. A. Stewart's *Myths of Plato*, Burke endorses its thesis that the philosopher's use of myth has the effect of "Revelation." "It takes us from the order of Reason to the order of Imagination." What is offered is "the unitary vision of 'the Good,' which is the 'mythic' ground of Reason, itself beyond Reason" (IM 199). Burke's own proposal, in this light, is that, even if we broaden our ideology to include "political or social motives," we have to allow that those motives "cannot be ultimate, since they must in turn be grounded in motives outside or beyond the political or social" (IM 199).

Yet Burke is all too aware that the "transcendental feeling" provided by myth is, by itself, liable to be interpreted as ideological in the restrictive, modern sense. Plato's vision is not sufficient evidence for the necessity and integrity of the mythic dimension of human thought, so that his advocacy of transcendence is open to the charge of special pleading. The myth/ideology dialectic still needs clarifying, particularly as Burke's definition of myth in "Revolutionary Symbolism in America" as a "social tool" that "deals with a *secondary* order of reality" does not fully dispel the dimension of "illusion." So here Burke, in order to be as comprehensive as possible within the short scope of an article, now turns to the anthropology of Bronislaw Malinowski to help him deal more explicitly with the relationship between the terms of his title: namely, "myth" and "ideology."

Suppose, Burke conjectures, that members of a society wished to justify the fundamental concerns that informed their way of life but had not developed a vocabulary of "essence." They had no terms such as "substance," "principle," and even "essence" itself. How would they fulfill their need to "justify" their "social practices and relations" without having to resort to the "philosophical idiom"? They would do so by telling a story. In "primitive" myth, according to Burke's reading of Malinowski, "principles" means "firsts." More exactly, "If you want to deal with *logical* principles, or 'firsts,' and don't have such a language, you get the equivalent by talking of *mythical* firsts. To derive a culture from a certain mythic ancestry, or ideal mythic type, is a way of stating that culture's essence in narrative terms" (IM 200). Burke cites the example of an origin myth narrated by the Trobriand Islanders, as recounted by Malinowski in his book *Myth in Primitive Psychology.* This narrative concerns "the tribe's descent from a mythic race of beings that lived underground, and that had led an existence similar in all respects to their present life on earth," illustrating Burke's point that "the 'mythic' past is a narrative terminology of essence" (IM 200).

This very point brings Burke back to the myths of Plato, which presuppose that "the pure forms or archetypes of all temporal things pre-exist in Heaven, and that the particular objects of this world exist only by participating in the absolute changeless being or essence of these perfect 'ancestral' ideas" (IM 200–201). If the idea that Plato is intellectually espousing is that of the "eternal form," the myth goes beyond it by drawing on the imaginative dimension of the "archetype." The link is memory, but the tales that Plato tells—of the cave, of the demiurge, of Eros—involve a recollection and a response that is more than rational.

Lest we begin to think that mythology is the prerogative of either the ancient or the "primitive" mind, as we might infer from reading both

Plato's myths and Malinowski's account of mythic thinking—Burke points out the evidence for the mythic imagination in modern thought:

> In proportion as historicist thinking came into fashion in the West . . . writers replaced philosophic terms by historicist terms, expressing the "logically prior" or the "essential" in terms of the "temporally prior." Thus, whenever they wanted to say that man is "essentially competitive" or "essentially good," they said that the "first men" were constantly at war or that men were "originally" good but were later corrupted by society. They postulated such "firsts" in some hypothetical past time, their thinking in this regard often being more mythical than they suspected, and no more based on actual scientific knowledge about that past than was the "mythical" doctrine of "original" sin (which, translated philosophically, would mean "essential" sin, that is, some ineradicable difference between individual and group which the individual, eager to socialize himself, might experience as a sense of guilt). (IM 200)

There is much in this speculation on the persistence of mythic thinking that will make more sense once we have given, in subsequent chapters, a fuller exposition of Burke's theory of myth. One aspect of his argument may already strike us as particularly provocative: the proposal that neither for the "primitive" nor for the modern mind are philosophical ideas and mythic images wholly distinct. This challenges the usual assumption of modernity that it is intrinsically superior to premodernity by virtue of having evolved from myth to reason. This is a question to which we must return. But for now we should perhaps register the import of Burke's central thesis: that myth precedes and informs ideology. To support this notion, Burke suggests that the Trobriand myth could not, strictly speaking, be defined as "ideology" because that term presupposes "a highly developed money economy, with its extreme division of labor and a maximum of abstract relationships for which the ideologist seeks to compensate by all the deliberate subterfuges for persuading people to 'identify themselves' with the factions, doctrines, or policies he represents" (IM 201). But he is also thinking of precedence in a more fundamental sense. Indeed, his tentative conclusion, prior to addressing the continuing need for myth in the contemporary cultural scene, is that "we may treat the mythic as the non-political ground of the political, not as antithetical to it, but as the 'pre-political' source out of which it is to be derived" (IM 201).

This declaration brings Burke forward to the requirements of the day. The "ideal myth" in the middle of the twentieth century, after a catastrophic global conflict that resulted from political failure, would be "a vision that transcended the political, yet had political attitudes interwoven with it" (IM 201). This hypothesis seems, if not downright contradictory, impossibly inclusive. How are we to find the source of such a vision? Burke, whose argument has already moved from Mannheim to Plato to Malinowski, proposes another return to an ancient spring. He looks to Virgil's *Aeneid* for inspiration.

Strictly speaking, Virgil's work belongs to the category of epic, but Burke's interest is in its literary use of the existing Greco-Roman mythology. The wanderings of the Trojan hero Aeneas after the war with Greece—his exploits include a descent into the underworld and culminate in the founding of Rome under divine approval—were familiar material to Virgil's audience. How did the author exploit this material? Noting how "so much of his mythology bears upon sleep, vision, prophecy, gods and the after-life," Burke explains:

> [T]he poet is writing of Roman power. It would be esthetically [*sic*] fitting that he place the subject in a context of other terms for power. Imperial power, in this poetic sense, would "go with" heroic power, divine power, the power of destiny, etc. Such surrounding of a theme with kindred images would be the only way in which one could develop it stylistically, and contextually. There need be no question of the "literal" hero. The poet is giving us a cluster of similar terms, joining empire, emperor, and the imperial destiny—whereupon we find his epic saying mythically that the emperor is divine "in principle." (IM 202)

This explanation of the function of myth only invites speculation about the ideological component. Burke anticipates this point and, having conceded that an important motive for Virgil was likely flattery (with a view to receiving the emperor's patronage), declares:

> As regards ideology and myth, the figure of the Roman emperor unites them. Here is the myth of the bringer of peace (to say as much is to understand why the Christians treated Virgil as *anima naturaliter Christiana*). Caesar Augustus is thus cast in the mythic role of a redeemer, a role that gains further in dignity by being put in the same context as Aeneas, whose heroic piety and gravity thus serve

as the "principle" of Augustus. Augustus' role is seen in terms of Aeneas' perfect, or archetypal, role. Poetically, mythically, Augustus is Aeneas.... In the *Aeneid*, this *mythic* form, or the bringing of peace, was given its *ideological* anchorage in the vision of Rome as the particular worldly state which brought this condition about. And the real emperor, made mythically resonant, was thus the bridge that brought forth both a myth and an ideology together. (IM 202)

This is a nice distinction, and an elegant reconciliation, but the reader might yet suspect that Burke has evaded the question of whether myth is ideology in narrative form, or even a mere body of images designed to enhance ideology. His conviction, we know, is that myth is more than ideology, but his chosen example raises issues that perhaps contradict that conviction. Moreover, he appears to be in danger of idealizing antiquity (given that he makes no mention of Augustus's reputation for corruption and cruelty), and offering it as a panacea to the contemporary crisis. It is true that Burke concludes his article with a case for a modern version of Virgilian myth, but his juxtaposition of Roman peace and Nazi aggression is perhaps not so naive as it may at first appear.

Burke's basic assumption concerning the age in which he writes is that "our own yearnings for a condition of world peace" have only attained "a loose ideological expression in the United Nations." They "still lack any appropriate grounding in myth." It is in this light that he comes to ponder the Roman "pacification," by which is meant "peace after victory." Rome's practice was, of course, to impose peace on subject peoples, a practice that Burke is neither condemning nor approving but simply acknowledging. His more important concern is that such pacification is not an ideal that can comprehend the full horrors of "the Nazi theory of racial domination, which would have made a peace of pacification impossible for many peoples, who simply could not submit, since they were marked for a systematic destruction or great weakening in accordance with the Nazi theories of genocide." Thus the global situation he addresses necessitates our deciding what is required that is radically different. "But even with the Nazi methods eliminated (though we must not be too sure they are)," he writes, "how could we enjoy the Roman peace, the peace of pacification? Does not the nature of our modern weapons inexorably demand that, if we are going to have peace at all, it must be a peace without pacification, that is, a peace without war, a peace *before* war?" (IM 202).

The implicit answer to this rhetorical inquiry is that we need a myth that will help us move beyond both Augustus and Hitler, even if the model chosen as an example dates back to the period of Augustus' rule. Burke ends by stressing the urgency of the task, his paragraph culminating in further tactical questioning as to the possibility of the vision of "a peace *before* war." For "The new myth, to be the ideal myth, must give us that new vision, and not merely in its purity, as with the Christian vision of peace on earth, but in its ideological implications as well. . . . And maybe it must do this very very soon [*sic*]. Or must the myth wait for quiet times, as Virgil's myth celebrated the *end* of the wars? And if it must, what will there be for the new myth to celebrate, if the magic number three is to have its sway, if there is to be a third world war?" (IM 203).

Burke's hypothetical myth would incorporate past myths and present ideologies. It would be prompted by the "motive" stated two years earlier in his epigraph to *A Grammar of Motives* (1945): *Ad bellum purificandum* ("toward the purification of war"). To this ideal the skeptical reader might object that in the real world "myth" all too often means "ideology" and little more. But though Burke is evidently finding difficulty in articulating his conviction at this early stage of his thinking, and though he is rather evasive at times, he makes a bold attempt to differentiate the two terms in unpropitious times.

As to the "motivational ingredients" of his projected myth, Burke proposes no fewer than twelve. In each case the Virgilian source would be restated, while inspiring a move beyond the current political crisis. We need not list all twelve of them here, but perhaps a selection of three will convey the flavor of Burke's "recipe," to use his own term. The first ingredient involves the idea of the nation: if Virgil's was a national myth, then the new myth must "transcend nationalism." However, the new myth must include it rather than suppress it, must "survey the pageant of nationalism's emergence, the quality of its exaltation, even while considering it inadequate as an over-all political motive." For the "mission" and "supremacy" of national strength could be fulfilled "only in the attempt to go beyond it, not by mere decay (the usual way in which it is 'transcended'), but by a positive new step" (IM 204).

The fourth ingredient, to take another example, involves a questioning of the Roman claim to have superseded Greek culture in a spirit of temporal triumphalism. The ideal myth today "must consider the modern world, not as 'superior' to other ages, but in terms of first and last things, motives which confront all ages, though in ways varying with the conditions of time and place" (IM 205). A new humility is commended, based on an acceptance of a common humanity and of common concerns that are transhistorical. Birth and death, peace and war, creation and catastrophe—these figure in all times and places, even if they are expressed in particular contexts.

The sixth ingredient, to conclude our selection, involves a revision of the ancient notion of heroism. Burke summarizes how heroism might be deepened and extended. The new myth "must celebrate the feats of heroes, great deeds in battle and council and government, such as had lent immortal greatness to the *Iliad* and *Odyssey*"—Virgil having himself benefited from Homer's example. But praise, while necessary, is no longer sufficient: "Above the sincere praise of great deeds, should hover the thought of human folly, the concern ever with the ironic possibility that much courage, power, ambition have been misdirected: not the 'explaining' of this so much as the constant meditating upon it" (IM 205). Humility directs us not only to see our culture in historical context, as in the last ingredient, but also to acknowledge the inevitable contradiction of all human endeavor, whereby apparent progression often turns out to be regression. Our advantage over the Greeks and Romans is simply that we have more evidence of this irony.

It would perhaps be accurate to say that Burke has succeeded in this essay in establishing, in an era obsessed by the ideological, that "myth" and "ideology" are not simply synonyms. Indeed, as in "Revolutionary Symbolism in America," he has put forth an impressive case for not only maintaining a healthy interest in the inevitably mythic dimension of culture but also promoting the progressive potential of myth. Throughout his career Burke may be seen as returning to the myth/ideology complex, always trying to find a slightly different perspective upon it. On some occasions he may seem to be conceding too much to the ideological side of the debate, acknowledging how myth may be used as a mechanism of social control. On other occasions he may seem to enthuse about the transcendent power of myth, attributing to it a quasi-mystical status beyond its cultural context of expression. His continuing ambivalence does not, of course, disqualify him as a myth theorist. On the contrary, it makes reading him a fascinating exercise. What we have to do, however, is keep alert to his shifting perspectives and allow for the possibility that we may never get the final, inclusive statement we want.

RELATED STATEMENTS

Burke's emphasis on the social function of myth has seemed the most logical place to start, given that he is so widely regarded as a "sociological" theorist. But even a superficial reading of the two essays discussed should prevent one from concluding that he regards myth as a mere reflection of the social order—any more than he regards art, language, or thought itself as a mere reflection. In his volume *The Philosophy of Literary Form* (1941), consisting of essays written in the 1930s, Burke explicitly states that, while he is concerned with the nature of "social acts in general," his "sociological" approach is not confined to "content." He refuses to view the imaginative work (or "act," as he prefers to say) as "a kind of unmethodical report on a given subject-matter": for "the content is functional," and statements about the "subject" of the work (novel, poem, myth, or whatever) will be also statements about "form" (*PLF* 102).

The formal aspect of myth is a topic to which we return in the next chapter—though, even now, it might be evident that the topic is one that Burke finds hard to set aside. Meanwhile we might bear out Burke's notion of the social element in myth as something more than a reflection of society by reminding ourselves of how useful he found the anthropology of Malinowski in the second of the two essays discussed in this chapter. The insight drawn there was that myths have a pragmatic function in the present social order, even—or especially—when they appear to be descriptions of what happened in the distant past. In *A Rhetoric of Motives* Burke concurs in Malinowski's interest in primitive speech as an attempt "to produce an action and not to describe one." Burke proceeds to draw on Malinowski's essay on "The Problem of Meaning in Primitive Languages" to support his own view that it does not diminish the mythic reference to the "ultimate" ground (the sphere of deities or revered ancestors) to say that "it itself arose out of a temporal ground, available to sociological description." Myth for both Burke and Malinowski helps create social reality even while it presupposes society. Its function is to provide the imaginative structure that makes social institutions meaningful. In creating an origin for social institutions, myth gives shape and significance to social experience. Burke elaborates upon Malinowski's essay as follows:

> Malinowski is describing a problem he encountered when attempting an English translation of some texts assembled in the course of his research among Polynesian tribes of New Guinea: "magical

formulae, items of folk-lore, narratives, fragments of conversation, and statements of my informants." He found that there was no direct equivalent for much of this material. Hence, instead of translating by "inserting an English word for a native one," he found it necessary to describe the customs, social psychology, and tribal organization that were implicit in a given utterance. To generalize this requirement, he proposed the expression, "context of situation," which, he says, indicates "on the one hand that the conception of *context* had to be broadened and on the other that the *situation* in which words are uttered can never be passed over as irrelevant to the linguistic expression." (*RM* 205)

Malinowksi confines these principles to primitive, oral communication. Burke, by contrast, wishes to extend them to all mythology and to "symbolic action" generally. Every text has a "context"; every word implies a "situation." Every utterance is an attempt to achieve something within that context, that situation. Thus it is always possible to discover a social dimension to every use of symbol, most obviously in myth.

We might illustrate Burke's thesis by taking an example that he himself uses later in his *Rhetoric*, when outlining the basis for a "socio-anagogic" interpretation of literature.[2] This term denotes the reciprocal relation between the "temporal" and the "ultimate" grounds of utterance. It indicates how a literary work may evoke the transcendent in terms of the immanent, and vice versa. The example he uses is particularly relevant for our purposes because it is a text that retells a familiar myth: it is William Shakespeare's poem *Venus and Adonis*. We may recall that in the original story, or at least in the version given in Ovid's *Metamorphoses*, the goddess Venus warns the handsome youth whom she loves, Adonis, against hunting dangerous animals. After ignoring her warning, he is gored to death by a boar.[3] For Burke, Shakespeare's handling of the mythic material makes sense only if we see it in the context not just of Greco-Roman mythology but also of Renaissance notions of courtship and of social hierarchy. It is significant, then, that Shakespeare slightly adapts his material, so that Adonis not only ignores Venus' warnings but also dismisses her amorous advances so that he may hunt. His poem thereby invites us to ponder the nature of their relationship more closely. Thus there is an "underlying proportion" to the poem: "goddess is to mortal as noblewoman is to commoner." That is, "The 'divine' attributes here are but those of social preferment." Burke stresses that a full interpretation, elaborating on the implications of this equation of divinity and social superiority, would have to be careful to respect the formal qualities of the poem. But he insists that it makes sense to conjecture that "Venus would stand for the upper class, Adonis for the middle class, the boar for the lower classes (as seen though middle-class eyes using courtly spectacles). The horses [used in the hunt] might represent the potent aspect of the middle class, though ambiguously noble (like all love-making, because of its 'divine' elation). The figure of the boar could, roundabout, identify the lower classes with the dregs, with moral evil" (*RM* 216).

We might infer, then, that the context of *Venus and Adonis* is simultaneously ancient myth and Shakespeare's contemporary society. The situation is the divine/human polarity, as expressed in a particular class system. As with Malinowski's account of Polynesian myth, Burke finds in Shakespeare's revision of Ovid a sanctioning of the given hierarchy, albeit an indirect one. According to Burke, the poem is not merely an erotic work, for its "rhetorical element ... treats of a hot-and-cold relation between persons of a different class, here figured as divine and mortal, while the real subject is not primarily sexual lewdness at all, but 'social lewdness' mythically expressed in sexual terms" (*RM* 208). Ostensibly a story of sexual courtship, the poem is really about social courtship, itself a figure for social hierarchy.

It was such ingenious readings of literary texts as this that led to Burke's being hailed in the 1980s as a precursor of "new historicism," that movement in literary criticism which, focusing primarily on the Renaissance, sought to discover the hidden meanings of a culture through analysis of its discourses.[4] But even without pursuing his influence on later literary critics, it should be clear from the essays discussed in this chapter how careful Burke is to avoid a conventionally economic reading of texts. In particular, no doubt guided by his interest in the anthropology of Malinowski, he seeks to dissociate himself from the "vulgar" Marxism that became so influential in the middle decades of the twentieth century. Consider the care that Burke displays in differentiating his view of ideology from more narrowly political ones in the following statement, again from his *Rhetoric of Motives*. Typically, he moves from ideology to theology, thence to mythology (implicit in his allusion to Eden), and so on to rhetoric, in the space of a sentence or two:

> Ideology cannot be deduced from economic considerations alone. It derives from man's nature as a "symbol-using animal." And since the "original economic plant" is the human body, with the divisive

centrality of its particular nervous system, the theologian's concerns with Eden and the "fall" come close to the heart of the rhetorical problem. For, behind the theology, there is the perception of generic divisiveness which, being common to all men, is a universal fact about them, prior to any divisiveness caused by social classes. Here is the basis of rhetoric. Out of this emerges the motives for linguistic persuasion. Then, *secondarily*, we get the motives peculiar to particular economic situations. (*RM* 146)

The intuition of a division and of the urge toward union is taken to be both universal and innate. The sphere of ideology is the particular, class-oriented, economic manifestation of this intuition. Burke could not make his distance from the determinist element in Marxism more clear. He carefully negotiates between the "ultimate" and the "temporal" spheres.

Perhaps one more relevant passage on ideology might be cited here, to confirm the independence of Burke's approach. The passage occurs in the course of his "Definition of Man," which begins a later volume of essays, *Language as Symbolic Action* (1966). Here he discusses, as he frequently does, the relation between words and the world. He emphasizes that language helps create social reality rather than merely reflects it, for "motivation" comes from "symbolicity" itself:

Do we simply use words, or do they not also use us? An "ideology" is like a god coming down to earth, where it will inhabit a place pervaded by its presence. An "ideology" is like a spirit taking up its abode in a body: it makes that body hop around in certain ways; and that same body would have hopped around in different ways had a different ideology happened to inhabit it. I am saying in one way what [Saint] Paul said in another when he told his listeners that "Faith comes from hearing." He had a doctrine which, if his hearers were persuaded to accept it, would direct a body somewhat differently from the way it would have moved and been moved in its daily round under the earlier pagan dispensation. (*LSA* 6)

We note again the ease with which Burke moves between theology and ideology, with a mythic image as the mediating factor ("like a god coming down to earth"). The problem—and it is one all too common in his work—is that, for the sake of dramatic effect, inconvenient issues are left aside. Here we might well regret that the relationship between myth and ideology, spelled out so painstakingly elsewhere, is sidestepped, as is the precise nature of the myth evoked. But we might yet concur with Stephen Bygrave when he praises Burke for his insistence that ideology functions "more pervasively than is allowed within a crude base-superstructure model."[5] Contemporary Marxism may take such an insight for granted, but the fact that it can do so is in no small measure thanks to Burke's pioneering speculations. Ideology cannot be simply argued away as a superstructural phenomenon that will be made redundant by political revolution. It is no less a permanent feature of the human imagination than is myth, with which it has so much in common but from which it must be carefully differentiated.

However, it is not Burke's intention to recommend submission to the dominant ideology of the day. By now, he might have lost most of his sympathy with the communist cause, but he still sees it as his duty to challenge the abuse of power. Referring to the definition of ideology given previously, with its idea of a god or spirit "taking up its abode in a body," another commentator on Burke's ideas, James Kasteley, comments that "No one can escape such possession, but one might be able to interfere with the operation of this god."[6] In "Ideology and Myth" we have seen how Burke could use myth as critical intervention, where one dubious ideology had possessed so many people. Against the menace of Nazism, he proposed an "ideal myth" in a "neo-Virgilian" mode. More generally, we can see Burke as responding to the three "deities which control us," according to Kasteley: those of "capitalism, technology, and hierarchy": "The first two of these gods have arisen because of particular social and economic circumstances and hence are historical deities; the third stands outside history and inheres in the very nature of language. Although it may be possible to vanquish or at least weaken the first two gods (for what has come into being can pass away), the third god is beyond such possibility and indeed sets the very conditions under which symbolic creatures are determined to confront any set of historical circumstances."[7]

Taking our cue from Kasteley, we conclude this chapter by concentrating on "the third god." Hierarchy is for Burke an indispensable element in any human society, given that no complex community can function without "the regularities of *order.*" "The more closely you scrutinize the conditions required by order, the surer you are to discover that order is impossible without *hierarchy* (a ladder of authority that extends from 'lower' to 'higher,' while its *official functions* tend towards a corresponding set of *social ratings*)." It is then a matter of deciding whether a given hierarchy offers proper scope for human realization or encourages inhuman oppression: "Call this design 'hierarchy' when you are feeling friendly towards it. When you are feeling unfriendly, call it the 'hierarchical psychosis'—or, more simply, the Rat Race, which is what the conditions of empire add up to, in their drearier manifestations" (*ATH* 374). Burke's previous case for myth in the context of revolutionary politics has suggested that he sees resistance to the ideology of competitive economics as an imperative. But as for the principle of hierarchy itself, he is in no doubt of its necessity. As we shall see in subsequent chapters, he is fascinated by the idea of an ultimate, cosmic order against which our "Rat Race" may be judged.

If hierarchy will always be with us, then there will always be some degree of "ideological mystification" because the "ideological priority of spirit" is inherent in the fact that we are "symbol-using animals." Where language is concerned, "spirit" comes before "body" in the sense that the capacity for language must precede its use. In a symbol-using animal, there must be a feeling for the principles of language: "The tribe that could spontaneously manipulate a Greek verb was implicitly a tribe of 'grammarians' " (*RM* 176). Language allows "man" to experience "a difference between *this* being and *that* being as a difference between *this kind of* being and *that kind of* being." Thus "man" is not so much a "class animal" as a "classifying animal" (*RM* 282–283).

In this light we note that, within a particular mode of production, each class is a "mystery" to the others, just as male and female are mutually inexplicable. "Social estrangement" may, then, find expression in the perennial "mystery" that resides in the distinction between the sexes. The relationship is rhetorical: "A persuasive communication between kinds (that is, persuasion by identification) is the abstract paradigm of *courtship*. Such appeal, or address, would be the technical equivalent of love. . . . But courtship, love, is 'mystery.' For love is a communion of estranged entities, and strangeness is a condition of mystery" (*RM* 177).

The next—more important—point to make is, of course, that if language sets up divisions, it also has the power to unify and reconcile. Myth in particular has the power of "pontification," or "bridging," of healing estrangements that have become disruptive (*ATH* 359). Thus, though Shakespeare's retelling of the Venus and Adonis story may foreground division, it might be possible to read the narrative in such a way that the goddess and her beloved are reconciled in the transformation symbolized by the rebirth that Adonis undergoes. Hierarchy would not be abolished, given that the distinctions between divine and human, female and male, are essential, but the dubious divisions and inequalities that one particular class has an interest in maintaining can be transcended. This brings us back to Burke's declaration, in his essay of 1935: " 'Myths' may be wrong, or they may be used to bad ends but they cannot be dispensed with. In the last analysis, they are our basic psychological tools for working together. A hammer is a carpenter's tool; a wrench is a mechanic's tool; and a 'myth' is the social tool for welding the sense of interrelationship by which the carpenter and the mechanic, though differently occupied, can work together for common social ends. In this sense a myth that works well is as real as food, tools, and shelter are" (RSA 267–268).

"A myth that works well"—but how exactly does a myth work? We have noted Burke's persistent interest in mythic form, and noted also his insistence that form complements function. As we move to consider the advantage afforded him as myth theorist by virtue of being a literary critic, we should thus bear in mind the continuity between the social and the symbolic aspects of myth.

2

MYTH AND LITERARY CRITICISM

In his own foreword to the second edition of *The Philosophy of Literary Form*,[1] Kenneth Burke writes: "Despite the fact that anthropology and literary criticism share the realm of 'myth' in common, purists will often frown upon a word such as 'scapegoat' on the grounds that it does not belong to the theory of tragedy (which is, etymologically, the 'goat-song'!). I would hold, on the other hand: Many sociological and anthropological concepts have their analogues in literary criticism proper. With the rise of aesthetics, such concepts got *unnecessarily* exiled; and they found a home in these supposedly alien fields" (*PLF* x). The assumption that literature should be studied as an esoteric kind of utterance, in isolation from the wider language of the culture, is for Burke a dubious one. The "aesthetic" approach to literature, which has involved attention to form in its narrowest sense, has excluded a proper attention to myth, and in particular a proper attention to its social function. For Burke, myth is a symbolic "tool," and literary criticism can help us understand how it works.

In this chapter we will consider two essays on myth from the later stages of Burke's writing career. In both, he demonstrates that "poetics," the study of literary activity in general, may illuminate the workings of myth. If for Burke aestheticism errs by virtue of isolating form from function and of narrowing down language to a specialized kind of speech, anthropology commits the contrary error. It concentrates on function to the exclusion of form, and it overlooks the fact that the power of myth relies on the power of language.

It is important to bear in mind both sides of this critique as we proceed. A superficial reading of these essays, and a cursory contrast to the two discussed in the first chapter, might suggest that Burke has abruptly shifted attention from the extrinsic perspective (the context of society) to the intrinsic (the nature of form). True, the later Burke becomes more explicitly concerned with symbol, style, and structure. But his continuing interest is in the dialectic of the extrinsic and intrinsic spheres.

The first essay discussed in this chapter, "Myth, Poetry and Philosophy," shows us Burke during his late-middle period. It was written in the mid-1960s, by which time nearly all of his major books had been published and he was at last able to offer a more considered—if by no means final—account of the nature of myth. But again, ideas posited earlier may be seen to take a more distinct shape, as he now proposes examining myth from the perspective of poetics, and taking narrative form as the basis of social function. The second essay, "Doing and Saying: Thoughts on Myth, Cult, and Archetypes," published at the beginning of the following decade, might be seen as an extension of the themes addressed in "Myth, Poetry and Philosophy," as well as an extension of the material covered in Chapter 1. Burke maintains his view of myth as fulfilling a permanent human need for symbolic expression, while he also explores its inevitable involvement in the social order. Here we can tell that Burke's perspective is that of the literary critic, but one with an ambitious notion of criticism: he seeks to comprehend the workings of the secular imagination in the context of both religious and cultural dimensions.

"MYTH, POETRY AND PHILOSOPHY" (1966)

Though Burke began defining myth in the context of historical concerns and political conflicts, we have seen that his concern was always to stress its persistent, formal features, which allow it to communicate to people and to consolidate communities. If we now move forward two decades and consider a mature essay, we can see that the nature of language, both literary and nonliterary, has become increasingly important to Burke, as he attempts to construct the philosophy he calls "logology," or "words about words." "Myth, Poetry and Philosophy" is one of the most important essays to be included in his *Language as Symbolic Action,* a volume that collects some of his major statements on the human being as the "symbol-using animal." We need not know the intricacies of logology to appreciate it, however.

In a footnote to "Doing and Saying," Burke refers back to "Myth, Poetry and Philosophy," summing up its thesis as an attempt "to distinguish between sheerly *historical derivations* of the 'combat myth' and origins considered in terms of *narrative principles*" (DS 112). Here I would stress the word "distinguish." He is not claiming that the formal analysis is the only way to interpret myth, to the exclusion of the historical; that would for Burke be an error analogous to that of aestheticism. Rather, as we shall see, he is trying to show how problems posed and resolutions offered by the tracing of "derivations" may find their ultimate resolution in formal "principles." Though we can indeed note a shift of perspective in this essay from that of political engagement to a more detached, descriptive stance, there are thus obvious continuities.

In one sense the essay is an extended review, based on Joseph Fontenrose's scholarly work *Python: A Study of Delphic Myth and Its Origins* (1959). In another sense it is an ambitious attempt to correct—or rather, to complete—what Burke takes to be the "anthropological" approach to myth by demonstrating the more comprehensive potential of a literary approach. How far the classicist Fontenrose can be characterized as an anthropologist is another matter. Perhaps Burke might be accused of using him as a foil in the development of his own argument. He may come closer to characterizing Fontenrose's approach when he uses the term "folkloristic" rather than "anthropological" (*LSA* 382). However, it must be admitted that Burke risks semantic confusion by treating these two epithets as synonymous.

Python is the name of the monstrous serpent that hatched from the mud of the deluge and was slain by the god Apollo at Delphi. Fontenrose is concerned not so much with this specific myth as with the general category of "combat myth," and with the cult derived from it. His starting point, logically enough, is the problem of origins, and Burke addresses this problem, too. However, Burke suggests that it is likely to be viewed differently, depending on whether our premises are informed by anthropology or by poetics. He assumes that, as the word *mythos* may be translated as "word," it is important to view a myth as a linguistic expression, for it involves an expansion from one word (*mythos*) to a tale composed of many words (again, *mythos*), just like "the step whereby the title of the play *Hamlet* becomes expanded into all the words and simulated actions, characters, and situations in which the play is composed. The title is in effect an 'essence' " (*LSA* 380–381).

Burke does not draw any conclusions from this observation until he has assessed the account of the development of mythology given in the book under review. How, then, did a "combat myth" originate? Fontenrose proposes that there was an earlier myth, involving the struggle between two deities, one in the form of a dragon and one in the form of a sky warrior; the warrior triumphed. Though neither Fontenrose nor Burke says so, it would seem that the kind of myth referred to here is what we call "cosmogonic": it is a recurrent pattern in various cultures, recounting the creation of the universe from a primal struggle between equally divine forces, one representing light and the other darkness. An obvious example, but another surprising omission here, is the Babylonian creation myth, which centers on the conflict of Marduk, the emergent lord of the heavens, and Tiamat, the preexistent female deity who, depicted as a monstrous, dragonlike creature, embodies the primordial waters.[2] Fontenrose's own interest is rather in how this myth of "origins" itself becomes the "origin" of that later category of tale he calls "combat myth." This kind of story concerns the struggle between an "older" god and a "new" god, with the "new" god emerging triumphant. The defeat of Python by Apollo fits this pattern. Fontenrose adds a third stage to these two stages of development: the establishment of a cult, centered on the triumphant deity.

The essence of this whole thesis is stated simply by Fontenrose, and Burke finds the statement to be worth quoting: "The combat-myth is a myth of beginnings, a tale of conflict between order and disorder, chaos and cosmos" (quoted in *LSA* 386). But if Fontenrose wishes to identify the myth with the very subject of origin, he also wishes to know the origin of the myth. Hence, integral to his thesis is his speculation about sources, which leads him to conjecture that the "combat myth" must be rooted in the early tribal experience of the struggle against nature, wild beasts, and human enemies. His complementary concern is with the purpose of the myth: the function of the story is "to account for the cult of services associated with it" (*LSA* 390). In other words, the myth provides an explanation for the existence of rituals dedicated to a particular deity—in this case, to Apollo at Delphi.

Burke's response is to question the nature of Fontenrose's concern with the origin of the combat myth. Rather than "Where did it come from?" Burke wants to ask, "To what extent does the paradigm give us, not some 'first story' from which the many variants were derived, but rather a 'perfect' form towards which a story would 'naturally' gravitate?" In other words, "In order to be a 'perfect combat myth, what form 'ought' the story to have?" (*LSA* 384). If Fontenrose lists the various "clauses" of the myth that he has discovered by documentation, Burke wants to consider the more abstract issue of narrative fulfillment, according to the principles of poetics. For example, Fontenrose gives us clauses 5 through 9 as follows:

5. The Enemy conspired against heaven.
6. A divine Champion appeared to face him
7. The Champion fought the enemy.
8. The Champion nearly lost the battle.
9. The Enemy was finally destroyed, after being outwitted, deceived, or bewitched. (quoted in *LSA* 383)

Focusing on clause 8, Burke declares that, according to the demands of effective narration, we need that moment of tension, followed by success against the odds. Without it, we are disappointed, and the preceding and succeeding events make little sense. He even surmises that it is "as if the primitive narrators of the 'combat myth' had read Aristotle on the dramatic value of plots complicated by reversal ('peripety')" (*LSA* 386).

We are not surprised to find Burke speculating about the "perfect combat myth" in literary terms. After all, his differentiation between ideology and myth culminated in the hypothesis of an "ideal" narrative for the mid-twentieth century based on Virgil. The difference here, however, is that Burke is not arguing pragmatically in response to a semantic confusion and a historical situation but is becoming ever more inclined to propose general principles in pursuit of a complete philosophical system, based on his own understanding of language. Burke calls that system "logology," which we address at length in Chapter 4. For now, all we need to register is that where an anthropological account of myth might need to attend to the question of origins, Burke's literary-critical account is more interested in the way that words, which are the basis of myth (*mythos* as speech), dictate the direction of the narrative (*mythos* as story).

Thus Fontenrose traces the earliest possible examples of tales involving the struggle against a monster and infers that they must originate in the human experience of physical conflict. But Burke finds his answer in "the genius of the negative" (*LSA* 390), which resides in language itself. He writes:

Though both types of the combat myth, in their simplicity, proceed *from* disorder to order, there is no such progression in the relation between the terms themselves, considered as logical opposites (or "polar" terms). We can say with equal justice either that "order" implies "disorder" or that "disorder" implies "order"—and the same will be found of "chaos" and "cosmos," insofar as they stand opposed. We would derive this state of affairs not from such *historical* "origins" or "firsts" as men's primitive battles with nature, wild beasts, and one another, but from the nature of that peculiarly linguistic marvel, the *negative.* The negative as such offers a basis for a tendency to think in terms of antithesis (yes–no, good–evil, true–false, right–wrong, order–disorder, cosmos–chaos, success–failure, presence–absence, pleasure–pain, clean–unclean, life–death, love–hate—or, recombining these last two sets, Eros–Thanatos). (*LSA* 387)

How, then, do we explain the combat myth, with its temporal form? "Insofar as negatives imply their opposites, the opposition between them is in effect 'timeless,'" insists Burke. But his main point, italicized for emphasis, is this: "*When translated into terms of mythic narrative . . . such opposition can become a quasi-temporal 'combat' between the two terms,* with the corresponding possibility that one of the terms can be pictured as 'vanquishing' the other" (*LSA* 387). The very narration of events thus implies purpose, and "once you have translated the logical principle of antithesis into terms of narrative combat, by the same token you have set the condition for a *purposive* development" (*LSA* 387). That is, we cannot help but envisage the principle of disorder "aiming to win over the principle of order, and vice versa" (*LSA* 387–388). The very drive of narrative toward its own completion makes for a "teleological scheme" (*LSA* 388). The drive is that identified by Plato's pupil, Aristotle, as "entelechy."

David Blakesley clarified the Aristotelian term, explaining that "it referred to the inner potentiality that could make matter into form. It comes from the Greek word, *entelechia*, whose roots are *telos* ('end') and *echein* ('to have'). Put most simply, entelechy is the actualization of form, which is in turn the fulfillment of an act of becoming. It is 'to have an end.'" Burke, he writes, borrows the concept from Aristotle to "explain the function of a terminology as a repository of potential meaning," or, more simply, "to describe a terminology's generative capacity."[3] If we seek further elucidation, we might ponder one of the aphorisms that Burke includes in the "Flowerishes" that punctuate his *Collected Poems*: "At the very start, one's terms jump to conclusions" (*CP* 299). The relevance of entelechy to myth is reemphasized by Burke when he declares that the principles of mythic form are to be located "not in the temporally past moments that a form develops *from*, but in possibilities of perfection which reside in the form as such and *toward* which all sorts of stories might gravitate" (*LSA* 390–391).

Burke's argument, which seeks to encompass Fontenrose's anthropological account, thus relies on the formal principles derived from the theory of literature. But it should again be emphasized that Aristotle, whom Burke invokes as an authority, was famously the author of a volume known as the *Poetics*, not the *Aesthetics*. It might seem to the casual reader of "Myth, Poetry, and Philosophy," from Burke's occasional exaggeration of statement, that for him language, structure, and style are his sole criteria—to the exclusion of history, origin, and function. This assumption would misrepresent him. Rather, we have to think of Burke's formal interest as an attempt to provide as full an account of combat myth as possible, incorporating Fontenrose's own—not denying the latter's right to attend chiefly to content and context but questioning the exclusive nature of his attention. Burke acknowledges that there is a question to be asked about the "perfection" of combat myth as an instrument in establishing the authority of a cult. However, he denies that the answer to this question is sufficient also to answer the question about the "perfection" of the story as a temporal treatment of the "logical" or "polar" opposition. For that has to do with the fact that a myth is constructed in language, that it has its very basis in words. The best answer would be one that encompassed both: it would deal with social and formal considerations alike. This, after all, was what the younger Burke was attempting in his corrective to the misrepresentation of myth by those with narrowly political agendas.

Burke's own speculation about the combat myth as *aition* ("cause" or "reason") will indicate how far his stance is from pure formalism:

> If the combat myth were nothing but a story of combat, designed to appeal simply as a story in keeping with the aesthetic canons of Art for Art's Sake, the study of its paradigm from the entelechial point of view would require only such considerations of internal symmetry. But a cult is a system of *governance*. Thus, its moral

authority is a direct or indirect means of influencing the dispositions and habits of the believers. And insofar as the myth of "origins" serves as a precedent on which to base this authority, it must be designed not merely to account for "origins," but also to account for them in ways that provide *sanctions* for the given order. (*LSA* 395)

Burke's interest is in how the very word "order" inevitably summons up its antithesis, given the dialectical structure of language.

Yet once again, the dialectic is not merely linguistic, as he goes on to explain:

Thus, whereas the mythic translation of opposition into terms of a contest allows ideas like order and disorder, cosmos and chaos to be represented by personified contestants that can triumph over each other or succeed each other, there still remains the fact that any system of order implies corresponding kinds of disorder. This persistence of the logical opposites despite the possibilities of mythic victory can best be handled in these two ways: (1) By a myth according to which, though one of the contestants has been vanquished (or, in the most thorough terms, "slain"), he still somehow survives (like Typhon buried by Zeus beneath Sicily and fuming through Aetna), with the constant threat that he may again rise in revolt. (2) By a myth according to which the vanquished principle does periodically take over, to reign for a season, and to be periodically replaced again by the opposing principle. (*LSA* 395)

Burke proceeds to make his choice between these options:

The design of human combat itself would seem to provide the basic imagery for the first of these versions, according to which one side conquers but can never remain wholly sure of his victory. And obviously, the periodicity of the seasons provides the basic image for the second version, which translates the principle of opposition into terms of cyclical succession. The second primarily concerns us now, since the paradigm calls for the victory of a sky-god or weather-god, and seasonal change is most readily associated with such a power. ... And in this sense, with the translation of polar opposition (order–disorder, cosmos–chaos, rule–misrule) into terms of powers whose jurisdiction fluctuated with the seasons, the combat myth was brought to a state of "aetiological perfection." (*LSA* 395–396)

The seasonal cycle has the advantage of carrying with it an air of inevitability, regardless of the fluctuations of individual seasons. For example, a priesthood that can associate its rites with such a cycle "has optimum conditions for establishing its authority." For no priestly rite could be more authoritative than "one which had obvious pragmatic sanction, since its services proved 'successful' year after year" (*LSA* 396).

Burke proposes that, in order to illuminate what is involved in this process, the methodology associated with literary criticism can and should complement the methodology associated with anthropology: "We can now see clearly the two kinds of 'perfection' that the 'entelechial' perspective must deal with, in the case of the 'combat myth.' There is its perfection simply as a story that translates polar opposition into terms of narrative. And there is its perfection as an instrument in the establishing of a cult's authority. For this second kind, we have suggested, there is the added factor of identification with seasonal *regularities*" (*LSA* 396). However, as he goes on to observe, "responsibility for seasonal *regularities*" means also "responsibility for the correcting of seasonal *irregularities*" (*LSA* 396). So there has to be, for both historical and formal reasons, a counterforce to balance the force, necessitating a conflict that would need to be seen to be resolved. This, of course, brings Burke back to the task of identifying the contestants in the combat myth as negative and positive. How do we decide which principle each represents?

Fontenrose applies the term "rebel gods" to the "older generation of gods" that the "victory-destined younger gods" displace. Burke comments: "In a sense it is always the younger gods who revolt, as with the Champion who goes forth to end the tyrannical reign of the Enemy; but the displaced gods are the rebels because, once the new order has become the norm, the old order stands for the corresponding principle of disorder which constantly threatens to regain control and can even be said to reign periodically (but not permanently, thanks to the efficacy of the cultic rites with which the myth is associated)" (*LSA* 402). Either side, strictly speaking, negates the other, but there is more to it, for "despite the fact that law is essentially negative (a structure of thou-shalt-nots), there is also the traditional tendency to associate the Negative with 'bad' and the Positive with 'good.' So we might arbitrarily use the Negative as the mark of the Enemy, though the negative [*sic*] would be in our attitude towards him" (*LSA* 402).

But even now, it seems, we have only begun to explain how exactly the narrative deals with the negative and the positive. Burke considers the process of the "embodying" of the two principles. He suggests that "our first step from sheer pattern to mythic particularization" would be: "Both sides should be 'gods.' " Thus "We have now translated our Negative and Positive into terms of body, though a kind of body which also shades off into ideas of the disembodied" (*LSA* 403).

Next it is necessary, if the myth is to be effective as narrative, for both principles—not just the positive principle—to be "amplified." Burke dwells on the need for "the Unfavored Principle" to be associated with a suitably demonic habitat, "some forbidden place where monsters and demons are traditionally thought to dwell," and with "a set of similarly unfavored physical traits (such as monstrous form)," all designed to be contrasted to those of "the Favored Principle," which he does not pause to specify. But the amplification will not be complete unless the demonic antagonist is invested with personality and characteristics:

> [H]owever monstrous, and however identified with superhuman or nonhuman powers, this principle, to be narratively "perfect," must be a person. Hence, amplification in terms of moral traits (powers and habits) upon which men look with disfavor. And this unfavored character must cap the climax by association with a purpose that is the most thoroughly (or "perfectly") disfavored. This should be his ambition for total tyranny, absolute misrule. If the narrative structure is to be as neat and its internal adjustments as possible, this culminating purpose on the part of the Unfavored Principle (or Principal) must serve as motive for the action of the rival Positive Favored Principle (endowed with correspondingly favored background, physical and moral powers and habits, all culminating in the intention to undo the Negative Principle's culminating intention). (*LSA* 403)

Burke plays with words here—"Principle (or Principal)"—to make a serious point. He is concerned with how logical conflicts, suitably embodied and amplified, may serve as "firsts," establishing precedent and authority in the very process of identifying narrative priority and attaining narrative completion. As with his hypothetical myth offered as an ideal for the postwar world of the late 1940s, he is compiling a structural paradigm of the ancient combat myth. In doing so, he seeks to reconcile the *mythos* with the *logos*, the "principal" with the "principle." True, this has necessitated some legerdemain, given the limited space afforded even by a substantial review essay. But in fairness to Burke, the need for reconciliation is a topic he deals with at length elsewhere, as we shall see in subsequent chapters.

Having argued for the importance of studying the structure of narrative, Burke in this essay must still indicate how the narrative itself will tend to be "amplified." We have already referred to Burke's response to Fontenrose's list of clauses, in which Burke suggests that the protagonist must appear to lose the battle for good reasons, which are the province of poetics. That is, an effective narrative will be one that includes a moment of "peripety," whereby defeat of "the Positive principle" is necessary before its success. "Given the nature of the contestants, the defeat can be expressed in the most thorough terms possible: The Positive principle can actually be said to 'die' (a proper juncture for lamentations on the part of those who favor the vanquished principle). For 'death' under such conditions is not incongruous with 'immortality' (and the two taken together make a perfect narrative equivalent for the underlying Paradox of the Negative whereby polar terms both exclude each other and necessarily require each other)" (*LSA* 403–404).

Again, an amplified narrative will also be an "embodied" narrative. There will be material in the myth that is there mainly to render it substantial and credible, and "[t]hus, a battlefield or a banquet hall will merit some details in its own right. In our search for explanations in terms of perfection, we must keep in mind the pressures that keep the contest from becoming too simply itself and that call for an underlying neutrality of details designed to help the narrative look real. This ambiguity is true of all characters in fiction. Some things they do because of their specific roles; but they do other things simply because they are 'people' " (*LSA* 404). In either case—either of peripety or of proliferation—the drive is entelechial: the narrative proceeds or expands toward its own "perfection."

As I have already hinted, there is much in this essay that cannot be covered here, as it relies on an understanding of ideas expounded in works by Burke that we have yet to consider. But perhaps sufficient material has been discussed for us to see how Burke's theory of myth has developed. Without abandoning his earlier sense of historical and social pressures, he has taken his notion of form to the point where it can encompass them. Poetics, in explaining "narrative principles," incorporates anthropology insofar as it is concerned with "historical derivations." Or rather, in the light of poetics, anthropology turns out to be much more formal than Fontenrose's version of it might suggest. Of course, Burke's decision to take Fontenrose as representative of an anthropological approach to myth, which for convenience he takes to be synonymous with a folkloristic approach, remains a problem. This decision would seem to be tactical, but it probably misrepresents Fontenrose, and it begs the question of the relationship between anthropology and folklore. Allowing for such doubts, we may provisionally conclude that if Burke believes anthropological insights can be incorporated into his own theory of myth, he by no means wishes to confine his attention to a narrowly literary account of the stylistic embellishments likely to be discovered in a given myth. The case for poetics is provisional and partially tactical: what Burke is after is greater and greater coherence. He seeks an increasingly inclusive philosophy that will do justice to the complexity of the human capacity for symbolism. In an essay published five years later, he makes further "notes towards" this end.

"DOING AND SAYING:
THOUGHTS ON MYTH, CULT, AND ARCHETYPES" (1971)

The essay "Doing and Saying" originated in Burke's response to a fellow contributor at an academic conference, God and Man in Contemporary Literature, which had been held at Temple University in 1969. Maurice Friedman had declared that religion and literature "meet in a matrix prior to both of them," since both begin "in a numinous awe of wonder." Burke's position, stated at the start of this essay, is that "if the relation between the sacred and the profane is approached thus, the issue is settled in advance, the 'matrix prior to them both' being automatically weighted on the side of the sacred." He believes that there is a need for a "more neutral" position and thus proposes to work within the theory of symbolism in general, taking that sphere to comprehend both secular and religious language. Burke's focus is on "man's symbolic expressiveness," as exemplified by myth (DS 100).

As we shall see in subsequent chapters, much of Burke's mature theory might be taken as an elaboration of his central definition of the human being as "the symbol-using animal" (*LSA* 3). For now, we need only accept the premise that there is a tendency in all human cultures for the more important activities to be given imaginative reinforcement, or what Burke calls symbolic "doubling," or "completion." He gives us the simple example of "the planting, cultivating, and harvesting of crops." The first thing to note is that "These material operations would be, in the strictest sense, a doing." The second thing to note is that "In the course of any such tribal performances, various amounts of saying would be involved, since the resources of speech can guide a cooperative enterprise (as the members of a football team go into a huddle to consult before each play)." But we have not yet exhausted the significance of the activity, for "over and above such strictly pragmatic use of speech, as a set of instructions, exhortations, admonitions directly related to the material operations in connection with which these resources are utilized, there is a further possibility" (DS 101).

To explain this possibility, Burke has to invoke the figure of what he calls "the myth-man." This is the person who, in each tribe or social grouping, would take responsibility for the "rounding out" of the given activity. He would be the one to supervise the ritual and recite the narrative appropriate to the task in hand. He would be the person accepted as "the mythic specialist" responsible for the "formal culmination" of others' material achievements. For example, this role might involve a "commemorating of the planting by, in effect, likening the process to an act of sexual impregnation." This action would in turn suggest further symbolic possibilities: "Since the state of the seasons is so important in planting, it would not require exceptional expertise for the mythic specialist to extend his similitude by correspondingly treating of the relation between Sky and Earth as copulatively fertile" (DS 104).

Burke's argument is informed by Samuel Taylor Coleridge, who, in chapter 13 of his *Biographia Literaria* (1817), makes an influential distinction between the "primary" and the "secondary" imaginations: "The primary imagination I hold to be the living power and prime agent of all human perception, and as a representation in the finite mind of the eternal act of creation in the infinite I AM. The secondary I consider as an echo of the former, co-existing with the conscious will. . . . It dissolves, diffuses, dissipates, in order to re-create; or where this process is rendered impossible, yet still, at all events, it struggles to idealize and to unify."[4] In other words, even though every human being may be defined by virtue of the creative capacity to affirm its own and the world's existence ("primary imagination"), it is the poet who manages to extend this capacity to a higher level ("secondary imagination"). The vital form of secondary imagination gives new shape and significance to reality. Burke draws a necessary parallel between the mythmaker and the poet, insofar as both go beyond rudimentary human awareness: "This line-up . . . is somewhat analogous to

Coleridge's distinction between 'primary' imagination (in terms of which we all experience the world), and 'secondary' imagination (that marks the special aptitude of artistic genius)" (DS 104). Again, we see that Burke's myth theory is developed within the literary paradigm, though with an overall concern which is more than literary as is the case with Coleridge's own speculations.

Who, however, would count as a "myth-man?" Burke offers an apparently random list to indicate the range of possibilities but also to query the assumption that we need to think of the symbolism involved as intrinsically sacred: "witch doctor, medicine man, shaman, oracles (such as the Delphic), poets, novelists, dancers, musicians, painters, actors, dramatists (artists in general). And here, above all, we should list priests and prophets, whatever their quarrels with one another" (DS 104). The range of likely candidates for the role of myth-man is designed to reinforce the idea of myth as a centrally human form of expression. His reference to "artists in general" serves to clinch his emphasis on the relevance of the secular sphere of aesthetics to this field of study:

> My paradigm would situate the impetus to myth in a sense of congruity, or propriety, the mythic specialist's feeling that, when something of a terminal or "boundary" nature takes place (such as a marriage, a birth, a death, an initiation, the acceptance of a new leader), the event must in effect be doubled, completed by a cere-monious, symbolic counterpart. Our nearest word for the origin of such a motive would probably be "aesthetic." It involves a sense of congruity, propriety, piety, quite as the myth-man might feel moved to sing a spring-song in the spring-time, or a lament at a burial. In brief, the very kind of attention which the symbol-using hominid would bring to such events, and which would lead him to distin-guish them from the course of experience in general, would also be the kind of response that would incite the expressively responsive myth-man to a purely symbolic perfecting of the event. (DS 105)

Though Burke draws attention to the "aesthetic" aspect of myth-making here, he emphasizes its basis in collective human need: "Further-more, note that such doubling would also in effect be a primitive mode of classification—for, insofar as the myth-man sings the same spring-song each spring or the same lament at each burial, his recurrent mythic utterance has, in effect, classified many different incidents under the same head, though such usages are developed long before men explicitly discussed the nature and problems of classification in the ways of philo-sophic or scientific methodology" (DS 105). Burke's conjunction of the aesthetic impulse with the basic capacity for classification should confirm that he is as radically opposed to aestheticism as ever before. As his use of Coleridge's terms indicates, the whole point of "rounding out," or symbolic "doubling," is that it is dependent upon—indeed, "secondary" to—the linguistic realm in which all members of the community participate. Art and myth differ from normal symbol using in degree, not kind.

In case we are tempted to suppose that anyone with a flair for the manipulation of symbols might count as a myth-man, we should note that Burke adds a rider to his magnanimous catalog: "Ad-writers, publicity men and the like are not perfect instances of the myth-man, since so much of their symbolizing does not aim at a kind of summa-rizing utterance that characterizes mythic completion" (DS 104). Their "instrumental" use of language, their imposition of "image," their exploitation of the "mythic motive" in "bastardized form"—these align them with what Burke cryptically calls "the unhappy nature of many tendencies towards interventionism in the realm of international relations" (DS 105).

One might wish that he had said more on this topic, but perhaps we can infer from these allusions that Burke is differentiating ideology from myth. He is not, however, any more inclined to sever the cate-gories here than he was in earlier pronouncements. The main thrust of his essay on "Ideology and Myth" is that the mythic transcends but does not exclude the ideological. This point is worth bearing in mind as he now turns to the question of the "cult." Here Burke surmises what is involved in the institutionalization of the act of symbolic "doubling." That is, he addresses the way myth inevitably becomes the focus of not only imaginative, but also social, power. On the one hand we have the neutral phenomenon of the "mythic specialist," respon-sible for the "perfection" of a shared cultural capacity. On the other hand we have the status attributed to those with that responsibility. Hence we find that the "votaries" of the cult, by which term Burke would seem to mean the elite officials rather than the average adher-ents, come to "enjoy special privileges or expectations of a quite prac-tical nature." He continues:

> When the shaman takes on his role as one who must symbolically
> respond to things in their season, or to the various troubles of his
> fellow tribesmen, this myth-man's role as a specialist obviously

involves privileges and responsibilities that relate directly to his status rather than being confined to our hypothetical derivation for the "pure" myth-man. One point at least is obvious: the very nature of the mythic vocation is *prima facie* evidence that the tribe is no longer homogenous, though such specialised rites may help hold it together. If the tribe were wholly homogenous, how could some members be thus "set apart" as experts whose special function as myth-men may be variously rewarded, but in any case is recognised and acknowledged by the community? (DS 106)

For Burke, myth may ultimately transcend ideology, but it would be naive to deny that the "myth-men" are as capable as any ruler of exploiting their own importance. We should not expect disinterestedness on their part; rather, they are likely to devote a good deal of energy to ensuring their own survival by persuading others of their own indispensability. This possibility leads Burke to entertain "a Darwinian kind of speculation" here, for the myth-man will spontaneously "perfect" his myth in ways whereby "what's good for the cult is good for the tribe." "Suppose," asserts Burke, "that the cult which a certain set of myth-men have evolved happens to fit especially well with the conditions of governance in general. If the state flourishes, the myth's services to the state help the cult to flourish correspondingly. In fact, the cult might even develop features that enable it not only to serve the state, but also to avoid too close an identification with the particular vicissitudes of political faction" (DS 106).

Such speculation, if extended, might have led Burke to develop a position analogous to the "cultural evolutionism" espoused by anthropologists with their roots in the eighteenth-century Enlightenment—notably, J. G. Frazer. However, Frazer is a thinker with whom Burke consistently disagrees, as we see in Chapter 3. Moreover, Burke's concern in "Doing and Saying" is not to offer a cynical reduction of myth but simply to counter its elevation to the realm of "numinous awe or wonder," as espoused by Friedman. Moreover, if Burke seems to be indulging in historical speculations to the extent that he might be accused of making the same error that in "Myth, Poetry and Philosophy" he accused Fontenrose of making, that is because Burke is here at pains to dissociate himself from the opposite error. He refuses to start from Friedman's assumption of a matrix that precedes cultural and imaginative expression. Friedman's "Darwinian speculation" does not represent Burke's own position.

As we shall see, Burke is a thinker who is exceptionally alert to how the adoption of a given paradigm necessarily involves selectivity, overemphasis, and even distortion, so that it is a theorist's duty to remain open to the possibility of error. His own solution to this danger is to recommend that theoretical orientations should include some scope for the critique of their own premises, that they should be knowingly provisional and partial, on the grounds that ultimate, integrated knowledge is a long-term aim rather than an immediate objective. Hence he concludes this section of his article on the "cult" with a short summary, followed by a moment of self-reflection: "The attempt to schematize these elements has led me into an oversimplified quasi-temporal statement of the case. For we are not discussing so clear a sequence of evolutionary stages as my account might suggest. But that takes us to our other route, which is above all concerned with the problem of a fallacy dear not only to the primitive myth-man, but also (twistedly) to present-day analysts of myth" (DS 109).

And so Burke returns to the question, hinted at earlier in this essay and addressed at length in the previous essay, of how myth turns "principles" into "principals": how it proposes a past even while it performs its function in the present. In short, he addresses the third term of his subtitle, "archetypes."

Burke explains that here he is concerned with "those myths which purport to gravitate about the subject of *beginnings* (the *Urzeit*, as when some rite and perhaps related cult are, as it were, 'derived' from events said to be connected with the tribe's original ancestors in some remote past)" (DS 109). We may infer, therefore, that he is not using the term "archetype" in the sense made famous by C. G. Jung, as a psychological pattern that arises from the "collective unconscious" and which finds expression in "archetypal images."[5] Rather, Burke takes "archetype" to mean "prototype." He gives the example of the ancient belief that Rome was founded by a legendary wolf-child, a belief that was presumably preferred to acknowledgment of the more mundane etymology through which Romulus was derived from Roma. Burke proposes to explain such "mythic reversals," which in effect turn the present into the distant past—"with their stress upon some event or situation ... [as] a kind of mythic 'first' "—by means of that principle of Aristotle's on which he drew in "Myth, Poetry and Philosophy"— namely, entelechy.

Burke gives the example of a tribal "rite of passage." Here the individual initiate is subordinated to "mythic elements ... primarily designed to solemnize such a process of transformation *in general*." "In their ritual recurrence from year to year, they are not shaped about the character and circumstances peculiar to any one particular tribesman. Rather, the ceremony in effect classifies all actual or possible initiates under a general heading that transcends their nature as individuals" (DS 109). It is in this process of generalization or classification, by which all participants are treated "*in terms of* a traditional recurrent ceremony," that the entelechial principle becomes evident:

> However varied may be the characters and experiences of the individual initiates, the given ceremony is designed to reflect their change of status (and thus in effect to *double* the condition that depends literally on their biological process of growing up). But is not such a rite also viewing the initiates in terms of a "perfection?" Regardless of what they *might* be, they are being considered from the standpoint of one particular absolute principle, namely: their identity, and corresponding reidentification, as initiates. A concern with "perfection" in this sense would be an instance of what I mean by an attempt to refurbish and re-adapt (at least for the study of mythic proclivities) the Aristotelian concept of the "entelechy," that is, the "aim" of an entity to fulfil the possibilities intrinsic to its nature. (DS 109–110)

As we have seen from his response to Fontenrose's model of "origins," Burke believes that this principle of entelechy allows for the possibility of what he is here calling "mythic reversal." For "given the narrative nature of myth, it follows that the mythic way of propounding a principle, or logical 'first' . . . can become transformed into a quasi-temporal equivalent" (DS 110). This is the process involved in the construction of what we call an "archetype," but it is all too often overlooked when that term is used. Burke states his case explicitly:

> Basically, the point is: The "proper" way to treat of principles (logical "firsts" or "beginnings") in terms of mythic narrative, is by translating them into terms concerned with quasi-temporal origin. For instance, the proper mythic way to represent the militaristic and fratricidal principles intrinsic to Roman society was exemplified in the mythic derivation of Rome from a son of Mars who slew his twin brother. Thus, insofar as mythic doubling is the formal perfecting of situations deemed central to the tribe's way of life, to

its social relations, and the like, it takes the form of a mythic first. Just as the search for paradigms leads one in the direction of such words as "prototype" and "archetype," so the essentializing nature of mythopoeia attains its terministic fulfillment in narratives which deal with things now, in terms of imputed origins from which the relevant manifestations now are said to be temporally descended. By this route, the entelechial nature of myths (their nature as bearing upon "first principles" of the tribe's condition) is manifested in terms of a mythically imputed past, in prehistory (or what the Germans resonantly call *die Urzeit*). (DS 110–111)

Burke here asserts that mythic beginnings turn out to have logical ends. If it is in the nature of narrative to postulate temporal origins, then it is the duty of the theorist of myth to recognize the project of "perfection" involved. The mythic principle that generates such "archetypes" is a source of fascination for Burke, even as he remains alert to its ideological function—that of justifying current social practice. We have seen how in "Ideology and Myth" he refers to the "Revelation" afforded by Platonic myth, which exemplifies the whole process very well, without offering any critique. However, Burke's more general perspective is to offer an affirmation of the strategy only by way of an initial suspicion.[6] Moreover, it is something of an obsession with him that, if one is to theorize about the nature of myth, one must be careful not to carry the mythic project over into the theory itself, lest various intellectual maneuvers be made surreptitiously.

In this context we may note that earlier in his essay Burke refers to the "fallacy" that is "dear not only to the primitive myth-man, but also (twistedly) to the present-day analysts of myth." It is one thing to claim that myth inevitably, by virtue of its narrative form, implies a temporal starting point; it is another thing to claim that myth itself is an instance of pure, sacred "origin." Burke refers to two theorists in particular who seem to fall into this trap, Adolf E. Jensen and Mircea Eliade, who both prompt Burke to state his own case with considerable vigor:

My general slant embodies a feeling that we should guard against an overly "universalizing" view of myth and its "archetypes." I would lay equal stress upon the fact that the myth-men are in notable respects "set apart" by their speciality. Both Jensen and Eliade begin with assumptions that implicitly confuse the "primal" with the "derived." I have discussed this matter at considerable length in my *Rhetoric of Motives*, with regard to the "socio-anagogic" dimension in the symbolizing of human relations. As I analyze the situation, much supposedly pious awe in the contemplation of the transcendently "divine" cannot be adequately interpreted unless we add (to any postulating of a generic mythopoeic awe) an element of sheerly social mystery, involving such administrative subjection as goes with response to authority that can levy taxes or pronounce magisterial sentences (decrees and judgments). It bears upon the ambiguous kind of "mystery" associated with the Roman emperor as *pontifex maximus*, a bridge between "celestial" mystery and the mystery of his role as august head of the state. (DS 111)

Burke's chief interest here is not to revive his general advice on the "revolutionary" use of myth, given to Marxists four decades earlier, but specifically to challenge Jensen's thesis. If Burke finds the notion that "the primary cause of mythic propositions is religious" to be insufficient, it is because it cannot explain how the sacred inevitably becomes involved with the secular. That does not discredit the idea of the sacred. In fact, Burke believes that his own starting point—the capacity of humans for symbolism—is more likely to do justice to the complexity of myth, whether in its secular or sacred aspects.

Turning to Eliade, Burke notes how he repeatedly stresses "the imputed relation of a myth to some event in the primordial past, *in illo tempore*." Those who have read any of Eliade's work will know that his overriding concern, as a student of mythology, is with narratives of origin, for these bear witness to the desire of *homo religiosus* to regain proximity to the gods—those responsible for creating our world—and to know the presence of the divine.[7] Rather than engage in a sustained critique of such a concern, Burke simply takes statement after statement by Eliade, translating them into the terms of his own language-based philosophy, which he calls "logology." Here is an example of a pronouncement of Eliade's that is closely followed by Burke's revision:

"All creation implies a wholeness that precedes it, an *Urgrund*. Hierogamy is only one of the forms of explanation of Creation from a primordial *Urgrund*; there are other cosmogonic myths beside the hierogamic; but they all presuppose the prior existence of an undifferentiated unity." … Interpreting this passage logologically, I'd say: The "unitary" ideal of myth is entelechially implicit in the fact that language can rise by ever higher powers of generalization, until all is headed in some title (most likely image-tinged) for the principle of "Everything." Nay more, given the genius of the negative, any such term for a universal ground of Being admits of one further step, to some term for "Non-Being," viewed in turn as Being's context and quasi-temporal source. Hence, beyond *Urgrund* lies the terministic possibility of *Ungrund* (that could be imaged in terms of Night as the maternal source of all). (DS 116)

Though Burke has little to say explicitly against Eliade's origin-orientated theory (the attraction of which is not in doubt), by translating it into other terms he invites us to view it from a more detached perspective than we might otherwise adopt. What we might have taken to be the final, authoritative pronouncement on the nature of myth turns out to be provisional, partial speculation.

The conclusion to the whole essay, a fourteen-point summary, confirms this need to read any given theory in a different perspective— that is, in other terms. Point 10 reads as follows: "In adapting the principle of fulfilment that is central to the genius of the Aristotelian 'entelechy', I propose what I would call a 'logological' critique of the mythologists" (DS 117). Though Burke slightly confuses his case by using the eighteenth- to nineteenth-century term for what became more widely known in the twentieth century as "mythographers," or interpreters of myth, his following point is clear enough. It is here that the second and third terms of his essay's subtitle are seen to be intimately related: "This critique also involves my claim that the mythically tinged cult of the 'archetype' over-universalizes the nature of such symbolizing in human relations" (DS 117).

"Doing and Saying" is, typically for Burke, more a sequence of insights than a coherent argument. The fact that the conclusion takes the form of notes is indicative of Burke's habit of anticipating, but never actually providing, a summation. Or rather, he is fond of inclusive statements, but usually presents them as provisional, supplemented by promises to explore their full implications at another time. But then, that is how he wishes us to read other theorists. The paradox is that, while few thinkers have been more concerned with unifying principles, Burke sees it as his duty to interrogate all models of integration. Hence his querying of the premises of Friedman, Jensen, Eliade, and (by implication) Jung. When Burke refers to the "cult" of the archetype, he seems to have in mind any theory of myth in which the theorist himself adopts the role of tribal "myth-man," claiming to offer a "rounding out," a "symbolic doubling," a "formal culmination" of mythology. The "mythic specialist," in other words, "over-universalizes," overriding "profane" contradictions in pursuit of "sacred" unity. How fair this kind of judgment is to the theorists just named is another matter: Burke's own theorizing tends to flourish in the context of polemic.

RELATED STATEMENTS

Once again, as in the first chapter, we conclude with some soundings from elsewhere in Burke's work. Perhaps the most important point to emphasize is how important is the concept of entelechy to Burke's thinking on literature and myth. In his "Definition of Man," which appears in *Language as Symbolic Action* (1966), the same volume that includes "Myth, Poetry and Philosophy," he declares: "The principle of perfection is central to the nature of language as motive. The mere desire to name something by its 'proper' name, or to speak a language in its distinctive ways is intrinsically 'perfectionist.' What is more 'perfectionist; in essence than the impulse, when one is in dire need of something, to so state this need that one in effect 'defines' the situation? And even a poet who works out cunning ways of distorting language does so with perfectionist principles in mind ..." (*LSA* 16).

Aesthetic deviation from the linguistic norm is certainly permitted. It is even taken to be a confirmation of that norm. That is, "perfectionism" is a principle that is confirmed by both everyday and self-consciously "poetic" utterance. It is aestheticism, the isolation of art from the rest of human endeavor, that is decidedly precluded. We have already seen how myth—which is traditional, collective, and anonymous—exemplifies for Burke the "perfectionist" impulse most clearly. The urge of mythic narrative toward culmination is taken by him to fulfill the Aristotelian concept of entelechy, here explicitly extended from the natural world (where acorns insist, as it were, on realizing their potential as oaks) to human culture (where even the most inarticulate speakers insist on groping for the right word). "There is," he explains, "a principle of perfection implicit in the nature of symbol systems; and in keeping with his nature as symbol-using animal, man is moved by this principle" (*LSA* 17).

Aristotle's term, as adapted by Burke, is essential to the argument against what Burke rather misleadingly sees as an "anthropological"—or "folkloristic"—approach to myth in "Myth, Poetry and Philosophy." Speculations about historical origins should not be at the expense of recognition of narrative destinations. Similarly, in "Doing and Saying," Burke seeks to question an "overly universal" emphasis on "archetypes." In both cases the error Burke advises us to avoid is that of overlooking the present symbolic action that is the myth in favor of ideas about some previous moment from which it precedes. In this respect he commends reading the myth against the grain, so to speak. If the myth has the effect of making the present past, the myth theorist should be alert to what is involved in this "mythic reversal."

Burke addresses the specific notion of the archetype in the second of the two lectures that comprise his *Dramatism and Development* (1972): " 'archetypes' or 'prototypes' can be mythic ways of formulating entelechical implications (or possible summings-up in principle) by translating them into terms of a vaguely hypothetical past" (*DD* 43–44). More to the point, "Myth (story) translates statements about principles into archetypal, quasi-temporal terms, quite as the Latin and Greek words, *principium* and *arche* respectively, mean 'beginning' in the sense of both temporal priority and logical priority (or 'first principles'). Hence, the mythic or narrative or archetypally quasi-historical ways of saying that 'the setting up of an order makes man *in principle* subject to temptation' is to tell how the first man [i.e., Adam] said no to the first thou-shalt-not imposed upon him by the first and foremost authority [i.e., God]" (*DD* 45).

Burke has much else to say about biblical myth in his *Rhetoric of Religion*, to be considered in Chapter 4. But for now, we are chiefly interested in two central statements that he makes in this second lecture in *Dramatism and Development* and that echo earlier arguments. On the one hand he stresses that mythology generally effects what he calls "the temporizing of essence" (*DD* 44). It translates the word "principles" as "firsts," in the sense of "principals." This is a procedure necessitated by the requirements of narrative, but with the possibility of strategic use. On the other hand he points out that myth theorists might use the same technique to render their theories as persuasive as possible. Burke explains the theoretical tactic by illustration:

As a current instance of how readily an uncritical use of the arche-typal can get things backwards, consider the dialectical distortion

in Norman O. Brown's book, *Love's Body*: Dialectics involves the
two principles of composition and division (unity and plurality,
generalization and specification, etc.). An instance of division would
be terms for distinguishing between the sexes, or a distinction
between earth and sky viewed as distinct motivational realms. But
here's how quickly Brown can twist that normal resource of terminology into quasi-vatic nonsense: "Division, duality, two sexes....
Dual organization is sexual organization.... The prototype of all
opposition or contrariety is sex. The prototype of the division into
two sexes is the separation of earth and sky, Mother Earth and
Father Sky, the primal parents." "Prototype" here does the trick.
Go along with such maneuvers, and you let yourself in for total
obfuscation. To say that "sex is dialectical" would pass well enough,
in the sense that an act of copulation in effect "unifies" the duality
of the sexual partners. But give Brown his way with the archetypes
(or prototypes, he uses both words), and things get reversed
whereby dialectics is sexual; specifically, "Every sentence is dialectics, an act of love." Thus in effect a quite viable proposition, "sex
is dialectical" gets archetypally transformed into "dialectics is
sexual." And whereas it would be reasonable enough to say that
sex relations can be discussed in terms of unity and division,
Brown's ideological reversal gives us what would amount to saying
that the principles of unity and division (applications of which are
available to all language-systems) are but special cases of sex, earth,
and sky. (*DD* 47–48)

Where Fontenrose was accused of narrowing combat myth down to
its supposedly historical origins, Brown is accused of expanding
fertility myth into an all-inclusive eroticism that is assumed to constitute the human essence. Both—according to Burke—miss the point
of myth, which is inseperable from its function as form, its status as
symbolic action.

Various commentators have remarked upon Burke's interest in the
necessity of maintaining the connection between form and function,
between symbol and action. Samuel Southwell sees his thought as
requiring "a continuous and more integral conjunction of becoming
and being (time and space, function and form, process and structure)."[8] This makes sense of Burke's interest in the coexistence of the
narrative and logical principles in myth. C. Allen Carter, reflecting on
Burke's theory in the light of Robert Ornstein's influential work *The*

Psychology of Consciousness (1972), writes of "the bicameral power of myth," where "bicameral" suggests a dual organization of the human mind: "Whether going backward to the ancestral or forward to the final, the language system (or its users) can translate any part of its 'timeless' relationships into the elements of a story—and then can collapse these back into a set of philosophical 'first principles.' If the former is the temporizing of the essence, the latter is the spatializing of the temporal.'" To use the structuralist terminology, we are always interpreting the world either synchronically or diachronically.[9]

The structuralist connection is made more emphatically by Frank Lentricchia, who refers to Burke's "anticipation of Lévi-Strauss and company." But Lentricchia also refers to Burke's implicit "critique of structuralism." For Lentricchia, Burke's work is about "diachrony, difference, and dialectic" rather than a pure "system," even though it frequently looks as though Burke is about to formulate such a system. Hence the best term to describe his project would be, Lentricchia thinks, "critical structuralism."[10] Timothy Crusius, however, makes a good case for *not* aligning Burke with the structuralist program, no matter the qualification, since by definition structuralism is an attempt to abstract the hidden code of language from its specific manifestations. "Distinguish *langue* from *parole*, and make *langue* the object of scientific study," writes Crusius. "Language is thus detached from use, and therefore from context of situation—and because detached from situation, detached also from society and history.... Language removed from communication and community is not language. Because language for him is always language in use, Burke is not a structuralist."[11] Nevertheless, Lentricchia's phrase has been influential. It might prove useful if we are sure to emphasize that epithet "critical," for we may say that Burke offers a critique of structuralist abstraction, even while anticipating its concern for the "grammar of myth." Crusius's emphasis on "language in use" is salutary.

If we are interested in pursuing this connection, the name of Jean-Pierre Vernant might be the appropriate one to consider. Vernant, founder of the Center for Comparative Research on Ancient Societies, reads Greek mythology in terms of structure, but not in the spirit of pure structuralism. That is, he is interested in the way a given myth makes sense within, and makes sense of, a specific culture. The question Vernant repeatedly asks is: "What is the link between the semantic space revealed by structural analysis as the myth's intellectual framework and the sociohistorical context in which myth was produced?"[12]

His answer usually involves a detailed exposition of the economic, political, social, and sexual context of the myth, with a particular eye on the cultural "contradictions" to which it applies its "cunning intelligence." Vernant resists the abstraction of Claude Lévi-Strauss, who sees myth as reflective of the structure of the mind rather than of society.[13] However, Vernant's attempt to reconcile the structural with the historical dimensions of myth is confined to the study of antiquity, and so it would be fair to say that he lacks the scope and circumference of Burke's theory.

But whichever epithet we choose, and whomever we care to compare him with, it should be clear enough that Burke is concerned with function and process as much as with form and structure and that his interest in these aspects is both wide and deep. When he opposes the paradigm of poetics to anthropological or archetypal approaches to myth, he is not thereby commending a narrowly literary analysis. Indeed, Burke's *Language as Symbolic Action* includes an essay entitled "Formalist Criticism: Its Principles and Limits," in which he unequivocally states that "the study of Poetics proper does not encompass the entire field of symbolic action; hence a theory of language in general can treat Poetics as but one aspect of the total subject matter" (*LSA* 485). This statement should clear up any misunderstanding about the nature of Burke's myth theory: though he consistently advocates a literary-critical approach to myth, this approach is only as a means to getting to the heart of what "symbol-using" involves.

The reader may, of course, decide that, if we are to avoid the term "formalism" in characterizing Burke's theory, we should avoid the term "structuralism," which is equally misleading. Many commentators have attempted to coin a phrase that will capture Burke's spirit, but few have succeeded. As one that comes very close, we might cite Robert Wess, who praises Burke for his "rhetorical realism," which he opposes to the "rhetorical idealism" of the North American disciples of Jacques Derrida. As Wess summarizes Burke's stance, "Language as action structures our lived relation to the real. . . . The real is gauged in the act, a prioritizing of this rather than that. The necessity of prioritizing is the constraint that rhetorical realism recognizes. Burke's premise is that language is action posits the act as the form in which language registers this constraint. As action, language inscribes rhetorical sayability rather than either enlightenment certainty or romantic authenticity. Charting that inscription is what Burke's dramatism is all about."[14]

This statement may help confirm some of the inferences we have made in the course of our exposition so far. However, the word "dramatism" requires further exposition. We next turn to Burke's notion of social life as a "ritual drama," which will allow us to make further sense of his "literary" theory of myth.

3

MYTH AND "RITUAL DRAMA"

The quoted phrase used in this chapter's title is Kenneth Burke's, but the conjunction of "ritual" with "drama" does not, of course, originate with him. It might be helpful to begin this chapter with a brief account of the modern development of interest in the *dromenon*. This is the Greek term for "rite," which literally means "the thing done"; and, as the "thing" is collectively "done," it is the root of our word "drama." Two names stand out in this development: those of J. G. Frazer and Jane Harrison.

The idea that mythology is best explained by reference to ritual is most widely associated with the work of J. G. Frazer, the classics scholar of the late nineteenth and early twentieth centuries.[1] His "comparative method," by which he tried to discover the meaning of ceremonies that seemed to vary only slightly from place to place and from time to time, and of the narratives that accompanied them, relied on the principle of "universalism," which assumed a common humanity; but the basis for this principle in turn was the rationalism that Frazer had inherited from the eighteenth-century Enlightenment. Thus inevitably, despite his exhaustive documentation of rituals, Frazer found some difficulty in entering into the spirit of "savage" custom and belief. However, with *The Golden Bough*, which reached twelve fat volumes in its third and final edition (1911–1915), he persuaded many writers of the modernist period that the origin of religion, civilization, and art lay in a certain kind of ritual, which was the enactment of a fertility myth. The ritual enacting the death and rebirth of the fertility god was an attempt to ensure the cycle of vegetation, and thereby the survival of the community. The myth was the story of the death and rebirth of the fertility god. Frazer's "myth and ritual theory" delineated a special connection between the god and the land itself, the link being fertility. As the god went, so went the crops. While arguing that the origin of civilization lay in fertility myth and ritual, Frazer believed that the future lay with rational, scientific progress.

Frazer's model of cultural evolution, a fusion of Charles Darwin's model of natural evolution with Enlightenment principles, works roughly in a series of stages. The first stage is that of sheer magic: here there is ritual but no myth, since the purpose is the manipulation of impersonal forces of nature. One imitates the falling of rain so that the rain will fall from the sky. The second stage is that of sheer religion: here the impersonal forces of nature have become personified as deities, so we have myth as well as ritual, but the connection between the two here is loose. One performs a rain dance to please the god and thereby persuaded him to send rain. It is only when magic and religion are combined that we get the kind of scenario described at length in *The Golden Bough*. As Robert Segal explains:

> [Here] myth describes the life of the god of vegetation, and ritual enacts the myth, or at least that portion of the myth describing the death and rebirth of the god. The ritual operates on the basis of the Law of Similarity, according to which the imitation of an action causes it to happen. The ritual does not manipulate vegetation directly. Rather, it manipulates the god of vegetation.... The assumption that vegetation is under the control of a god is the legacy of religion. The assumption that vegetation can be controlled is the legacy of magic. The combination of myth and ritual is the combination of religion and magic.[2]

In the interests of accuracy, we should add, as Segal does, that Frazer proffered two different versions of "myth and ritual theory." In the first version of the myth, the death and rebirth of the god of vegetation are ritually acted out. The king, who is a human being, at most plays the role of the god. In the second version the fate of the land depends on the king, in whom the god resides, rather than the god himself. Thus the myth, which recounts the death and rebirth of the god, has now only a tenuous connection with the ritual. However, though this second version had a profound influence on later mythographers such as S. H. Hooke and Lord Raglan, it is the first version that is normally taken to be Frazer's position.

The third full stage is that of science, which Frazer takes to mark the evolution of humanity beyond magic and religion—and so beyond ritual and myth. Frazer associates magic and religion with the infancy of humanity's evolution or, where surviving, with the residual "savagery" of contemporary peasants. Frazer assumes that they are incompatible with modernity, magic being the primitive counterpart to science, which simply does not work, and religion being a further mystification of the relationship between humanity and nature. Magic, he tells us, is "a spurious system of natural law as well as a fallacious guide of conduct; it is a false science as well as an abortive art."[3] Religion "involves, first, a belief in superhuman beings who rule the world, and, second, an attempt to win their favour"; thus, unlike magic, it "clearly assumes that the course of nature is to some extent elastic or variable, and that we can persuade or induce the mighty beings who control it to deflect, for our benefit, the current of events from the channel in which they would otherwise flow."[4] However, though the religious attitude contradicts the magical attitude, "savage" thinking has always tended to confuse the two. If in the archaic past "the functions of priest and sorcerer were often combined or, to speak perhaps more correctly, were not yet differentiated from each other," Frazer notes that "the same confusion of ideas" crops up among "the ignorant classes of modern Europe."[5] He regards this residual "ignorance" as an offense to his own faith in the rational project of the Enlightenment: "It is not our business here to consider what bearings the permanent existence of such a solid layer of savagery beneath the surface of society, and unaffected by the superficial changes of religion and culture, has upon the future of humanity. The dispassionate observer, whose studies have led him to plumb its depths, can hardly regard it otherwise than as a standing menace to civilization. We seem to move on a thin crust which may at any moment be rent by the subterranean forces slumbering below."[6]

How "dispassionate" this is as a judgment on the mass of humanity may be left for the reader to decide. Consider also the following reflection on the consequences of the combination of magic and religion: "If mankind had always been logical and wise, history would not be a long chronicle of folly and crime."[7]

Yet despite Frazer's observations about the "ignorance" and "savagery" represented by magic and religion, and in particular their combination, his documentation of rituals and myths of fertility—those of Adonis, Osiris, Tammuz, and other ancient deities—proved hugely influential. In particular, the "Cambridge Ritualists" set out to explore the implications of the central *agon* of the dying and reviving god, while tempering his rationalist assumptions. It was with them that the implications of the word *dromenon* were explored. They applied the pattern to a study of literature, and drama in particular, which allowed them to draw many parallels between archaic culture and the "mature" civilization of the ancient Greeks. The key ritualist was Jane E. Harrison.

Accepting Frazer's basic account of the connection between myth and ritual, Harrison sought to go beyond him. Inspired by thinkers as diverse as Henri Bergson, Emile Durkheim, and Friedrich Nietzsche, she sought to relate the ritual of fertility to the ritual of initiation into society. In doing so, however, Harrison made myth an effect of ritual, rather than that which gave it meaning. The idea of a divinity was the result of the sense of enthusiasm engendered by the ceremony. Subsequently, the god became a god of vegetation, and the myth told was one of death and rebirth, just as the ritual of initiation merged with that of the death and rebirth of crops. In due course, the initiation theme was subsumed by the fertility theme. However, while arguing that a merging of two kinds of ritual was the basis of myth, Harrison was chiefly concerned with how, once they were both fully established, ritual and myth comprised an imaginative unity.

Insisting that the two forms were inseparable, in her *Themis* (1912) Harrison asserts: "The primary meaning of myth ... is the spoken correlative of the acted rite, the thing done."[8] Later, Harrison went as far as to say that the two forms actually arose together, even though such a view contradicts her earlier speculations.

One of Harrison's most important influences was on literary studies. This was because she not only sought to explain ritual in relation to myth but also sought to relate both to drama. The key work here is *Ancient Art and Ritual* (1913), in which she seeks to demonstrate that art and ritual "have a common root, and that neither can be understood without the other. It is at the outset the same impulse that sends a man to church and to the theatre."[9] Taking her cue from hints in Aristotle's *Poetics,* and encouraged by her reading of Frazer and Nietzsche in particular, she conjectures that as the power of myth waned, ritual developed into art, which inherited its central, collective function. Thus the ancient Greek drama was rooted in the archaic ritual of the dying and reviving god. The pattern of death and revival was the source of the complementary genres of tragedy and comedy. (This insight was particularly influential on the classicists Gilbert Murray and F. M. Cornford, scholars of tragedy and comedy, respectively.) Harrison concludes, however, that ritual and art must finally be distinguished, since the ritual always has a practical end—whereas the art does not. While both involve an imitation of life—that is, while both may be deemed "mimetic"—art is not intended to issue in a tangible result: "The end of art is itself." Ritual, however, *"makes, as it were, a bridge between real life and art,* a bridge over which in primitive times man must pass."[10] Thus, despite being less of a doctrinaire rationalist than Frazer, Harrison continued to work within his evolutionist model, whereby the "savage" soul was thought to stand in need of refinement, which art—more "sophisticated" than ritual—would in due time provide.

It is not my intention to suggest that Frazer and Harrison influenced Burke, though he could hardly have been unaware of them in his early writing years. As far as Frazer is concerned, we see that Burke certainly considers himself obliged to question the model of cultural evolutionism. As far as Harrison is concerned, we may say that Burke appears to be cognizant of her insights into the function of the *dromenon* in Greek civilization. However, what we will be interested in is the way Burke develops his own theory of "ritual drama," which rejects the idea that rites are "things done" only in the distant past or, if in the present, only in the context of the church or theater. Burke's philosophy of dramatism sees humanity as always and everywhere engaged in ritualistic behavior.

RITUAL AND REVELATION

Burke's first theoretical work, *Counter-Statement* (1931), consists of essays written during the later 1920s, revised and ordered so as to represent the broad development of his early thought. As we shall see, it is especially illuminating about the nature of ritual. But first we need to register its significance as a representatively Burkean enterprise.

In the preface to the second edition, published in 1952, Burke notes with "unqualified delight" that "the book begins on the word 'perhaps' and ends on the word 'norm' " (*CS* xi). That is, it is characterized by tentativeness, but it knows where it is going. This observation evinces a trend characteristic of Burke: an exploration of human potential in the act of defining certain indispensable human standards. William Rueckert sees the title of the book as implying a rhetorical intervention in a world that seems to have lost touch with its humanity: "Burke's central point is that the poet, and his interpreter, the critic, are ... counter-agents who perform a vital social function by perceiving the most serious deviations from the sane moral norm and combating them with the counter-forces and counter-statements of poetry."[11] In other words, the present historical conditions must, according to Burke, be challenged from a perspective that aspires to be transhistorical.

A shallowly progressive view of human understanding will not suffice, for Burke sees it as his duty to resist the assumption that the past is always to be he thought of as inferior to the present. For instance, reflecting that whereas in medieval times beliefs were founded mainly on religion they are now increasingly founded on science, he refuses to choose between them: "There is perhaps no essential difference between religious and scientific 'foundations' ... as religion is probably only the outgrowth of magic, itself a 'science' based on theories of causation which were subsequently modified or discredited" (*CS* 163). "Magic, religion, and science are alike in that they foster a body of thought concerning the nature of the universe and man's relation to it. All three offer possibilities for the artist in so far as they tend to make some beliefs prevalent or stable" (*CS* 163). Clearly, Burke is aware of Frazer's scheme, but he rejects Frazer's assumption that the stage of science necessitates the rejection of the stages of magic and religion. Similarly, where Frazer sees myth and ritual as effectively outmoded, Burke is arguing for their permanent power.

In these, his earliest speculations on the nature of ritual, Burke is deliberately extending the notion beyond the specific context of magical or religious practice. Thus, in considering in more detail the question of what constitutes "aesthetic truth," he speculates that "The relation between 'scientific' and 'aesthetic' truth might be likened to the relation between revelation and ritual. Revelation is 'scientific,' whether its 'truth' be founded upon magic, religion, or laboratory experiment. Revelation is 'belief,' or 'fact.' Art enters when this revelation is ritualized, when it is converted into a symbolic process" (*CS* 168).

This alarmingly sweeping statement runs the risk of conflating too many ideas at once. Still, let us try to trace its logic. Ritual has always sought to influence people's attitudes, even while it claims to be having a causal effect on nature. The participants in the ceremonies documented by Frazer were being brought together as a community in anticipation of the beneficial result of an act representing cyclical renewal. Art, even more obviously, involves an appeal to the needs of its audience. In that respect it is inseparable from rhetoric.

Burke's next move is to argue that form itself needs to be understood in the context of rhetoric. An essay in *Counter-Statement*, "Psychology and Form," offers, on a modest scale, an understanding of the nature of literature as a social, communicative phenomenon. It begins with an account of the first scene of William Shakespeare's *Hamlet*, reflecting on the anticipation likely to be felt by the audience as it waits for the appearance of the ghost of the prince's murdered father. This anticipation demonstrates for Burke that "psychology" and "form" are best defined vis-à-vis each other. "That is, the psychology here is not the psychology of the *hero*, but the psychology of the *audience*. And by that distinction, form would be the psychology of the audience. Or, seen from another angle, form is the creation of an appetite in the mind of the auditor, and the adequate satisfying of that appetite" (*CS* 31).

This process makes form almost identical with ritual, since both can be said to be *doing* something for those who witness the event: their ultimate justification is pragmatic. Thus the *revelation* of art and the change of mood wrought by *ritual* suggest to Burke that they both come under the broader category of "rhetoric," which is the underlying preoccupation of the whole book. In "Psychology and Form," rhetoric is treated under the aspect of "eloquence." Far from being defined as "showiness," Burke proposes that eloquence be thought of, in the aesthetic context, as the result of "that desire in the artist to make a work perfect" by adapting it to "the racial [i.e., the human race's] appetites" (*CS* 41). For the psychology of form indicates that the "truth" revealed by art, as with that of ritual, is "not the discovery of facts, not an addition of human knowledge in the scientific sense of the word" but rather, "the exercise of human propriety, the formulation of symbols which rigidify our sense of poise and rhythm" (*CS* 42).

Burke is proposing that "form" is the key to psychological fulfillment. But as yet this suggestion is tenuous. In the following essay, "The Poetic Process," his case becomes stronger. Art, he declares, has always appealed to certain "forms of the mind" that are "constant" and "innate." In a religious context they are comparable with Plato's "archetypes, or pure ideas, existing in heaven." But for Burke, the principle of a permanent form makes sense even if we do not feel inclined to attribute it to a supernatural source:

> For we need but take his universals out of heaven and situate them in the human mind (a process begun by Kant), making them not metaphysical, but psychological. Instead of divine forms, we now have "conditions of appeal." ... The researches of anthropologists indicate that man has "progressed" in cultural cycles which repeat themselves in essence (in form) despite the limitless variety of specific

details to embody such essences, or forms. Speech, material traits (for instance, tools), art, mythology, religion, social systems, property, government, and war—these are the nine "potentials" which man continually re-individuates into specific channels, and which anthropologists call the "universal pattern." And when we speak of psychological universals, we mean simply that just as there is inborn in the germ-plasm of a dog the potentiality of barking, so there is inborn in the germ-plasm of man the potentiality of speech, art, mythology, and so on. And while these potentialities are continually changing their external aspects, their "individuations," they do not change in essence. (*CS* 48)

Though there appears to be something cavalier about the apparently arbitrary listing of the nine "potentials," the inclusion of mythology is important. For if myth appears negative by virtue of its association with war, it is associated also with speech, tools, and art.

We can expect, then, that the tension between "the universal pattern," or "psychological universal," and the "individuation" will be evident in the "channels" of mythology and art alike. In both cases the essential form will be "an arousing and fulfilment of desires," to use the definition given in the "Lexicon Rhetoricae" that constitutes the final essay of the book. To this definition Burke appends an explanation: "A work has form in so far as one part of it leads a reader [or audience] to anticipate another part, to be gratified by the sequence" (*CS* 124).

The most obvious example of such a process is narrative, which only enforces for Burke the importance of mythology. If the form of a narrative involves anticipation and gratification, then myth retains its link with ritual. Both are pragmatic in that they seek to induce an effect. While it may be confusing to see the early Burke move without explicit transition from myth to ritual to literature, sometimes in the course of one short paragraph, it is important to understand the underlying assumption: there are universal patterns; there is a basic human need for formal resolution. As Burke puts it in this final essay: "There are some stock patterns of experience which seem to arise out of any system of living." He provides his own list of examples: "the return of youth (Faust legend, the man who came back); persecution at the hands of those whom one would benefit (Christ legend) . . . Judas psychology (poignancy of harming a friend—Agamemnon sacrificing his daughter—Brutus conspiring against Caesar for the good of the state)," and so forth. He uses one other instance, "*per aspera ad astra* (attainment through difficulty)," to illustrate how the appeal of the universal pattern will depend on its individuation. For though "the many avid readers" of "our modern 'success literature' ... would find little to entice them in ... *The Quest of the Golden Fleece*," that does not discredit the pattern, and it indicates the need for varied expression (*CS* 171). As we read earlier in the "Lexicon": "Each work re-embodies the formal principles in different subject-matter" (*CS* 143). This process never ends.

Indeed, Burke surmises that the best proof that there is an "individuation of forms" is the fact that there is a "re-individuation of forms." "Perhaps the most elaborate re-individuation in all history is James Joyce's *Ulysses*. But whereas in most instances the purpose of the new individuation is to make changes which reproduce under one set of conditions an effect originally obtained under another set of conditions, in the case of *Ulysses* each individuation is given a strictly 'un-Homeric' equivalent. The new individuations intentionally alter the effect. The *Ulysses* is the Anti-Odyssey" (*CS* 149). Burke proposes here that the universal patterns are especially associated with ancient narrative—that is, with myth, rather too vaguely treated here as synonymous with derivative forms such as epic and legend. But he is also arguing that myth will survive through literary adaptation. Mythology, far from being outmoded, as it is for Frazer, acquires greater significance in time. Joyce's novel renews the Homeric model even as it confirms it—just as Homer did, presumably, with the mythic material he himself inherited. Of course, literature for Frazer is not myth, but at most only the legacy of myth.

MAGIC AND PIETY

In his next book, *Permanence and Change* (1935), Burke begins to elaborate on some of the conjectures contained in *Counter-Statement*. The affirmation of magic and religion and the skepticism toward the claims of science are reaffirmed at some length. Indeed, magic, religion, and science are regarded as alternative "orientations," or general views of the world relying on the human capacity for "symbol-making," all three of which are indispensable. Alternatively put, magic, religion, and science are three "orders of rationalization" that Burke summarizes as follows: "Magic as the schema which stressed mainly the control of natural forces, religion stressing the control of human forces, and science stressing the control of the third productive order, the technological" (*PC* 59). This last definition may seem to put the proverbial cart before the horse, given that technology is usually taken to be the appliance of an existing science, but the point is that in the modern world they seem inseparable. Burke's proposal is that the very idea that magic and religion could simply be superseded in the name of the third makes no sense, given that each "orientation" is equally a manifestation of the urge toward symbolic expression. For Frazer, we recall, the fact that magical and religious thinking survives into modernity may be a fact, but it is also a cause for rationalist regret.

The basis for Burke's argument is that, if artistic form is analogous to ritual, and if ritual is an indispensable human need, then neither art nor ritual can be denied without distortion and damage to humanity. Here the argument is consolidated by the introduction of a new term, "piety." Burke writes: "Santayana has somewhere defined piety as loyalty to the sources of our being. Such a notion should suggest that piety is not confined to the strictly religious sphere. It would as well be present when the potter moulds the clay to exactly that form which completely gratifies his sense of how it ought to be" (*PC* 71). The modern, mature, rational adult may hope to live without piety, but it is impossible. Burke explains that "should he take an axe and fell a great tree, we need not be surprised to find a strange misgiving permeate him as the noble symbol of shelter comes crashing to the earth. For however neutral his act, though the tree had been felled to satisfy the simple utilitarian needs of firewood, there may also be lurking here a kind of symbolic parricide. Not only firewood, but a parent-symbol, may be brought down in the crash" (*PC* 71).

There is, Burke implies, a residual reverence that we can still trace back to the infancy of humanity, even when we wish to assert that piety makes no rational sense. Given the link between ritual and art, we can rely on artists to intuit the continuing need:

> It is possible that much of the anguish affecting poets in the modern world is due to the many symbolic outrages which a purely utilitarian philosophy of action requires us to commit. In primitive eras, when the utilitarian processes were considerably fewer, and more common to the entire group, definite proprietary rituals seem to have arisen as a way of canceling off these symbolic offenses. In the magical orientation (so close to that of poetry), if the felling of a tree had connotations of symbolic parricide, the group would probably develop a corresponding ritual of symbolic expiation. The offender would thus have a technique for cleansing himself of the sin he had committed. (*PC* 72)

Hence an apparently outmoded orientation may turn out to have distinct advantages for the human psyche, and thus prove permanent. Magic cannot be dismissed any more than ritual itself can be. Rather, it is the implicit contention here that piety will manifest itself in some form or other, even in the most secularized context.[12]

Burke reflects further on the link between poetry and the first of the three orientations later in the book. He claims that the rituals of "homeopathic magic" by which "the savage attempts to coerce the processes of the universe" are precisely those of the "pathetic fallacy." (That term, coined by the nineteenth-century art critic John Ruskin, refers to the anthropomorphising of natural phenomena: skies weep, flowers blush, and so forth.) Going further, Burke seeks to make the jump from ritual (archaic in origin, and still evident in modernity) to rhetoric (ancient in formulation and still evident in modernity): "In the magical rationalization, the verbal and mimetic devices whereby men induce one another to respond in sympathy were transferred to the field of inanimate operations—and in keeping with the logic of this attitude, the operations themselves were taken to be animatedly motivated" (*PC* 216) If this seems obscure let me refer to a later and clearer formulation of the same idea, from *A Rhetoric of Motives* (1950). Here there is no doubt that Burke is saying that magic derives from rhetoric. "Originally, the magical use of symbolism to affect natural processes by rituals and incantations was a mistaken transference of a proper linguistic function to an area for which it was not fit. The realistic use of addressed language to *induce action in people* became the magical use of addressed language to *induce motion in things* (things by nature alien to purely linguistic orders of motivation)" (*RM* 42).

Again, we might object that Burke seems to be contradicting his own affirmation of the legitimacy of magic against the claim to superiority by science, for he is now in effect treating it as an erroneous adaptation of language. But we have already seen that he defends the magical dimension of ritual by way of a parallel with the imaginative dimension of poetry: both are essential activities of the "symbol-using animal." The object of his scorn here would seem to be those who attempt to dismiss rhetoric as mere "verbal magic," by which phrase both of these activities are dismissed as irrational. Burke's argument is consistent, if we are prepared to make the necessary concessions and inferences.

It is true that Burke is guilty of smuggling in large assumptions and of making breathtaking associations—as when he goes on, in the section from *Permanence and Change* quoted, to assert, "In the field of psychology, homeopathic magic is effective and necessary. A persuasive work of art is nothing else" (PC 216). But a flair for hyperbole and provocative connotation is not, of course, a reason to reject the essential ideas, for underlying the insistence on seeing magic at work everywhere is not so much a desire to demean modern rationality as a desire to remind the reader of the dangers of hubris. We should think twice before rejecting a primitive, childish past in the name of a sophisticated, mature present. Just when we consider ourselves to be most clear and coherent, there may well lurk residual interests, anxieties, and errors.

Burke draws on the American pragmatist philosopher John Dewey's concept of "occupational psychosis" to support his point of view:

> Professor Dewey suggests that a tribe's ways of gaining sustenance promote certain specific patterns of thought which, since thought is an aspect of action, assist the tribe in its productive and distributive operations.... Once this [occupational] psychosis is established by the authority of the food-getting patterns (which are certainly primary as regards problems of existence) it is carried over into other aspects of tribal culture. Thus, a tribe which lives by the hunt may be expected to reveal a corresponding hunt pattern in its marriage rites, where the relation between man and woman may show a marked similarity to the relationship between huntsman and quarry. The woman will be ritually *seized*. (PC 38–39)

Burke extrapolates from this example to make some cultural comparisons. "As further corroboration of this, we might note the contrasting emphasis upon the traditional, in the art and thought of agrarian cultures, which would naturally stress the periodically recurrent, the lore of the seasons, the astronomical fixities, etc., as basic to their productive system. And today, our psychotic openness to fads, the great cry for innovation engendered by competitive capitalism, could seem to be in keeping with the marked unstableness of our economic and social expectancies" (PC 39).

These historical observations culminate in a bold attempt at a transhistorical summation. Burke reflects on the ambiguity involved in all human action and all human thinking. "Any performance," he explains, "is discussible either from the standpoint of what it *attains* or what it *misses*. Comprehensiveness can be dismissed as superficiality, intensiveness as stricture, tolerance as uncertainty.... A way of seeing is also a way of not seeing—a focus upon object A involves a neglect of object B" (*PC* 49). In light of Burke's earlier reflections on magic, religion, and science as "orientations," we might say that he is inclined to accept that they each involve a "way of seeing" that is also a "way of not seeing," and that the best strategy to adopt is to give each of them its due. However, Burke has more to say on the question of how we become conscious of our human limitations and how this consciousness bears on certain mythic or ritualistic forms.

COMEDY AND REBIRTH

The back cover of the 1986 paperback edition of *Attitudes Toward History* (originally published in 1937) claims that it "marks Kenneth Burke's breakthrough from literary and aesthetic criticism into social theory and the philosophy of history." This is a fair claim, but the literary context still remains. Burke is here thinking through the implications of the various literary genres—in particular, that of comedy. One of the most important elements in Burke's thesis is his advocacy of what he calls the "comic frame," a necessary corrective to human arrogance.

The "comic frame," Burke tells us, would "enable people *to be observers of themselves, while acting. Its ultimate would not be passiveness*, but *maximum consciousness*. One would "transcend" himself by noting his own foibles. He would provide a rationale for locating the irrational and the non-rational" (*ATH* 171). Hence even Frazer, who was so eager for science to supersede "savage" delusions and so regretful about the persistence of superstition and credulity, would find himself enlisted in the cause:

> The materials for such a frame by no means require a new start. They are all about us.... The comic frame is present in the best of psychoanalytic criticism. It is highly present in anthropological catalogues like that of Frazer's *Golden Bough* which, by showing us the rites of magical purification in primitive peoples, gives us the necessary cues for the detection of similar processes in even the most practical and non-priestly of contemporary acts.... Yet, while never permitting itself to overlook the admonitions of even the most caustic social criticism, [the comic frame] does not *waste* the world's rich store of error, as those parochial-minded persons waste it who dismiss all thought before a certain date as "ignorance" and "superstition."

> Instead, it cherishes the lore of so-called "error" as a *genuine aspect of the truth*, with emphases valuable for the correcting of present emphases. (*ATH* 172)

Frazer would become an unwitting exponent of a projected "folk criticism," the complement of "folk art." Burke is not hereby adopting an "aesthetic" approach: the appeal of these phrases for him is not, he assures us, their "picturesque" value. Rather, he is referring to "a collective philosophy of motivation, arising to name the relationships, or social situations, which people have found so pivotal and so constantly recurring as to need names for them" (*ATH* 173). By making "metaphorical migrations" from the sphere of primitive magic to the sphere of modern thought, Burke demonstrates the "translative act" that is at the heart of "the comic frame." For frame "considers human life as a project in 'composition,' where the poet works with the materials of social relationships. Composition, translation, also 'revision,' hence offering maximum opportunity for the resources of *criticism*" (*ATH* 173). Considering human life in this way affords a "*charitable* attitude towards people," thus facilitating cooperation while at the same time maintaining our "shrewdness." That is, to give the benefit of the doubt is not to become wholly gullible (*ATH* 166). We have already seen Burke's working within such a "frame" in his questioning the idea that it might be possible to leave the magical "orientation" behind. Instead of accusing Frazer of arrogance, he simply translates Frazer's thesis into "comic" terms.

The notion of human life as "a project in 'composition'" allows Burke to look at cultural and philosophical positions in a new light by shifting perspective and placing them in surprising contexts. A good example of "metaphorical migration" occurs in a discussion in the book of techniques of "transcendence." Burke argues that both art and philosophy provide evidence of an essentially human urge to transcend a situation by the resolution of dialectical opposites. This pattern may be seen as originating in ritual or, in complementary fashion, it may be seen as a "psychological universal" of the kind that we discover in myth. For example, Burke refers to "the tragic rejoicing of the *Liebestod*" in Richard Wagner's opera *Tristan and Isolde* as "a bit of magic whereby the composer transcendentally puts life and death together" (*ATH* 89). This magic results in the translation of "love" into "life," of "life" into "death," and of "death" into "new life." He then goes on, in a typically Burkean leap of speculation, to discuss G. W. F. Hegel and Karl Marx, noting that "Hegel 'transcended' by using a dialectic of *historic* process as a way of resolving metaphysical opposites.... Marx secularized the Hegelian pattern (though retaining unavowed vestiges of godhead, a covert 'god-function,' in the idea that social antitheses would be reconciled by a 'higher' synthesis). Marx's attacks upon the established symbols of authority seem likewise to have stimulated some sense of guilt, for he identifies himself in 'pastoral' fashion with a suffering proletariat, who must redeem the world by blood-sacrifice" (*ATH* 90)—an echo of the death of Frazer's king.

One important effect of these startling shifts of perspective is to demonstrate the persistence of the kind of thinking that positivism would say we should have left behind. Marxism, as in Burke's essay "Revolutionary Symbolism in America," is depicted as a modern myth based in archaic ritual. However, even though we have seen Burke trying to put the term "ritual" into some sort of context in *Counter-Statement,* he decides that the nature of ritual merits even more explicit attention toward the end of *Attitudes Toward History.* As might be expected, the context is literary:

> The organization of a [literary] work can be considered with relation to a "key" symbol of authority. The work is a ritual whereby the poet takes inventory with reference to the acceptance or rejection of this authority.... Authority symbols of the mature adult involve such intellectualistic or philosophical concepts as church, state, society, political party, craft. They are largely "forensic." (*ATH* 209)

"Forensic" is an important term for Burke. Referring specifically to courts of law, and thus to crime, its etymology is wider: derived from the Latin *forum,* it reminds us of the dramatic quality of experience. Burke even sees society as a drama, as we shall see.

For Burke, each new situation, being implicitly dramatic demands the adoption of a new relationship to forensic structures. Once again, literature is our guide: the literary work involves a ritual of "rebirth," the enactment of a change of identity. This change involves "symbolic regression" to the "pre-forensic, pre-political ('autistic') level of informative experience, even when symbolizing [the author's] concern with purely forensic matter" (*ATH* 210). For example, the relations between king and subject might be figured in the relations between parent and child: "The bearing of the forensic upon the autistic introduces such ingredients as symbolic parricide (when rejection is uppermost) and incest-awe, with symbolic castration (when acceptance is uppermost)" (*ATH* 210).

The change of identity of a character in a literary work, whereby "he is at once the same man and a new man," will often be seen to give him a new perspective on reality, perhaps even powers of foresight. For example, in Thomas Mann's *Joseph and His Brothers*, we see that "Joseph is not equipped to be a 'prophet' until he has been reborn in the pit" (*ATH* 210). This idea leads Burke to a wider speculation: "Rebirth is a process of socialization, since it is a ritual whereby the poet fits himself to accept necessities suggested by the problems of the forensic. It will also, as regression, involve concern with the 'womb-heaven' of the embryo, and with the 'first revolution' that took place when the embryo developed to the point where its 'shelter' became 'confinement.' Hence, when you examine this ritual, you find such symbols as the 'pit,' a symbolic return-to, and return-from the womb" (*ATH* 210–211).

The necessary ambiguity of the rebirth pattern is that the ascent into lightness and life only makes sense given the descent into darkness and death: comedy and tragedy are intimately linked. It is perhaps surprising that Burke chooses not to invoke Frazer again, since the pattern of the dying and reviving god of vegetation would confirm this idea that the tragic and the comic are two aspects of the same myth. Moreover, the myth being rooted in ritual, Burke might have made much of the fact that tragedy and comedy are the two main forms of literary drama in the west. Harrison and her fellow "Cambridge Ritualists" such as Murray and Cornford had demonstrated the debt owed by the two main genres of Greek theater to the twofold pattern of the archaic myth and ritual pattern worked out by Frazer. Certainly, this kind of speculation informs the work of a later myth theorist who was greatly influenced by both Frazer and Burke, namely Northrop Frye.[13] Instead, Burke chooses to explore the social function of these forms, in accordance with his forensic emphasis.

The great tragedians of ancient Greece, from whom Aristotle derived his ideas about the name and nature of tragedy, wrote drama based on the *agon* of the courtroom. As Burke points out:

> Their plays, we might say, are complex trials by jury, with plaintiff, defendant, attorneys, judges, and jury all rolled into one—or, otherwise stated, we get in one piece the offence, the sentence, and the expiation. The magical concept of fatality [evident in the earlier

forms of myth and epic] remain (the *participation mystique* whereby divine dispositions are concerned with human destinies), but they must be fused with the new forensic materials.... The rise of business individualism sharpened the awareness of personal ambitions as a motive in human acts, but the great tragic playwrights were pious, orthodox, conservative, "reactionary" in their attitudes towards it; hence they made pride, *hubris*, the basic sin, and "welcomed" it by tragic ambiguity, surrounding it with the connotations of crime. Their frame of acceptance admonished one to "resign" himself to a sense of his limitations. They *feared* good fortune, as the first sign of punishment from the gods. Among contemporary psychologists, schooled to the norms of bourgeois thought, this attitude is usually considered as an aspect of pathology. (*ATH* 38–39)

If we bear in mind that a "frame of acceptance" is a means of maintaining individual and social health, the myth and ritual pattern of death and rebirth still underlines Burke's thinking here. But again, turning from the tragic to the comic, he resists the temptation to overplay the Frazerian card of myth and ritual, confining himself to the sphere of values: "Like tragedy, comedy warns against the dangers of pride, but its emphasis shifts from *crime* to *stupidity*" (*ATH* 41). As he explains: "The progress of humane enlightenment can go no further than in picturing people not as *vicious*, but as *mistaken*. When you add that people are *necessarily* mistaken, that *all* people are exposed to situations in which they must act as fools, that *every* insight contains its own special kind of blindness, you complete the comic circle, returning again to the lesson of humility that underlies great tragedy" (*ATH* 41). As Burke puts it in *Permanence and Change*, any "way of seeing" is also a "way of not seeing"; every "insight" involves its own "blindness."[14]

This lesson is learned differently, however, depending on the dramatic context. Tragedy tends more toward the "fatalistic," says Burke, whereas comedy tends more toward the "forensic," though both tendencies are evident in either form. "In the tragic plot," Burke explains, "the *deus ex machina* is always lurking, to give events a fatalistic turn in accordance with the old '*participation*' pattern whereby men anthropomorphize nature, feeling its force as the taking of sides with them or against them. Comedy must develop logical forensic causality to its highest point, calling not upon astronomical marvels to help shape the plot, but completing the process of internal organization whereby each event is deduced 'syllogistically' from the premises of the informing situation. Comedy deals with *man in society*, tragedy with the *cosmic man*" (*ATH* 42). In short, "Comedy is essentially *humane*" (*ATH* 42). That is why Burke chooses to adopt it as the more appropriate "frame" for his own perspective on the world.

But Burke's interest in universal forms, rooted as they are in myth and ritual, does not offer an easy way out of the travails of worldly experience. To adopt a comic "attitude to history" is not to ignore the tragic *agon* of history. Burke ends his case for the "comic frame" as follows:

> It could not, however, remove the ravages of boredom and inanition that go with the "alienation" of contemporary society. The necessities of earning a living may induce men actually to compete "of their own free will" to get the most incredible kinds of jobs, jobs that make them rot in the dark while the sun is shining, or warp their bodies and their minds by overlong sedentary regimentation and grotesque devotion to all the unadventurous tasks of filing and recording that our enormous superstructure, for manipulating the mere abstract symbols of exchange, has built up. The need of wages may induce men "voluntarily" to scramble for such "opportunities," even plotting to elbow themselves into offices which, in earlier economies, would not have been performed at all except by slaves and criminals under compulsion. For alienations of this sort ... the comic frame could not, and should not, offer recompense. Its value should only reside in helping to produce a state of affairs whereby these rigors may abate. (*ATH* 174–175)

The truly comic sense is not conservative, not complacent, and not callous.

RITUAL DRAMA AS HUB

"Critical and imaginative works are answers to questions posed by the situation in which they arose. They are not merely answers, they are *strategic* answers, *stylized* answers" (*PLF* 1). Thus begins the long title essay that forms nearly a quarter of Burke's *The Philosophy of Literary Form* (1941). Once again, we note a tendency to extend the context, so that literature becomes a means of making sense of mythology and related topics. Thus the discussion of "strategic" or "stylized" utterance soon involves a reconsideration of magic and religion. Burke is inclined to defend these two "orientations" as having a continuing validity, despite the doubts thrown upon them by science, but in the last chapter we found Burke discussing magic to the exclusion of religion. Now he juxtaposes them, in a manner surprisingly reminiscent of Frazer:

> Magic, verbal coercion, establishment or management by decree, says, in effect: "Let there be—and there was." And men share in the magical resources of some power by speaking "in the name of" that power.... The magical decree is implicit in all language; for the mere act of naming an object or situation decrees that it is not to be singled out as such-and-such rather than as something-other. Hence, I think that an attempt to *eliminate* magic, in this sense, would involve us in the elimination of vocabulary itself as a way of sizing up reality. Rather, what we may need is *correct* magic, magic whose decrees about the naming of real situations is the closest possible approximation to the situation named (with the greater accuracy of approximation being supplied by the "collective revelation" of testing and discussion). If magic says, "*Let there be* such and such," religion says, "*Please do* such and such." The decree of magic, the petition of prayer. (*PLF* 3–4)

As we know, Frazer argues that, though magic preceded religion, the two modes of thought were subsequently combined so that ritualistic magic was enacted on the basis of an elaborate myth concerning the fate of a god. Burke, again unembarrassed by his debt to Frazer, of whom he has been elsewhere so critical, now goes on to affirm that magic and religion, while properly differentiated in principle, are frequently integrated in practice. The difference is that Burke sees this integration as an essential feature of modern culture, not just archaic or residually "primitive" culture: "It is difficult to keep the magical decree and the religious petition totally distinct. Though the distinction between the coercive command and the conducive request is clear enough in its extremes, there are many borderline cases. Ordinarily, we find three ingredients interwoven in a given utterance: the spell and the counter-spell, the curse; the prayer and the prayer-in-reverse, oath, indictment, invective; the dream and the dream gone sour, nightmare" (*PLF* 5).

The discovery of three ingredients in one utterance, whether magic or religious, allows Burke to propose "three subdivisions for the analysis of an act in poetry." Now, however, the "spell" becomes (for no clear reason, but with a magisterial sweep of association) "chart."

Any poem might thus be read under the aspect of "dream," "prayer," or "chart." The aspect of dream involves "the unconscious or subconscious factors in a poem." The aspect of prayer involves "the communicative functions of a poem, which lead us into the many considerations of form, since the poet's inducements can lead us to participate in his poem only in so far as his work has a public, or communicative, structure." The aspect of chart involves "the realistic sizing-up of situations that is sometimes explicit, sometimes implicit, in poetic strategies" (*PLF* 5–6).

Burke's distinctions of dream, prayer, and chart seem to be restatements of a traditional distinction with a modern twist—for example, bringing in the psychoanalytic notion of the unconscious, or using the streetwise phrase "sizing-up." According to the literary historian M. H. Abrams, most theorists of literature, from Plato to Samuel Taylor Coleridge, have considered themselves obliged to choose one of the following three dimensions to emphasize: the "expressive" (the poem is about its author's inner life), the "pragmatic" (the poem is designed to have an effect on the reader), or the "mimetic" (the poem represents, or tells us something about, the world).[15] Burke is unusual in insisting on all three, suitably updated. Moreover, while his explicit subject is literary form, he finds himself compelled to make extraliterary conjectures.

We see Burke digress further on the nature of magic and its relevance to contemporary society in his reflections on what "charting" might involve, whether in poetic or everyday language. (Poetry, we recall, is for Burke inseparable from the social discourse of its day.) For though "It may annoy some persons that I take the realistic chart to possess 'magical' ingredients, but [the] choice here is not a choice between magic and no magic, but a choice between magics that vary in their degree of approximation to the truth." For example, whether one is "sizing up" the economic situation in the vocabulary of "regimentation" or in that of a "planned economy," in both of these "magics" there is usually "an assumption (or implied *fiat*) to the effect that increased industrial production is itself a good." But "when we recall that every increase in the *consumption* of natural resources could with equal relevance be characterized as a corresponding increase in the *destruction* of natural resources, we can glimpse the opportunity for a totally different magic here, that would size up the situation by a different quality of namings" (*PLF* 6–7). Positivism and facile notions of progress are thus repudiated, and Burke's consistent concern for ecology, to be discussed in a later chapter, is evinced.

Burke now sums up his argument thus far by declaring that "poetry, or any verbal act," may be considered a "symbolic act," which may further be defined as "the *dancing of an attitude*" (*PLF* 8–9). The dance always takes place within a specific context, knowledge of which helps us understand the impulse behind the act. In other words, "*situation is but another word for motives*" (*PLF* 20). The consequences of this insight are spelled out when later in the essay he observes that poetry is "produced for purposes of comfort, as part of the *consolation philosophiae*. It is undertaken as *equipment for living*, as a ritualistic way of arming us to confront perplexities and risks. It would *protect* us" (*PLF* 61). But this reflection is itself based on a presupposition which Burke articulates as follows: "[I]mplicit in the idea of protection there is the idea of something to be *protected against*. Hence, to analyze the element of *comfort* in beauty, without false emphasis, we must be less monistic, more 'dialectical,' in that we include also, as an important aspect of the recipe, the element of *discomfort* (actual or threatened) for which the poetry is 'medicine,' therapeutic or prophylactic." Taking his supposition further, and drawing on traditional speculations as to the nature of the "sublime," he asserts that "the *threat* is the basis of beauty" (*PLF* 61).

Looking around for a myth to typify the function of poetry, Burke decides on the Greek tale of Perseus and Medusa. Perseus, he notes, "could not face the serpent-headed monster without being turned to stone, but was immune to this danger if he observed it by reflection in a mirror. The poet's style, his form (a social idiom) is this mirror, enabling him to confront the risk, but by the protection of an indirect reflection" (*PLF* 63). Again, considering tribal culture, Burke proposes that we think of the poet as a medicine man who deals with poisons. Though broadly subscribing to a comic frame, Burke is aware of the power of tragedy in this regard: "The poet, in his pious or tragic role, would immunize us by stylistically infecting us with the disease." He supports this medical analogy not only by referring the reader to Frazer's "homeopathic magic" but also by quoting John Milton's own justification of his tragedy *Samson Agonistes*: " 'for so, in physic, things of melancholic hue and quality are used against melancholy, sour against sour, to remove salt humors' " (Milton, quoted in *PLF* 65).

Discussion of the power of tragedy brings Burke eventually to his central statement:

The general perspective that is interwoven with our methodology of analysis might be summarily characterized as a *theory of drama*. We propose to take *ritual drama* as the Ur-form, the "hub," with all other aspects of *human* action treated as spokes radiating from this hub. That is, the social sphere is considered in terms of situations and acts, in contrast with the physical sphere, which is considered in mechanistic terms, idealized as a flat cause-and-effect or stimulus-and-response relationship. Ritual drama is considered as the culminating form, from this point of view, and any other form is to be considered as the "efficient" overstressing of one or another of the ingredients found in ritual drama. An essayistic treatise of scientific cast, for instance, would be viewed as a kind of Hamletic soliloquy, its rhythm slowed down to a snail's pace, or perhaps to an irregular jog, and the dramatic situation of which it is a part usually being left unmentioned. (*PLF* 103)

"Ritual drama" is the form with which Burke had been most concerned in the decade preceding the publication of this book. Moreover, when he comes to defend his notion that his chosen form is the "hub," he anticipates the point which he will make against a too-narrow view of origins, in his later essays on myth ("Myth, Poetry, and Philosophy" and "Doing and Saying"), though in a more forthright manner:

The objection may be raised that "historically" the ritual drama is *not* the Ur-form. If one does not conceive of ritual drama in a restricted sense (allowing for a "broad interpretation," whereby a Greek goat-song and a savage dance to tom-toms in behalf of fertility, rain, or victory could be put in the same bin), a good argument could be adduced, even on the historical, or genetic, interpretation of the Ur-form. However, from my point of view, even if it were proved beyond all question that the ritual drama is not by any means the poetic prototype from which all other forms of poetic and critical expression have successively broken off (as dissociated fragments each made "efficient" within its own rights), my proposal would be in no way impaired. Let ritual drama be proved, for instance, to be the *last* form historically developed; or let it be proved to have arisen anywhere along the line. There would be no embarrassment: we could contend, for instance, that the earlier forms were but groping towards it, as rough drafts, with the ritual drama as the perfection of these trends—while subsequent forms could be treated as "departures" from it, a kind of "aesthetic fall." (*PLF* 104–105)

This provocative proposal is typical of Burke's relish for debate—itself a "dramatic" enough mode of argument—with the implication that it is now up to his putative antagonist to come up with a better argument.

Burke is not being cavalier. Even though he does not invoke Aristotle at this point, he is really only extending the principle of "entelechy" as far as it can go—in itself a good demonstration of the entelechical impulse. He is asserting that ritual drama should be seen as a form that, as it were, demands its own completion and perfection. He further explains his "lack of embarrassment" by insisting that he is "upholding this perspective" as "a *calculus*—a vocabulary, or set of coordinates, that serves best for the integration of all phenomena studied by the *social* sciences" (*PLF* 105). A paradigm that foregrounds "symbolic action" is more likely to do justice to distinctively human characteristics than a mechanistic model, which would be based on mere "motion."

In this context, it is by paying due attention to the act and its effects that we appreciate the validity of magic, even in the face of science:

A ritual dance for promoting the fertility of crops was absurd enough as "science" (though its absurdity was effectively and realistically corrected in so far as the savage, along with the mummery of the rite, planted the seed; and if you do not abstract the rite as the essence of the event, but instead consider the act of planting as also an important ingredient of the total recipe, you see that the chart of meanings contained a very important accuracy). It should also be noted that the rite, considered as "social science," had an accuracy lacking in much of our contemporary action, since it was highly *collective* in its attributes, a *group dance* in which *all* shared, hence an incantatory device that kept alive a much stronger sense of the group's consubstantiability than is stimulated today by the typical acts of private enterprise. (*PLF* 108–109)

Burke's thesis relies, then, on an understanding of human meaning as intersubjective. Primitive ritual may remind us of this disposition, whereby the fragmentary nature of much modern experience appears aberrant. His interest is in the symbolic act as necessitating a reaction: the situation is always charged with creative tension. Thus we may equate the "dramatic" with the "dialectical." In doing so, "we automatically have also our perspective for the analysis of history, which is a 'dramatic' process, involving dialectical opposi- tions" (*PLF* 109).

This equation brings Burke to his own culminating metaphor, by which he seems to justify his model. It is transhistorical in that it claims to have an overview of human endeavor, even while admitting that what is offered is only a hypothesis, projected from a historical situa- tion. Burke now offers the image for which he has become widely known outside the fields of either literary or myth theory, that of the endless discussion in the "parlor":

> Where does the drama get its materials? From the "unending conver- sation" that is going on at the point in history when we are born. Imagine that you enter a parlor. You come late. When you arrive, others have long since preceded you, and they are engaged in a heated discussion, a discussion too heated for them to pause and tell you exactly what it is about. In fact, the discussion had already begun long before any of them got there, so that no one present is qualified to retrace for you all the steps that had gone before. You listen for a while, until you decide that you have caught the tenor of the argument; then you put in your oar. Someone answers; you answer him; another comes to your defense; another aligns himself against you, to either the embarrassment or gratification of your opponent, depending upon the quality of your ally's assistance. However, the discussion is interminable. The hour grows late, you must depart. And you do depart, the discussion still vigorously in progress. (*PLF* 110–111)

DISCOUNTING

Besides setting out the model of society as intrinsically dramatic, based on the efficacy of magic and ritual, *The Philosophy of Literary Form* itself contributes to the "unending conversation" that is the theory of myth. Burke might have chosen to conduct this dialogue in the spirit of what he calls "debunking" or "unmasking" of someone's motives, revealing them to be deceptive and oppressive. But Burke favors the term "discounting," which, being more accommodating, more inclu- sive, it is synonymous for Burke with "making allowances for" (*PLF* 129). Discounting is in the spirit of the "comic frame" discussed in

Attitudes Toward History. The comic frame, we recall, "does not *waste the world's rich store of error* ... Instead, it cherishes the lore of so-called 'error' as a *genuine aspect of the truth*, with emphases valuable for the correcting of present emphases" (*ATH* 172). For Burke, discounting applies just as much in response to modern readings of myth as to archaic ritual and belief. The dialogue is maintained by the "charitable" gesture of discounting, and the added bonus is that the discounter is likely to learn something by not having presumed from the outset to have all the answers.

For example, the volume contains a review of *The Hero: A Study in Tradition, Myth and Drama* (1936) by Lord Raglan, a disciple of Frazer's. Raglan, inspired by the second version of "myth-ritualism" developed in *The Golden Bough*, proposed that the protagonist of hero myth was a later variation upon the figure of the sacred king who had in turn been identified with the figure of the god of vegetation. Raglan rejected the possibility that Theseus, Perseus, and Aeneas actually existed. Rather, these figures were wholly fictional—or, in Raglan's terms, mythical. Thus Raglan was concerned with origin in a general sense rather than with specific historical facts. He claimed to have found the key to hero myth by a process of inference about the divinity of kingship.

Burke begins his review of *The Hero* by acknowledging that Raglan's notion that "the figures and events of myth have no basis in history" is a persuasive one. He then shows himself willing to go along further still with Raglan's thesis, even though it involves inferences about origin that he himself is not prepared to make. Burke summarizes Raglan's thesis as follows: "It is his contention that the figures and events of myth owe their origin to the ritual dramas of initiation and propitiation (rites for the installation of kings, for rain-making, fertilization, and victory in war). The origin of myth, therefore, is in drama, and in drama of a purely *ceremonial* sort.... He traces the role played by king-god-hero in these magic rituals for the securing of prosperity" (*PLF* 412).

Burke, however, denies that it is possible even to conjecture about what "really" happened when myth began, about who the referent of the founding ritual would have been. In suggesting his alternative, he is able to propose that both myth and ritual are fulfillments of permanent human needs:

Noting that the details of the hero's life are not realistic, but ritualistic, he seems to underestimate the role of the people in the development of mythic figures. The author seems to assume that, since the details of the dramatic rituals deal with kingly ceremonies rather than with everyday life, the people beheld them merely as onlookers, their participation residing mainly in the fact that they had a share in the successful outcome of the rite. This emphasis would, I think, imply a false relationship between drama and audience. The spectator, I believe, could not have been attached to these dramas merely because they were spectacular but mistaken ways of doing what is now done by irrigation and reforestation. The dramas could retain their hold only in so far as the spectators were "glued" to them—and one is glued to a work of art only when that work is reliving for him some basic pattern of his own experience, with its appropriate "medicine." (*PLF* 412–413)

Burke proposes that what was involved in the dramas was a "heroic-ritualistic translation" of the people's own life processes. Hence Raglan's theory may be accepted in principle but stands in need of adaptation. "Thus the author accounts for the fact that so many of the ritual dramas have a doorway or gateway as setting by attributing it to a mere technical convenience of stage presentation; but could we not rather note the relevance of this 'Janus' symbol for objectifying rebirth, such changes of identity as investigators have noted in totemic initiation? From this standpoint we might hold that, despite absence of realistic, everyday detail in the rituals, they symbolized the experience of even the most lowly, though expressed 'transcendentally,' in 'stylistic dignification' ..." (*PLF* 413).

Once this theoretical accommodation has been made, Burke can affirm what he has taken away from his encounter with Raglan. Whether he has done full justice to the complexity of Raglan's position, which seems to involve an attempt to combine an evolutionist model with an interest in recurrent mythical motifs, is another matter. But perhaps this review might yet be taken to illustrate Burke's instinct that discounting allows for more meaning to be gained than a high-handed debunking would have permitted.

If the thesis of *The Hero* is opposed to "Euhemerism," the theory (named after its originator, Euhemerus of Messene) that each god of each myth was originally a human being who came to be divinized after death, Burke is largely in agreement with Raglan. But he reserves the right to reconsider Euhemerus' position, thus giving scope for the question of "motive" in myth:

The author [i.e., Raglan] is strongly antagonistic to Euhemerus and all his modern variants. He does not believe with that genial old debunker of 300 BC that the gods and heroes of mythology were merely deified mortals, with their real acts amplified by the imagination. Perhaps my reservation is but another brand of Euhemerism, though with a difference. I am suggesting that, despite the absence of realistic details in the rituals, it was not the *king's* life but their *own* lives that the onlookers were reliving—and these lives were being made acceptable, or "negotiable," by transmogrification into royal attributes. (*PLF* 413)

This genial corrective to Raglan's theory should not suggest that Burke is defending the principle of historical origin. Rather, he is insisting that myths arise because humanity, always and everywhere, has an undeniable drive to symbolic completion, or "transcendence." If this position is implicit in Raglan's theory, then discounting has only served to bring it out, for Burke seems even to allow for the possibility that authors may know more than they state.

The term he uses elsewhere in *The Philosophy of Literary Form* to describe this discounting stance is "neo-euhemerism." He again refers to Raglan:

In his stimulating study of the ritual drama, *The Hero,* Lord Raglan overstresses, it seems to me, the notion that these dramas appealed purely as spectacles. Would it not be more likely that the fate of the sacrificial king was also the fate of the audience, in stylized form, "writ large?" Thus, their engrossment in the drama would not be merely that of watching a parade, or the utilitarian belief that the ritual would insure rainfall, crops, fertility, a good year, etc.; but also, the stages of the hero's journey would chart the stages of their journey (as an Elizabethan play about royalty was not merely an opportunity for the pit to get a glimpse of high life, a living newspaper on the doings of society, but a dignification or memorializing of their own concerns, translated into the idiom then currently adapted as the proper language of magnification). (*PLF* 276–277)

"Neo-euhemerism" is not the most apt of neologisms. If we take the prefix to signify a mere updating of an old method, then it does not do justice to what Burke is trying to say. If, however, "neo" is meant to indicate a radical revision of an outdated principle, he appears more arrogant than he is actually being. This is a good instance of Burke's first coining ideas along with his phrases, and then being forced to justify them. What matters is that he is willing to engage in the "unending conversation" with other theorists of myth, both ancient and contemporary, in the spirit of discounting.

THE PHILOSOPHY OF DRAMATISM

Burke's work of the 1920s and 1930s, culminating in the essays gathered in *The Philosophy of Literary Form*, might be regarded as an attempt to outline a theory of human life as essentially dramatic. As we have seen, his discussions of myth and ritual, as well as of literature, have all been hovering around this emergent insight. But it was only in 1945, with *A Grammar of Motives*, that he made an explicit statement of his "dramatistic" principle. A more useful exposition of Burke's theory is given in the essay entitled "Dramatism," written more than two decades later for inclusion in Lee Thayer's anthology *Communication: Concepts and Perspectives* (1967). While this essay concerns myth only intermittently, it is indispensable for a full grasp of Burke's theory of myth. As we have noted, whenever Burke writes about myth, it is almost always in a context that demands prior understanding of his terms and references.

Burke begins the essay by addressing the human urge to translate the "logically prior" into "the temporally prior" (D 327). This topic will come as no surprise, given Burke's previous reflections on the tendency of myth to treat "principles" as "principals." He here reprises a generalization: "many such motivational matters can be adequately handled from the standpoint of language *here and now*, not language as 'derived' from some earlier condition" (D 328).

To illustrate his point, he draws on a volume he has recently read, *The Power of Satire: Magic, Ritual, Art* (1960), by Robert C. Elliott:

> It's an extremely suggestive book, particularly his appendix on magical cursing, the role of the railer in many primitive cultures. But two quite different procedures are possible when one is considering the relation between the primitive magical curse and modern aesthetic satire. You may treat modern aesthetic satire as "derived" from such earlier practices. Or you can ask how both are "derived" from the resources "natural" to language at any time. The second approach allows us to retain a historical account, yet without "deriving" aesthetic satire from the magical curse. It starts from the fact that invective is an intrinsic resource of language. If you start

language all over again tomorrow, you would have the means of praise and blame (*laus et vituperatio*). Such resources are "natural" to language *now*. And from this thought we get a totally different kind of derivation. Given invective as a resource of language, we can go back and see how this aptitude worked in eras when a magical world view prevailed, and men thought that the ritual curse could contribute to the prosperity of the tribe. But under modern conditions the stylistics of vituperation will be manifested differently, as in aesthetic satire. (D 328)

Burke explains that he is not against the idea of writing a history of the development of vituperation, but that we would be best to avoid the "genetic fallacy": "Rather than showing that the last stage 'derives' from the first, you should show how the resources 'natural' to language manifest themselves at different stages along the way" (D 328).

If praise and blame are intrinsic to human language, then we can infer that human language is an activity that takes place in a "situation." Prior to defining "dramatism," Burke wishes to insist that the "symbolic action" that characterizes humanity cannot be reduced to "motion": "The man who designs a computer is *acting*. The computer that he designs can but move" (D 329). The difference is that the "symbolic action" takes place in the social sphere of intersubjective meaning: "As regards Dramatistic tests, the point is that once you have an organism in the realm of sheer motion, a mere physical body, if you add the mature ability to use symbols, thereby you bring in all such motives as are involved when you ask about its merging with groups, or whatever you want to consider in the way of motivation" (D 330).

Shakespeare's drama, and in particular his *Coriolanus*, is used to illustrate this principle, by which biological entities are rendered social, and so begin to play their parts through symbolic action:

Symbolicity, by assigning proper names and attesting to the rights of property, strongly punctuates this physical kind of individuality— and an author like Shakespeare adds his momentous contribution. I think it is safe to say that Coriolanus most thoroughly meets this description. Yet even his name is not his own, but derives from the conquest of a city, Corioli. Such a play illustrates what I call the "paradox of substance," the way in which the nature of individuals is involved in their group relationships. I think that the study of plays from this angle is revealing. You get what I call the "paradox of substance" in the sense that no character in a play can "be himself" unless all other characters help him to enact the role for which he was designed. (D 330)

In other words, the human being is not so much "substantial" as "consubstantial." Individuality is possible only by differentiation; differentiation is possible only given the existence of other individuals in relationship.

Human beings thus "act" symbolically within the "situation" of the social context. *Things* "move" against an impersonal background. But Burke anticipates that his readers may not yet be convinced by the fundamental opposition he is proposing. He, therefore, considers himself obliged to rehearse it further: "My concerns center in the question: Is my distinction between action and motion valid?" Burke answers himself by noting that his principle of dramatism involves "the need *to include a step beyond communication*" (D 330). Most of the social sciences remain content with the communicative model, but he suspects that this model is inadequate for explaining the full force and distinctive quality of symbolic action. Certainly, it does scant justice to the process of art—or, we might infer, of ritual, of myth, or of myth theory itself.

Burke asks us to consider the last quartets of Ludwig van Beethoven. There we will find that, beyond communication, "Beethoven saw certain possibilities, and he carried them out. Thus there is a principle of *consummation*, the carrying out of possibilities" (D 331). Burke declares, with an appropriately dramatic flourish: "I think that the principle of consummation is fundamental to an understanding of the world today. Every single one of our specialized nomenclatures suggests a set of consummatory possibilities peculiar to its field" (D 331). For consummation here we may, if we prefer, substitute another term we have already discussed at some length—"entelechy," the fulfillment of potential. Human beings not only act but also feel compelled to bring their acts to completion or perfection—as we have seen, in myth and myth theory.

Now we are ready for a definition of "dramatism." Fortunately, the term, invented by Burke, had already become widely current by the time he wrote this essay. Thus he quotes *Webster's Dictionary*: " 'a technique of analysis of language and thought as basic modes of action rather than as means of conveying information' " (quoted in D 332). However, he feels the need to elaborate here, using a neologism of his own that involves some typically Burkean wordplay, by which the "terminological" (from the Latin for "term") elides into "terministic" (from the Latin for "end, boundary, limit"):

> Dramatism is a method of terministic analysis (and a corresponding critique of terminology) designed to show that the most direct route to the study of human relations and human motives is via a methodic enquiry into the cycle of terms and their functions implicit in the key term, "act." "Act" is thus a terministic center from which a whole universe of terms is "derived." ... Dramatism centers on observations of this sort: For there to be an *act*, there must be an *agent*. Similarly, there must be a *scene* in which the agent acts. To act in a scene, the agent must employ some means, or *agency*. And there cannot be an act, in the full sense of the term, unless there is a *purpose*.... In *A Grammar of Motives*, I specifically labeled these five terms (act, scene, agent, agency, purpose) the Dramatistic pentad—and the aim was to show how the functions which they designate operate in the imputing of motives. (D 332)

Burke further allows for the possibility of extending the pentad into a hexad, by admitting a sixth term, "*attitude* (as an ambiguous term for *incipient* action)" (D 332).

It is not necessary to explore each of these dimensions here. Burke chooses to illustrate one of them by way of a paragraph that glides effortlessly from the ancient to the modern, from the sacred to the secular. This kind of "symbolic act" is representative of Burke's own practice as theorist:

> Obviously, for instance, the concept of *scene* can be widened or narrowed (conceived of in terms of varying "scope" or circumference). Thus, an agent's behavior ("act") might be thought of as taking place against a polytheistic background; or the overall scene may be thought of as grounded in one god; or the circumference of the situation can be narrowed to naturalistic limits, as in Darwinism; or it can be localized in such terms as "Western civilization," or "Elizabethanism," "capitalism," or "D-Day," or "10 Downing Street," or "on this train ride," and so on, endlessly. The main point is that any change of the circumference in terms of which an act is viewed implies a corresponding change in the quality of the act's motivation. Such a loose yet compelling correspondence between act and scene is called a "scene-act ratio." (D 333)

Similarly, when Burke comes to reflect that, strictly speaking, "Dramatism is a theory of terminology," he observes that "a nomenclature could be called Dramatistic only if it were specifically designed to talk, at one remove, about the cycle of terms implicit in the idea of an act." But he allows for a wider sense, explaining that "any study of relations in terms of 'action' could be called 'Dramatistic' " (D 337–338). This definition leads him to even more ambitious associations:

> A major difficulty in delimiting the field of reference derives from the fact that common sense vocabularies of motives are spontaneously personalistic, hence innately given to drama-laden terms. And the turn from the naïve to the speculative is marked by such obviously "action-words" as *tao, karma, dike, hodos,* Islam (to designate a submissive *attitude*), all of which are clearly "Dramatistic" when contrasted with the terminological ideals proper to the physical sciences. The Dramatistic nature of the Bible is proclaimed in the verb (*bara*) of the opening sentence that designates God's creative act; and the series of fiats that follows identifies such action with the principle of symbolicity ("the Word"). (D 338)

We will return in Chapter 5 to Burke's invocation of the *tao*—or "the Tao," as it is more frequently transcribed. But for now, we note how readily he moves from a linguistic or cultural principle to its cosmic connotations. Dramatism goes down deep into communal life, but for Burke it is simultaneously the way humanity and the universe relate to each other.

The last quotation, with its appeal to the Tao, to God, and to creation, may seem rather too ambitious in the context, taking us too far beyond the specific insight that the generation of meaning is implicit in the very notion of an "act." As if to assuage the more suspicious reader, Burke offers a more specific, detailed, extended example—that of the psychological theory of Sigmund Freud. He offers a dramatistic analysis of the "internalities of Freud's nomenclature." By way of testing his thesis, he proposes "to 'prophesy' what is likely to follow from Freud's generative proposition that 'repression' is an 'unconscious' process" (D 343). What he will seek to do is construct a series of rules that are implicit in the psychoanalytic orientation. But prior to that undertaking, he pauses to dwell on the significance of the fact that repression is an act. As an act, it must take place in a scene or situation of some sort. Hence in the dramatistic perspective the unconscious may be envisaged as "a kind of *place*, as were one to say not just that repression *is* unconscious, but that it takes place '*in* the unconscious' " (D 344). Further, "When introducing the term 'unconscious,' we set up the terministic conditions for a complementary term, the 'conscious.' " "Once you get two terms as far apart as positive and negative, you set up the conditions for an intermediate term of some sort." If in the religious context we see how "terms so greatly different as 'God' and 'man' set up the conditions for an intermediate term, the 'God-man,' " then we will be able to anticipate "the corresponding intermediate term in the Freudian nomenclature is 'preconscious' " (D 344).

Having mentioned the "preconscious" with its translation of a spatial principle into a temporal principal, Burke is able to move on to his table of Freudian rules:

Rule 1: When seeking to define the etiology of a psychic symptom, one should always look first of all for a way to interpret a patient's problems in terms of the temporally prior (childhood, infancy, the womb, or even "prehistory"). (The force of this rule would be manifest in the choice of "preconscious" to name the realm intermediate between "conscious" and "unconscious.")

Rule 2: This is the principle of "Dramatistic thoroughness" whereby friendship is to be conceived in terms of homosexuality, family affection in terms of incest, disagreement in terms of hostility, resistance to the father (or to authority generally) in terms of the desire to kill, and so on....

Rule 3: Inquiries into the nature of "symbolic action" in general should be presented in terms of "symbolic action" in the more specific sense of the "neurotic" or "symptomatic."

Rule 4: Viewed as a *philosophy of life*, a *Weltanschauung*, inquiries to do with psychotherapy via the couch of secular confession should be considered and presented in the spirit of what might be called the "principle of individualistic libertarianism." (D 345)

Burke here treats psychotherapy in the same way that he treats myth itself. Taking them both as symbolic acts, he seeks out the points where they may be seen to move toward consummation. Hence his four rules. But it is with the first rule in particular that we see the parallel between

Freudian theory and myth most exactly: both translate principles into principals; both convert a projected state of affairs into a story.

Burke's shorthand term for this strategy, coined toward the end of *A Grammar of Motives*, is the "temporizing of essence" (*GM* 430). Explaining that the process involves expressing "the logically prior" in terms of "the temporally prior," Burke remarks that it may take the form of "symbolic *regression.*" He goes on to offer an illustration: Freud's speculation about the "primal crime" of the "primal horde," as adapted from Freud's own reading of Darwin in the pages of *Totem and Taboo* (1913). Here Freud assumes that the origin of religion was the guilt felt by the young males of the earliest human groupings after they had murdered the father in order to gain access to the females of the horde. Freud is applying the Oedipus complex to the infancy of humanity itself. Burke comments:

> If you recall that Darwin's evolutionism vowed him to a wholly historicist vocabulary, you will begin by taking it for granted that Darwin could not possibly state a theory of essence in his characteristic terms except by attributing to this essence some stage of existence in the past. And Freud, in response to the Darwinian vocabulary, would be led to a similar mode of expression. Hence, if you take the theory of the "primal horde" as a statement about *existence* rather than about *essence*, you find it proved or disproved by anthropological research. Anthropologists seem to have done it quite a lot of damage. There seems to be no evidence that any such "primal horde" ever existed. But if we interpreted the concept as a statement about *essence*, we might find it quite useful despite the anthropologists' discrediting of it. For it may well be that the human relation which the concept of the primal horde designates really is *essential* to some social structures, such as the society of his own day which Freud was studying. (*GM* 431)

This final reflection may seem an exceptionally magnanimous treatment of the psychoanalytical strategy, given the way Burke has previously sought to demystify the Freudian rules. Yet it would seem that Freud is being discussed here not as a "myth theorist" but as a "mythmaker," in which case psychoanalysis would be seen as involving both a narrative (the "family romance" of patriarchy, based in turn on the Oedipus myth) and a rite (the "talking cure" of the treatment). The clue is in Burke's aside about Freud's insights being essentially true of his own society. That is, Burke is seeking to enter into the spirit of psychoanalysis in the same way that Bronislaw Malinowski sought to enter into the spirit of the Trobriand Islanders' creation story.

Thus what we see here is Burke discounting, or making allowances for, Freud's narrative hypothesis about the distant past—that is, Freud's own myth—in that Burke allows the "essence" it temporizes to make sense in (and of) the present. There is much in Freudian theory as such, as distinguished from its founding myth, that Burke would be more inclined to debunk: for instance, the tendency to "individualistic libertarianism" noted in rule 4, above. But the process of translating present "essence" into past "existence" is not refuted insofar as it is a modern illustration of the persistence of mythic thinking. Burke finds a sanction for it in theology: "the doctrine of 'original sin' should be converted from historical terms (i.e., the 'historical' terms of legend) to essentialist terms, if we translated it as 'essential sin' (that is, man as 'essentially a transgressor')" (*GM* 432). No matter what the context, whether secular or sacred, we find the same process at work: logical principles tend to get expressed in narrative terms. They seem to make little sense otherwise.

"Discounting," "unending conversation," "dramatism," "ritual drama as hub": these are different ways of saying something essential to Burke's thinking. We have noted that his first book begins with the word "perhaps" and ends with the word "norm." We have traced his attempt to find a norm that would make sense of human interaction. In the very act of throwing into question the commonsense notion that we are each of us substantial, he has sought to demonstrate that we are consubstantial. If individual identity is inseparable from the drama of human relations, then it is necessary for us to respect one another as "symbolic actors" on the worldly stage. For a major implication of the philosophy of dramatism is that one should not reduce people—whose realm is "symbolic action"—to the sphere of mere motion. At one point in *Language as Symbolic Action*, Burke debates whether it is ever possible for this ideal to be practiced. By way of an example, he cites the reported behavior of German officers in the First World War when organizing an attack against a Belgian fortress. "The approach to the fortress was known to be mined." "And the mines had to be exploded. So wave after wave of human flesh was sent forward, as conditioned cattle, to get blown up, until all the mines had been touched off. Then the next wave, or the next two or three waves thereafter, could take the fort. Granted, that comes close to sheer motion, doubtless conceived in the best war-game tradition" (*LSA* 54).

Burke is able to judge such offenses because he has a clear idea of what it means to be human, thanks to the fundamental opposition between action and motion. Dramatism may be said to approximate to a universal norm in that it asserts the intrinsic rights and responsibilities that go with the capacity for symbolic action. This "representative anecdote" demonstrates that, in the realm of language and thought, it is for Burke necessary and desirable always to move toward transcendent, transhistorical principles. His whole corpus of work is testimony to that conviction. Indeed, William Rueckert has even taken Burke's central idea of ritual drama as indicative of his integral vision: "In typical fashion, Burke reduces the many to the one, and all verbalization is reduced to symbolic action; symbolic action is then reduced to its most perfect or ideal form, which is poetic symbolic action; all poetic symbolic action is then reduced to its essence, which is the purgative-redemptive ethical drama; ethical drama is then reduced to its most perfect or ideal form, which is ritual drama; Burke then takes the final step and equates the point of departure—linguistic action—with the terminal point—ritual drama—and ends with the proposition that the essence of all linguistic action is to be found in ritual drama."[16]

As for dramatism, Rueckert explains it succinctly as the conjunction of this idea of ritual drama with another of Burke's insights—namely, that of the human being as "symbol-using animal." If one puts these points together, one has a whole philosophy of life.[17] Moreover, according to C. Allen Carter, that philosophy is crucially relevant, though hard to label:

> Here Burke serves as an intersection of contemporary critical theories. Like some structuralists, he rejects any notion of a substantial self. The Burkean self is a social or linguistic construction shaped by its interactions with others. The self does not pre-exist its distinguishing of itself from others; it *is* this series of diacritical acts. There is no fixed or essential self; if the self can be said to have an essence, its essence is constant transformation. But, unlike some poststructuralists, Burke does not completely decenter the self. The Burkean self is a center of experience. No one encounters exactly the same admonitions in exactly the same situations. The Burkean self is a unique site at which the process of identity takes a dramatic turn.... If the self is diacritical (defined in relation to others) and dialectical (subject to shifts of meaning), it is also ethical (defined in relation to the rules). Burke's is an ethicist version of the structuralist self.[18]

This insistence on responsibility as well as reciprocity makes Burke's understanding of society as a dramatic phenomenon so important. We shall see how important it is to maintain a critical distance from the workings of ritual drama when we come to consider in the next chapter its tendency toward the "scapegoat mechanism."

4

MYTH AND "VICTIMAGE"

From "ritual drama" to "victimage" is a small step rather than a giant leap, but in order to make it we will need to walk over some theoretical ground. The last chapter ended with the notion of an ethical self that is more consubstantial than substantial. The importance of the epithet "ethical" (from the Greek, *ethos*, or "character, disposition") should not be overlooked. Kenneth Burke's philosophy of dramatism visualizes the human being as playing a role, yet not as indulging in a game. The comic frame is "charitable," yet not irresponsible. Burke sees hierarchy and mystery as intrinsic to the world of symbolic action, but he thinks it possible to discriminate between the necessities of "order" and the abuses of privilege. He knows that all rhetorical "identification" tends to exclude some symbolic actors from this or that "scene" of the total drama, but he thinks it possible to resist the temptation to what he calls "congregation by segregation."

This notion of exclusion brings us to "victimage." As with dramatism, we must begin with some account of the ideas that lie behind the concept. Moreover, as should have become evident now, Burke has a fondness for elaboration and for connotation. Although our goal is visible enough, we need to take a few philosophical diversions, as we come close to the Burkean position on the violence implicit in myth.

"PERSPECTIVE BY INCONGRUITY"

Readers of Burke accustom themselves to his habit of prefacing the various sections of his books with cryptic statements that seem to render a given topic even more strange than it would have been if he had neglected to write anything at all. An example is the page that heralds the start of Part II of *Permanence and Change* (1935), the title of which is "Perspective by Incongruity." Having addressed, in Part I, the subject of "orientation," or the way we see and interpret the world by means of symbols, Burke announces that he will now be concerned with how we move beyond an existing orientation to a new one. Part II, he tells us, "will deal with the state of transition itself." What immediately follows will make sense insofar as we already know the term "piety," but the associative leaps he makes may yet surprise us:

> Since the conditions of such transformation involve not merely intellectualistic problems, but also deeply emotional ones, the analysis is centered on a discussion of "piety" and "impiety." Piety, as the yearning to conform with the "sources of one's being," is shown to be a much more extensive motive than it is usually thought to be. Conversely, even the most conscientious of new doctrines necessarily contains an element of impiety, with a corresponding sense of guilt (though the doctrine may later become an orthodoxy, with its generally accepted code of proprieties and improprieties). The intermediate stage involves a shattering or fragmentation, analogous to the stage of "rending and tearing" (or *sparagmos*) in tragic ritual.... Here reasons are offered for calling it "perspective by incongruity" (with the placing of special stress upon the kinds of hermeticism, or stylistic mercureality, that are got by the merging of categories once felt to be mutually exclusive). This is the realm of gargoyles. (*PC* 69)

The instinctive way that Burke opts for the analogy with ritual is instructive. The parallel makes sense if we are already alerted to his emergent dramatism, but if we are not, it may seem a bizarre way of talking about a shift of attitudes, ideas, or beliefs. It is probably best to go along with Burke's mode of expression, in the expectation that we will find that the whole matter becomes clear in time, as is usually, though not always, the case with Burke.

The context in which we first came across Burke's use of the term "piety" before was that of the psychological advantage of primitive rituals of appeasement to nature over the modern indifference, or even downright hostility, to nature. As the phrase "sources of one's being" indicates, Burke's premise is that a sense of piety is essential to the realization of our humanity. This position underlies his conviction that, despite the poverty of modern utilitarianism, we may expect that the piety that is repressed—for example, in the felling of a mature tree—will still somehow find expression. This expression may be in the realm of the unconscious, or of poetry, or perhaps both. Before we consider the advantages of "impiety," we have to acknowledge the need for the initial condition. For as Burke explains:

> [P]iety is a system-builder, a desire to round things out, to fit experiences together into a unified whole.... Piety is *the sense of what properly goes with what*. And it leads to construction in this way: If there is an altar, it is pious of a man to perform some ritual act whereby he may approach this altar with clean hands. A kind of symbolic cleanliness goes with altars, a technique of symbolic cleansing goes with cleanliness, a preparation or initiation goes with the technique of cleansing, the need of cleansing was based upon some feeling of taboo—and so on, until pious linkages may have brought all the significant details of the day into coordination, relating them integrally with one another by a complex interpretative framework. (*PC* 75)

Piety has religious connotations, as indicated. But Burke's point is that we need not confine the term to denoting a sense of the sacred. Even in secular contexts, even in everyday discourse, we find evidence of piety.

In an amusing illustration Burke asks us to imagine the Victorian pundit and defender of "high culture," Matthew Arnold, who always "assumed that exquisiteness of taste was restricted to the 'better' classes of people," in an alien context:

> [I]f we can bring ourselves to imagine Matthew Arnold loafing on the corner with the gashouse gang, we promptly realize how undiscriminating he would prove himself. Everything about him would be inappropriate: both what he said and the ways in which he said it. Consider the crudeness of his perception as regards the proper oaths, the correct way of commenting upon passing women, the etiquette of spitting. Does not his very crassness here reveal the presence of a morality, a deeply felt and piously observed sense of the appropriate, on the part of these men, whose linkages he would outrageously violate? Watch them—and observe with what earnestness, what *devotion* these gashouse Matthew Arnolds act to preserve themselves, every minute of the day, true members of their cult. Vulgarity is pious. (*PC* 77)

Piety, then, is an inescapable element of all cultures—and, we might add, subcultures. Even if the modern world seems to be lacking in explicit rituals through which to express reverence for a felled tree, or to approach an altar, it still has a variety of ways of demonstrating "what goes with what." As David Blakesley explains, "Burke does not restrict its use to religious contexts but instead sees piety as a kind of ordering principle governed by an ideological system or a set of principles that exert control on symbolic action."[1]

Yet no culture, no way of life, and indeed no "way of seeing" can resist change. The very establishment of a pious protocol invites revision. Otherwise, for example, we would see no development in the matter of faith. In short, there would be no history of religions. If we extend the notion of the religious, we can see that all orthodoxies end up being challenged:

> In this sense, any new way of putting the characters of events together is an attempt to convert people, regardless of whether it go by the name of religion, psychotherapy, or science. It is impious, by our definition, insofar as it attacks the kinds of linkage already established. It attempts, by rationalization, to alter the nature of our responses. Thus, in the Jewish and Christian rationalizations, we see the earlier pagan practice of sacred prostitution reoriented as a sin.... In Marxism, we find new meanings serving to draw forth, for special attention, specific factors in the vast complexity of our productive, distributive, and moral network. (*PC* 86–87)

Burke calls this kind of shift in emphasis, which unsettles the prevailing wisdom, "perspective by incongruity." His very application of the word *piety* to the conduct of the "gashouse gang" is a good example of this procedure. The world as previously understood is defamiliarized by transposing terms from one cultural sphere to another. To take another of the examples given, what was a pious ritual for the Babylonians becomes a demonic offense according to the Jews and Christians. Or again, the social hierarchy ordained by the Victorian capitalists' God becomes exploitation of proletarian labor power for Marxists (see *PC* 87). If the principle still eludes us, we might reflect that one of Burke's more striking pieces of advice in *Counter-Statement* is in the spirit of perspective by incongruity: "When in Rome, do as the Greeks" (*CS* 119).

Insofar as "impiety" takes on a more sustained form, we can write of "planned incongruity." Burke has already referred to "the realm of gargoyles." Indeed, he does argue later in *Permanence and Change* that those medieval church carvings may be seen, in their cultural context, as "violating one order of classification" and "stressing another"—an order that had yet to be understood by the orthodox mind. More broadly, he writes that this kind of innovation belongs to the sphere of the "grotesque," which really came into its own in secular art some centuries later (see *PC* 112). At first glance it seems to involve little more than a sense of fun, but Burke sees in it more than that, noting that: "The grotesque is a much more complex matter, and gradually merges into something very much like mysticism. Humor tends to be conservative, the grotesque tends to be revolutionary. Aristophanes was a humorist, excoriating new ways with reference to traditional tests of propriety. Aristophanes was pious, but Socrates had leanings towards the grotesque and impious" (*PC* 112).

This typically Burkean reflection links together apparently unrelated ideas, thereby meriting the description of perspective by incongruity. Nor does Burke rest content there. He now moves effortlessly from mysticism back to Marxism. The revolutionary motive aligns it with the gargoyle or grotesque impulse of planned incongruity. "Marx's formula of class-consciousness is a social therapeutic because it is *reclassification-consciousness*," he writes. "It is a new perspective that realigns something so profoundly ethical as our categories of allegiance. By this reinterpretative schema, members of the same race or nation who had formerly thought of themselves as *enemies* become *allies*. The new classification thus has implicit in it a new set of ideas as to what *action* is, and in these ideas are implicit new criteria for deciding what means-selection would be adequate" (*PC* 113). By an audacious pattern of association, Burke thus demonstrates that Karl Marx turns out to have been preaching a kind of "secular mysticism," also to be found in the work of those artists working at the time of the book's publication, namely the Surrealists—or, as Burke calls them, the "Super-Realists" (*PC* 113).

If finding a new terminology is essential to achieving perspective by incongruity, then even a phrase can effect this achievement. We have already seen in Chapter 3 that Burke draws on John Dewey's unusual conjunction of terms. "Occupational psychosis" has the same kind of effect as does the Marxist vocabulary, forcing us to see that "a society's environment in the historical sense is synonymous with the society's methods of production." If a tribe lives mainly by hunting, then all aspects of its world will be viewed obsessively in the perspective of the hunt. Burke is fond of such paradoxical phrases as "occupational psychosis."

Another phrase that he refers to—indeed, one he relies on for a large part of his argument in *Permanence and Change*—is the social theorist Thorstein Veblen's "trained incapacity," which Burke likes principally because the two words together seem so radically incongruous. In its original formulation, as summarized by Burke, it is restricted to "the case of business men who, through long training in competitive finance, have so built their scheme of orientation about this kind of effort and ambition that they cannot see serious possibilities in any other system of production and distribution" (*PC* 7). For Burke, it means more generally "that state of affairs whereby one's very abilities can function as blindnesses." For example, "If we had conditioned chickens to interpret the sound of a bell as a food-signal, and if we now rang the bell to assemble them for punishment, their training would work against them" (*PC* 7). Burke's point is that if there will always be those who have an investment in remaining oblivious to the need for adaptation, so likewise there must always be those who manage to refuse such an investment, and who can therefore gain a critical distance from the sphere of trained incapacity.

Society thus always exists in a tension between the emergent orientation; and the emergent orientation is anticipated in the act of perspective by incongruity. Burke explains what is involved as follows, drawing on the distinction made by the sociologist Max Weber between priests and prophets:

> Even if one ascribes the rise of an orientation to its usefulness, one cannot conclude that it necessarily serves the ends of use. It may survive from conditions for which it was fit into conditions for which it is unfit (*cultural lag*). And its fossilized existence may be prolonged, after it has become dangerous to the social body as a whole, if some group which profits by it controls the educative, legislative, and constabulary resources of the state (*class morality*). The members of a group specifically charged with upholding a given orientation may be said to perform a *priesthood function*. If we define a priesthood in the technical sense, we find that in the priesthood of today the clergy take a minor part: The function is mainly performed by our college professors, journalist, public relations counselors, sales promoters, writers of advertising copy, many of

whom will usually fume at the hypocrisy of the medieval Church while excusing their own position on the grounds of necessity. The decay of a priesthood (when they more or less definitely resent the work that is asked of them) leads to a division between *priests* and *prophets*. The priests devote their efforts to maintaining the vestigial structure; the prophets seek new perspectives whereby this vestigial structure may be criticized and a new one established in its place. In this sense, Marx could be said to have performed a prophecy-function, as distinct from a priesthood-function. (*PC* 179)

As usual, no sooner does Burke mention Marx than he starts thinking of Judaism and Christianity, and vice versa. This instinct is, again, evidence of his own disposition toward perspective by incongruity: secular and sacred myths are treated interchangeably. Here Burke takes up the priest/prophet division in the context of the Bible itself: "The desire to re-characterize events necessarily requires a new reading of the signs." Thus prophets such as Ezekiel introduce "a new principle of interpretation, a new perspective or point of view, whereby the picture of 'things as they *really* are' is reorganized" (*PC* 180). They can achieve this shift in viewpoint because they believe themselves to have transcended the present time and place, their transcendence often being symbolized by their ascent of a high mountain.

Burke's examples of perspective by incongruity are many, but we have given enough indication of how useful the term might be. Yet it would be misleading to leave the topic at that, with the implication that, prior to the new orientation, only the challenge to piety by impiety is involved. For any such achievement is, for Burke, likely to be a mixed blessing. In his next book, *Attitudes Toward History*, he coins a phrase—again, another example of perspective by incongruity in its own right—to describe what happens when an ideal that seems audacious and liberating when voiced in opposition is actually put into practice. He calls this occurrence "the bureaucratization of the imaginative," noting that "[André] Gide has somewhere said that he distrusts the carrying-out of one possibility because it necessarily restricts other possibilities. Call the possibilities 'imaginative.' And call the carrying out of *one* possibility the *bureaucratization* of the imaginative. An imaginative possibility (usually at the start Utopian) is bureaucratized when it is embodied in the realities of a social texture, in all the complexity of language and habits, in the property relationships, the methods of government, production and distribution, and in the development of rituals that re-enforce the same emphasis" (*ATH* 225).

Burke's "bureaucratization of the imaginative" may seem at first to be reminiscent of Weber's "routinization of charisma." But Weber is referring chiefly to the distinction between tribal communities, which have a respect for magical powers as invested in special individuals, and complex societies, which follow the dictates of rationality.[2]

By contrast, Burke is referring to a procedure observable in all collective enterprises. An interesting case study of the bureaucratization of the imaginative offered by Burke is that of monasticism, which tells us much about the nature of transition. The impulse behind such a movement would most likely be a radical dissatisfaction with the current religious orthodoxy, found to be too lax or too corrupt. This impulse would be the attraction for those wishing to become monks in this particular monastic order. At times, notes Burke, when "orders are sincere, and have not degenerated into opportunities for business men in a theocratic state, they tend to enlist their members at a *point of crisis.*" In a suitably extreme response to this point of crisis, self-punishment through asceticism is offered as the ideal way of life. With the passing of the crisis, one might expect the mood to change, but what actually happens is that "the monastic order *institutionalizes the mentality prevailing at the point of crisis.*" That is, monasticism "fixes the transitional"; it remains "suspended between heaven and earth"; and "in the name of *there*, it organizes it as *here.*" "Finding a man who stands between two worlds, it offers him a world formed of this midway state. And since the spiritual features are given their material grounding in a collective technique of living (the 'imaginative' ingredients being 'bureaucratized' by the economic order) the 'grotesque' becomes 'natural,' with conventional norms. The subjective state is embodied in a public order, a society-within-a-society" (*ATH* 69–70).

Again, Marxism seems the appropriately complementary example. Marx's "class morality" implies a sect that has rejected the values imposed by the ruling class in favor of an alternative vision of social relations, one that has yet to be realized. This new morality has the effect of "organizing the individual mind to confront a present imperfect world by the co-ordination of a subsequent better world." But "until the day of redemption arrives with the establishment of a socialist state, it is essentially ideal rather than realistic." It has to rely on "the concept of a *beyond.*" Burke now is able to make his comparison between Marxism and monasticism: "[T]he monastic order begins with 'spirituality,' and in the course of 'implementing' it with relation to all human necessities, arrives at 'material' organization. The treatment of the transitional emphasis in Marxist 'class morality' begins with materiality, and in the course of implementing it, arrives at 'spiritual' organization, or 'consciousness' " (*ATH* 74).

More generally, what is envisaged is a dialectical process by which piety is opened up to perspective by incongruity, by the imaginative possibilities implicit in a new use of terminology, to be replaced by a new order or rationalization that is the bureaucratization of those possibilities. This process in turn becomes subject to disorientation. And so the dialectic proceeds: "In sum, we contend that 'perspective by incongruity' makes for a *dramatic* vocabulary, with weighting and counter-weighting, in contrast with the more liberal ideal of *neutral* naming in the characterization of processes" (*ATH* 315). We are reminded of Burke's more general case for ritual drama as social hub, or for dramatism as a philosophy that explains human relations.

From ritual to myth is a logical progression for Burke, though their respective orientations may differ. There must be a narrative that serves as motivation for people either to serve or to resist the dominant piety: "As the imaginative becomes bureaucratized, the bureaucratic body brings up new problems of its own." The persons who must "devote all their genius" to its "incidental by-products," such as "complex filing systems," are thereby threatened with either "inanition" or "alienation," or both. "They are robbed of the world, since their efforts are expended in so cramped a territory. And they must struggle to repossess the world" (*ATH* 314–315). A myth of liberation will be their medium. There will most likely develop a "class struggle" between those benefiting from the bureaucracy and those alienated by its maintenance:

> A rationalization of history is the first step whereby the dispossessed repossess the world. By organizing their interests and their characters about a purpose as located by the rationale, they enjoy a large measure of repossession (a spiritual property that "no one can take from them") even though they are still suffering under the weight of the bureaucratic body oppressing their society. Maximum alienation prevails when the oppressed suffer oppression without a rationale that locates the cause of the disturbance and the policies making for its removal. By a rationale of history, on the other hand, they own a "myth" to take up the slack between what is desired and what is got. (*ATH* 315)

Burke's notion of the interval, and the whole subject of transition that he may be seen to explore throughout his writing career, has proved extremely influential. One of the more obvious examples is the anthropology of Victor Turner. In *The Ritual Process* (1974) Turner even echoes the insight of dramatism when he discusses ritual as social drama, though he never cites Burke. His own stated source for his speculations on the nature of ritual is Arnold van Gennep. Van Gennep's model of the "rite of passage" observes the ethnological importance of the "liminal" period, during which the initiate has a profound experience of moving from one state to another. That is, the initiate crosses a "threshold" (Latin: *limen*). For Turner, this phase becomes the key to all ritual. In spelling out this insight, he can be seen to qualify van Gennep's model in terms very close to Burke's paradigm.

Turner's basic distinction is between two ways of living socially: "structure" and "communitas." Having distinguished them, he is interested in how communitas marks a move beyond the threshold of the structure. "All human societies implicitly or explicitly refer to two contrasting social model. One ... is of society as a structure of jural, political and economic positions, offices, statuses and roles, in which the individual is only ambiguously grasped behind the social persona. The other is of society as a communitas of concrete, idiosyncratic individuals who, though differing in physical and mental endowment, are nevertheless regarded as equal in terms of shared humanity."[3]

"Structure" is the everyday social world, with all its ranks and restrictions. "Communitas," inspired by the vision of a sacred alternative, is transitional, promoting equality and fellowship. Looking around for contemporary examples, Turner praises the counterculture of hippies. He remarks on their inclination toward marginal, tribal living, nonpossessive personal relationships, and eccentric appearance and behavior: "The Hippie emphasis on spontaneity, immediacy, and 'existence' throws into relief one of the senses in which communitas contrasts with structure."[4] Nor does Turner lack more traditional illustrations. He sees many mystics and founders of religious orders, such as St. Francis of Assisi, as representing devotional experience rather than abstract doctrine: religious radicals always embody communitas rather than structure.[5] Indeed, it is the religious aspect of the principle that makes it so radical, given the unimaginative, uniform nature of life in modern secular society. Still, Turner is under no illusions about the sustainability of communitas. He acknowledges that the transitional way of life, while originating in spontaneity and marginality, will usually become normative, institutional, and narrowly ideological—like "charismatic" authority for Weber.[6]

Burke anticipates Turner in various ways. First, Turner's liminality is reminiscent of Burke's perspective by incongruity—that is, in the process by which we move from one orientation to another. Second, when Turner refers to the given social order by the term "structure," he seems to mean something like Burke's "piety," though for Burke restricted to its secular manifestations. Third, by identifying structure with institution and authority, Turner may remind us of Burke's stress on the importance of the "forensic" as the background against which ritual rebirth might occur. Fourth, by linking communitas with liminality, marginality, and the blurring of hitherto rigid distinctions, Turner echoes Burke's interest in various forms of impiety—in the grotesque, the gargoyle imagination, revolutionary thinking, and mysticism. Burke foreshadows Turner's emphasis on both mysticism and monasticism. Finally, when we follow Turner's reasoning, we find that he allows for the institutionalization of the transitional, marginal, alternative way of life—precisely Burke's argument in the "bureaucratization of the imaginative."

At the same time Burke might want to amend Turner's model. Turner defines structure as secular, where Burke would want to say that piety comprehends both sacred and secular dimensions of the established order. Turner defines communitas as religious, but Burke would want to say that impiety crosses the threshold between the sacred and the secular, between the religious and the nonreligious. For Turner to maintain such a rigid distinction between his social models is in itself to lose sight of the dialectical vision that for Burke is synonymous with the dramatic model of human relations. Turner's anthropology, though clearly indebted to literary thinking, would for Burke simply not be literary enough. Burke would rightly consider his own pioneering case for impiety to be more comprehensive.

THE SCAPEGOAT RITUAL

No serious reader of Burke could view him as a complacent conservative. Yet we may detect also a good deal of skepticism toward the idea of progress. There are, he seems to say, certain traits in human nature that may not entirely be eradicated. Still, Burke seems to believe that it is our duty to devise means of correcting our worst tendencies: hence his case for the "comic frame."

But which is the most tragic of collective practices that humankind has devised, standing most obviously in need of a "charitable" corrective? There is a social mechanism that has the weight of religious tradition behind it and that has survived into a predominantly secular age. For Burke, it is deeply rooted in human guilt, a characteristic that has persisted despite the decline in Christianity. This practice is the scapegoat ritual, which developed in antiquity among the Hebrews and which was eventually established as part of "the Law." In the Book of Leviticus we are told how Moses comes to establish the Day of Atonement. Guided by God, he instructs his brother Aaron, who "shall take [the] two goats, and present them before the Lord at the door of the tabernacle of the congregation. And Aaron shall cast lots upon the two goats: one lot for the Lord, and the other lot for the scapegoat. And Aaron shall bring the goat upon which the Lord's lot fell, and offer him for a sin offering. But the goat on which the lot fell to be scapegoat, shall be presented alive before the Lord, to make an atonement with him, and to let him go for a scapegoat into the wilderness" (Leviticus 16:7–10).

Here the text requires some sort of context. It helps to know that the second goat, the scapegoat, was thought by the Hebrews to belong to Azazel, a demonic creature of the desert, later assimilated with the figure of Satan. While originally one goat was for God and one in effect for the Devil, in time the two goats became symbolically merged: the belief grew that the scapegoat, in being driven away from the community into the wilderness, in effect suffered a kind of death, and so incorporated the role of the first goat, the "sin offering."

In Christianity it seemed appropriate to refer to Jesus as the sacrificial figure who, after a similar pattern, had been sacrificed by the society of his day. Yet Jesus was, of course, known more frequently as the "lamb," given the recurrent imagery of the Gospels and of the book of Revelation. For example, in the Roman Catholic liturgy of the Mass, Jesus is the "Lamb of God, who takest away the sins of the world." Certainly in anthropology the scapegoat is a single figure that focuses many needs and anxieties. With J. G. Frazer, for example, the idea is that the dying god of vegetation carries away death itself by taking its burden upon himself, thus removing the threat of sterility from the land and of hunger from the community. The principle behind this removal is magic—here specifically "contagious magic." Were the god not to die as a scapegoat but rather to live on to degenerate in health, his sickness and impotence would contaminate the land and its inhab-itants.[7]

Burke's conviction early on was that, far from being outmoded, the scapegoat principle was central to the functioning of contemporary society. In the 1930s he saw it at work in Europe, and he set himself to explaining an apparent aberration of political thinking as the appro-priation of a recurrent myth. Burke read Adolf Hitler's *Mein Kampf*, shortly after its translation into English, just prior to the outbreak of the Second World War. His analysis was subsequently included in *The Philosophy of Literary Form* (1941). The essay "The Rhetoric of Hitler's 'Battle' " is a remarkably shrewd summation of the scapegoat principle in relation to the terrifying ideas being propounded by the self-styled savior of the German people.

The scapegoating that is at the heart of Hitler's apologia, and thus behind the whole project of Nazism, casts the Jew in the central role. For that project to flourish, it needs "the symbol of a common enemy." But far from the Jew taking the selfless role attrib-uted to Christ, he is thoroughly demonized: he is reconnected to Azazel and by association becomes "the Prince of Evil himself." Hitler is able to select an "international" devil in the form of the "international" Jew by which to unite the "Aryan" people because, from the Middle Ages onward, "the Prince was international, universal, 'catholic.' " He adds: "This *materialization* of a religious pattern is, I think, one terrifically effective weapon of propaganda in a period where religion has been progressively weakened by many centuries of capitalist materialism" (*PLF* 193–194). That is, secular unity is afforded to a disintegrating nation by means of the distortion of a sacred paradigm.

Burke traces four main features of the "unification device" employed by Hitler. The first of these is "inborn dignity":

In both religious and humanistic patterns of thought, a "natural born" dignity is considered to be an attribute of *all* men, if they will but avail themselves of it, by right thinking and right living. But Hitler gives this ennobling attitude an ominous twist by his theories of race and nation, whereby the "Aryan" is elevated above all others by the innate endowment of his blood, while other "races," in partic-ular Jews and Negroes, are innately inferior. This sinister secular-ized version of a Christian theology thus puts the sense of dignity upon a fighting basis, requiring the conquest of "inferior races." (*PLF* 202)

The religious aspect of Hitler's distorted model is one that fascinates Burke, and he returns to it at the end of his essay. But it is also implicit in the second feature of the Nazi "unification device," which Burke calls the "*projection* device." He defines as the "curative" process that which comes with "the ability to hand over one's ills to a scapegoat, thereby gaining purification by dissociation." Although at the time of writing this he had yet to make his philosophy of dramatism explicit, one can detect an anticipation of it here. We must envisage every "symbolic act" as taking place in a particular "scene," to which the "agent" responds:

> Hence if one can hand over his infirmities to a vessel, or "cause," outside the self, one can battle an external enemy instead of battling an enemy within. And the greater one's internal inadequacies, the greater the amount of evils one can load upon the back of "the enemy." This device is furthermore given a semblance of reason because the individual properly realizes that he is not alone responsible for his condition. There *are* inimical features in the scene itself. And he wants to have them "placed," preferably in a way that would require a minimum change in the ways of thinking to which he had been accustomed. This was especially appealing to the middle class, who were encouraged to feel that they could conduct their businesses without any basic change whatever, once the businessmen of a different "race" were eliminated. (*PLF* 203)

One might think that these two devices—"unification" and "projection"—convey the basic fault of Nazism, but Burke now traces a third feature, which arises from the conjunction of the first two and to which he gives the familiar name "symbolic rebirth." Once again, we need to see how a political doctrine can draw its appeal from appropriating religious principles:

> The projective device of the scapegoat, coupled with the Hitlerite doctrine of inborn racial superiority, provides its followers with a "positive" view of life. They can get the feel of *moving forwards*, towards a *goal* (a promissory feature of which Hitler makes much). In Hitler, as the group's prophet, such rebirth involved a symbolic change of lineage. Here, above all, we see Hitler giving a malign twist to a benign aspect of Christian thought. For whereas the Pope, in the familistic pattern of thought basic to the Church, stated that the Hebrew prophets were the *spiritual ancestors* of Christianity,

Hitler uses this same mode of thinking in reverse. He renounces this "ancestry" in a "materialistic" way by voting himself and the members of his lodge a different "blood stream" from that of the Jews. (*PLF* 203)

We may recall that, in his earlier writings, Burke had already pondered the nature of the rebirth ritual, which involves a "regression" prior to the gaining of a new "identity." Here he ingeniously reviews this process to describe what is involved when a whole nation is persuaded to undergo the same rite of renewal, according to spurious ideas of racial destiny. After all, suggests Burke, we have to keep reminding ourselves that the primary "scene" is the economic one, to which racial meaning has been attributed. In *Permanence and Change*, addressing the question of "the scapegoat mechanism" in passing, he defined it as an "error of interpretation," an instance of "trained incapacity" (*PC* 16). Now, in defining the fourth feature of the Nazi "unification device," he gives a specific example. He calls this feature "commercial use." He explains: "Hitler obviously here had something to sell—and it was but a question of time until he sold it (i.e., got financial backers for his movement). For it provided a *noneconomic interpretation of economic ills*. As such, it served with maximum efficiency in deflecting the attention from the economic factors involved in modern conflict; hence by attacking 'Jew finance' instead of *finance*, it could simulate an enthusiastic movement that left 'Aryan finance' in control" (*PLF* 204).

Yet Burke is saying something more profound than that Nazism allowed German capitalism to survive by creating a suitable scapegoat figure to explain away its internal contradictions. He is saying that, if a state has descended into financial chaos and is lacking in the dignity appropriate to a once-great country, it will tend to want to preserve the dignity first, at whatever cost. "A people in collapse, suffering under economic frustration and the defeat of nationalistic aspirations ... have little other than some 'spiritual' basis to which they could refer their nationalistic dignity. Hence, the categorical dignity of superior race was a perfect recipe for the situation. It was 'spiritual' in so far as it was 'above' crude economic 'interests,' but it was 'materialized' at the psychologically 'right' spot in that 'the enemy' was something you could *see*" (*PLF* 205). The whole point about a scapegoat, in other words, is that it must be visible and that the burden of sin or death which it bears on its back must be understood to have been taken away entirely.

Burke emphasizes the distortion of the sacred paradigm that all such persecution as the Nazi program of extermination involves:

> But above all, I believe, we must make it apparent that Hitler appeals by relying upon a bastardization of fundamentally religious patterns of thought. In this, if properly presented, there is no slight to religion. There is nothing in religion proper that requires a fascist state. There is much in religion, when misused, that does lead to a fascist state. There is a Latin proverb, *Corruptio optimi pessima*, "the corruption of the best is the worst." And it is the corruptors of religion who are a major menace to the world today, in giving the profound patterns of religious thought a crude and sinister distortion. (*PLF* 219)

Burke is quite obviously not setting out to expunge the survival of religious myth from modern political thought. Witness his earlier speculations on Marxism. On the contrary, he is arguing that a secular society that has lost touch with its religious roots, while retaining the characteristically human need for religious fulfillment, will be more vulnerable to the "crude and sinister distortion" outlined above.[8]

DIALECTIC OF THE SCAPEGOAT

So far, we have seen how Burke draws on the tradition of the scapegoat ritual to explain modern politics. But it is the very principle by which a figure may be excluded and punished by a community that fascinates him. Much of his middle and later work is dedicated to providing a satisfactory definition of the scapegoat itself, beyond its contemporary manifestations. In *A Grammar of Motives* (1945) he relates scapegoating to the theme of the dialectic. As is usual with Burke, the main context is linguistic. He is concerned with the kind of "symbolic action" of which human beings are capable.

Thus Burke first has to explain that by "dialectics in the most general sense" he means "the employment of the possibilities of linguistic transformation." He considers dialectics under three headings:

1. Merger and division. (There may be a state of merger, or a state of division, or developments from either state to the other.)

2. The Three Major Pairs: action–passion, mind–body, being–nothing.

3. Transcendence. (Transcendence likewise may be either a state or a development. Non-representational art, for instance, may be a state of transcendence with respect to representational art, as the artist thereafter dwells in the contemplation of relatively disembodied forms. But within the fixity of this stage, the particular things he paints will have development, quite as the lyric, while arresting some mood or attitude and making it the entire universe of discourse, yet has progression rather than mere succession.) (*GM* 402–403)

This three-stage description seems highly abstract. But we soon get our bearings when he expounds the "Dialectic of the Scapegoat." The scheme is again triadic, comprised, according to Burke, of "(1) an original state of merger, in that the iniquities are shared by both the iniquitous and their chosen vessel; (2) a principle of division, in that the elements shared in common are being ritualistically alienated; (3) a new principle of merger, this time in the unification of those whose purified identity is defined in dialectical opposition to the sacrificial offering" (*GM* 406).

This triadic scheme makes more sense if we read it in conjunction with Burke's speculations in the title essay of *The Philosophy of Literary Form*. There he notes the analogy between the rhetorical device known as synecdoche (the part that represents the whole, as when an employer may speak of a laborer as a hired "hand" when actually referring to the whole person) and the scapegoat (the figure who represents the fundamental anxiety of the whole community). Burke's comment is cryptic: referring to the "synecdochic function," he observes that "The 'scapegoat' becomes another kind of 'representative,' in serving as the symbolic vessel of certain burdens, which are ritualistically delegated to it" (*PLF* 27). C. Allen Carter provided a useful synopsis of Burke's thinking in light of both this statement and the discussion of the dialectic of the scapegoat. He makes explicit what Burke, while using the exact term, is content to leave implicit: that the scapegoat, like the rhetorical figure of synecdoche, is "a part that assumes the burden of the whole." Writes Carter: "At one moment the chosen victim is *a part of* the clan, being one of their number; a moment later it symbolizes something *apart from* them, being the curse they wish to lift from themselves. By the operation of dialectical change, they first identify with their victim; then they deny the connection altogether."[9]

As might be expected, Burke no sooner presents the dialectic of the scapegoat in terms of sequence than he qualifies it, allowing for "an ambiguous shuttling between concepts of logical priority and concepts of temporal priority":

> "Essences" or "principles" are among the logically prior, as an essence is logically prior to its accidents, or as a principle is logically prior to the instances of its workings. Hence the ancestral nature of the scapegoat as vessel of vicarious atonement. And by the same token the scapegoat can possess the divinity of a sacrificial king, since gods too are terms for the essence of motivation, as a tribe that regulates its life about the seasonal fluctuations of a river may sum up the whole complex of tribal motivations in the concept of a river god, which could be the "essence" of the tribal adjustments to the stream's behavior and utility. (*GM* 407)

In arguing that the tribe will always "temporize" its own "essence" by translating "essential" into "original," Burke here uses the examples of a king and a god. But he is not forgetting that a criminal will serve the function of scapegoat just as well, provided that his removal from society means that society "purifies itself" through "moral indignation" in the act of condemning him. Still, we have to recognize the paradox by which, no matter how antipathetic the chosen figure is, he achieves a certain "power," if only by being the focus of so much symbolic investment. Burke dwells briefly on the scapegoat as a "concentration of power, which may be for either good or evil until that stage of religious development is reached where power is dissociated into good and evil principles" (*GM* 407). Again demonstrating his own preoccupation with the religious impulse, he speculates further that "[t]his stage was more complete in the Manichean heresy than it is in orthodox Christianity, that sees in Lucifer a fallen *angel*, and which proclaims the divinity in Jesus by a revolutionary redefinition of the figure whom His crucifiers had classed with criminals. In the Christian dialectic of atonement, the vicarious sacrifice Who took upon Himself the burden of the world thus retains the ambiguities of power only in the sense that He suffered calumny" (*GM* 408).

If the essence of Christianity, at least in its Pauline form, is best approached through the scapegoat principle, then Burke is not inclined to dismiss it as a delusion. Rather, he seems to suggest that there is an underlying mystery at work which merits attention. He will return to this theme in his later work. Meanwhile, he notes again, as in the essay on Hitler, how Nazi anti-Semitism works upon an "essential" pattern, even while corrupting and debasing it. Thus he traces "a related process of dialectic: unification of a foe shared by a common enemy" (*GM* 408). But even in repeating this point from that essay, he cannot help but remind us of the linguistic roots of oppositional thinking, admittedly taken to extremes by Hitler: "On the purely Grammatical level, this is reducible purely to the *antithetical nature* of dialectical terms, like 'freedom,' 'perfection,' or the terms for social movements, that derive their significance from their relation to opposite terms." Burke is presumably thinking of socialism and communism, both of which define themselves against the prevailing individualism that is encouraged by the capitalist economy. At any rate, we must concede his point that there are some dialectically weighted words that, as it were, do our thinking for us. He contrasts these words to terms such as "house" and "apple," which "require no counter-words like 'anti-house' or un-apple' to define them" (*GM* 408). Whether we choose to emphasize antithesis (opposition) or, as mentioned, synecdoche (representation of the whole by a part), we can agree with Carter when he declares on behalf of Burke that the scapegoat "is thus in some ways a matter of terminology or a figure of speech, a figure of speech by which all live *and* by which some die."[10]

In stressing that the basis of the scapegoat mechanism is language itself, Burke anticipates his own later thinking. We have already referred in some detail to his important summarizing essay "Dramatism" (1967). What remains to explore is how in that essay Burke develops his analysis of language and thought as "modes of action rather than as means of conveying information" by addressing the issue of what he now calls "victimage." He takes as his starting point one of the two figures of speech implicit in the dialectic of the scapegoat—namely, antithesis. With Henri Bergson's *Creative Evolution* in mind, and specifically the chapter "The Idea of Nothing," Burke considers the nature of the negative. For Bergson, human language introduces the "not" into the world: "It is" is inevitably complemented by "It is not." For dramatism, however, the negative that is more important than this descriptive one is the "moralistic" or "hortatory" negative: "Thou shalt not." Thus, notes Burke, " 'Order,' being a polar term, implies a corresponding idea of 'Disorder,' while these terms in turn involve ideas of 'obedience' or 'disobedience' to the 'authority' implicit in the Order (with further terministic radiations, such as the attitude of 'humility' that leads to the act of obedience, or the attitude of 'pride' that leads to the act of disobedience, these in turn involving

114 ℘ *Kenneth Burke: From Myth to Ecology*

ideas of guidance or temptation, reward or punishment, and so on)" (D 341–342).

As always with Burke, where we discover a logical opposition or a grammatical antithesis at work, there will be larger cultural issues at stake. Add to antithesis the general linguistic device known as substitution, by which a word may stand for a thing, or one word for another word, and bear in mind that synecdoche is a variant form of substitution, and we now have the discursive basis of "victimage." The scapegoat is defined by opposition, and the scapegoat is that which stands for something else—namely, the pollution or guilt that the ritual is designed to remove from the community.

Given the "entelechial" urge that Burke believes to be intrinsically human, we find that the very play of positive and negative, together with the interchangeability of term with thing and of term with term, may move us toward a violent "culmination." Dramatism, then, will reveal "how the negativistic principle of guilt implicit in the nature of order combines with the principles of thoroughness (or 'perfection') and substitution that are characteristic of symbol systems in such a way that the sacrificial principle of victimage (the 'scapegoat') is intrinsic to human congregation. The intricate line of exposition might be summed up thus: If order, then guilt; if guilt, then need for redemption; but any such 'payment' is victimage. Or: If action, then drama; if drama, then conflict; if conflict, then victimage" (D 342).

Once again, Christian myth forms the context of Burke's "dramatistic" speculations, so much so that some of this last statement may appear rather too cryptic to the reader who is unfamiliar with the implicit theology. To explore victimage further, we must consider Burke's sustained analysis of Christian myth.

DRAMATISM OR LOGOLOGY?

We have been working within the context of dramatism, but *The Rhetoric of Religion* (1961) is not confined to this method of interpretation. The subtitle announces that Burke is concerned rather with "Studies in Logology." "Logology" is a term we have noted in passing, but it is with this work that Burke espouses the idea explicitly and systematically. Perhaps it would be worth pausing to see what he tells us about it in the opening pages. Fortunately, he wastes no time. The title of the introduction is "On *Theology* and *Logology*," and Burke declares in his first sentence: "If we defined 'theology' as 'words about God,' then by 'logology' we should mean 'words about words.'"

He explains that he is privileging neither religious nor secular premises. He writes: The Biblical avowal that *man* is made in *God's image* has made us wary of the reversed anthropomorphic tendency to conceive of God in *man's image*. But the present enquiry stands midway between those two positions, contending merely that, insofar as religious doctrine is verbal, it will necessarily exemplify its nature as verbalization; and insofar as religious doctrine is thorough, its way of exemplifying verbal principles should be correspondingly thorough" (*RR* 1).

The existence or nonexistence of God is not at issue for logology: the divine becomes, provisionally, a linguistic rather than metaphysical premise. Burke puts the case at the beginning of Chapter 1, which concerns the relation between "words" and "the Word." He has in mind the opening of the Gospel of St. John: "In the beginning was the Word" (John 1:1). He elaborates upon this passage as follows: "We are to be concerned with the analogy between 'words' (lower case) and 'The Word' (*Logos, Verbum*) as it were in caps. 'Words' in the first sense have wholly naturalistic, empirical reference. But they may be used analogically, to designate a further dimension, the 'supernatural.' Whether or not there is a realm of the 'supernatural,' there are *words* for it" (*RR* 7). For Burke, theology is complemented rather than contradicted by logology.

The absence of any initial mention of dramatism need not concern us. We need not fear that we now have to negotiate a whole new philosophy. Logology is simply the logical extension of the insights of dramatism. The later Burke, having coined both terms, seems at times to have abandoned one for the other. However, in his major essays of summation, written in his last three decades, he insists that both name the same theory. Thus in "Order, Action, and Victimage" (1968) he explains: "I call [my] position 'Dramatistic' because it features the concept of action (secondarily involving a strategic distinction between 'action' and 'motion'). I call the position 'Logological' because it lays primary stress upon the element of 'symbolicity' in the motivating of human action, man's *reflexive* ability, as a symbol-wielding animal, to use symbols about symbols, or words about words" (OAV 168).

A more philosophically orthodox distinction is made in "Dramatism and Logology" (1985): "My 'Dramatism' article ... is ontological. It stresses what we *are*: the symbol-using animal. I call logology epistemological because it relates to the initial *duplication* that came into the world when we would go from *sensations* to *words* for sensations." The nature of language, he elaborates, is such that "our *words* for sensations can be developed analogically," as with "the figurative use of terms for *natural* conditions, whereby nature supplies us with a source from which we could develop a vocabulary for the 'spiritual.'" Again, Burke adds: "The *discriminations* that we make by language constitute our realm of *knowledge*, thus being epistemological" (DL 91). To put the matter as starkly as possible, dramatism is concerned with what the human being *is* (namely, a symbolic actor in a specific scene); logology is concerned with what the human being *knows* (namely, the nature of symbolism, or the way "words" culminate in the absolute "Word," or *Logos*).

No sooner does Burke define logology then he begins to tie it to victimage. The introduction to *The Rhetoric of Religion* includes a short poem that might help elucidate the last quotation from Burke's essay "Dramatism." It spells out the logic of victimage without any explicit reliance on the dramatistic model and with greater stress on the theology that Burke is trying to rationalize by way of logology:

> Order leads to Guilt
> (for who can keep commandments!)
> Guilt needs Redemption
> (for who would not be cleansed!)
> Redemption needs Redeemer
> (which is to say, a Victim!).
>
> In short,
> Order
> Through Guilt
> To Victimage
> (hence: Cult of the Kill!). (*RR 4–5*)

We cannot help but note here a deep ambivalence on Burke's part. The feeling of the poem seems to be one of regret, even bitterness, over an urge toward scapegoating that is inherent in human nature. But the subject matter can also be seen as a matter-of-fact summary of Pauline Christianity, according to which the Son inevitably has to be sacrificed to atone to the Father for a sinful humanity. It is hard to assess Burke's tone—how he is addressing us, how he is expecting us to respond. On one hand it seems unlikely that he is asserting a fundamentalist case for redemption by violence, a process that he thereby expects to be applauded. On the other hand it seems doubtful that the tone is that of a skeptic talking to other skeptics: the theology is taken too seriously for that. Perhaps, then, the ambivalence is the key. Burke is not so much refusing to commit himself as refusing to ignore any possibility within the symbolic universe that human beings construct. Again, we have to go along with him while we see what he has to say further about victimage in relation to Christian myth.

The relevant part of the book is his comprehensive discussion of "The First Three Chapters of Genesis," which extends to more than one hundred pages. It begins by reflecting on the seventeenth-century philosopher Thomas Hobbes' obsession with the idea of a covenant. Burke proceeds to develop his own logological account of covenants as "motives." This approach demands that he "relate the ideas of Creation, Covenant and Fall" so that "they can be seen to implicate one another inextricably, along with ideas of Sacrifice and Redemption":

> Creation implies authority in the sense of power, sovereignty—the highest or most radical sovereignty in case the Covenant is made by God. The possibility of a "Fall" is implied in the idea of a Covenant insofar as the idea of a Covenant implies the possibility of its being violated. One does not make a covenant [*sic*] with stones or trees or fire—for such things cannot break agreements or defy commandments, since they cannot even understand agreements or commands. Also, the possibility of a "Fall" is implied in the idea of the Creation, insofar as the Creation was a kind of "divisiveness," since it set up different categories of things which could be variously at odds with one another and which accordingly lack the proto-Edenic simplicity of absolute unity. (*RR* 174)

Already the logological perspective is evident, as Burke considers how words imply one another, how words imply an essential or "entelechial" Word, and how the Word implies words through which it might find expression. The Bible does narrate a temporal, linear myth, but it is always possible to translate this into spatial, cyclical terms:

> Narratively, there was the Creation; then came the "Edenic" Covenant (which included the injunction against eating of the tree of knowledge of good and evil); then the Fall; and then the "Adamic Covenant" (3:14–19) which included punishments for Adam's first disobedience. But though this order is irreversible from the standpoint of narrative, there is a sense in which we can reverse the order. For instance, we could "begin" with the idea of punishment; next we could note that the idea of punishment implies the idea of some

infraction which makes the punishment relevant; and such infraction implies the need for a set of conditions that make the infraction
possible; and insofar as we looked for a "first" set of such conditions, the idea of them would imply the idea of the kind of Creation
that allowed for disobedience. (*RR* 175)

Already one can see that the poem featured in the introduction is being
augmented to the point of a fully logological account of the biblical
narrative.

Having inferred from the first two chapters of Genesis the rest of
that book, and the rest of the Pentateuch, with its saga of human sin
and divine wrath, Burke now proceeds to infer from those same two
chapters the whole of the Christian New Testament, with its promise
of salvation. In doing so, he draws also on the terminology of dramatism, and in particular its pentad of elements in any instance of
symbolic action:

> Insofar as punishment is a kind of "payment" for wrong, we can see
> flickering about the edges of the idea of punishment the idea of
> redemption. To "pay" for one's wrongdoing by suffering punishment
> is to "redeem" oneself, to cancel one's debt, to ransom or "buy
> back." Next, since the idea of an *agent* is implicit in the idea of an
> *act*, we can say that in the idea of *redemption* there is implicit the
> idea of a personal *redeemer*. Or, if you think of redemption as a
> condition or situation (a "scene"), then you may extract the same
> implication by thinking of a redeemer as an instrument, or agency,
> for bringing about the condition. And this step, you will note, auto-
> matically includes the idea of a substitution: the possibility that one
> character may be redeemed through the act or agency of another.
> (*RR* 175)

What the biblical myth presents in narrative terms—as a sequence
of sin and salvation, promise and fulfillment—Burke presents in
spatial, linguistic, and logical terms. Yet he still does full justice to the
temporal power of the myth:

> The idea of such substitution, or vicarage, neatly parallels at one
> end of the series an idea at the other: the notion that, as one char-
> acter can redeem another by suffering in his stead, so one character
> can impute guilt to another by sinning in his stead. This would be
> true of the Pauline logic whereby Adam's disobedience represents a

guiltiness in Everyman with regard to Covenants ("In Adam's fall, We sinned all"), and there is introduced a principle of representation whereby a "second Adam" can serve as sacrificial substitute for mankind when the categorical guiltiness is being "paid for." (*RR* 175–176)

Thus is the Christian myth translated into logological terms, yet not thereby emptied of its power. In espousing logology, Burke is not seeking the triumph of *logos* over *mythos,* of the word of rationality over the word of imagination. Burke is not a "demythologizer," if by that we mean someone who regards the mythic form of the Bible as the disposable husk that hides the kernel of meaning.[11] Rather, logology signifies the attempt to mediate between *mythos* and *logos*. This aim is valid, given that the Bible, which is the main text he focuses upon, recounts a myth, or a series of myths, that is informed by the life of the ultimate *Logos* ("In the beginning was the Word ...").

ORDER

It will not have escaped the reader's notice that, if logology is about the mutual implication of words—that is, about their cyclical relationship—and if the Bible refers all words to one Word, then the whole process is governed by tautology. That is what Burke addresses next, in a subsection entitled "Tautological Cycle of Terms for 'Order.' " In effect, he argues here that the whole narrative of the Bible may be deduced from the initial polarity: that of order-obedience versus disorder-disobedience. What essentially concerns Burke is the human capacity for negation. "The Biblical myth pictures natural things as coming into being through the agency of God's Word; but they can merely do as they were designed to do, whereas with God's permission though not without his resentment, the seed of Adam can do even what it has been explicitly told not to do. The word-using animal not only understands a thou-shalt-not; it can carry the principle of the negative a step further, and answer the thou-shalt-not with a disobedient No" (*RR* 186–187).

No matter how complex the theology, Burke is able to spell out the logological implications, which hinge on his fundamental distinction between human *action* and nonhuman *motion*: " 'Things' can but *move* or *be moved.* 'Persons' by definition can 'act.' In being endowed with words (symbols) by which they can frame responses to questions and commands, by the same token they have 'responsibility.' " Further if disobedience is an "act," then the corresponding "attitude" that precedes it is "pride." By way of balance, we can then associate obedience with "humility" (RR 187). However, there is a third, intermediate factor: the possibility of choice between the two, which we know as "free will." In a theological context we may say that "this locus of freedom makes possible the kind of personal choice we have in mind when we speak of 'Action.'" In a logological context, however, "the statement should be made the other way round. That is, whereas ontologically or theologically we say that by being endowed with free will man is able to act morally, the corresponding logological statement would be: Implicit in the idea of an act is the idea of free will." Burke adds parenthetically, but significantly, another version of the formula: "Implicit in the idea of an act is the idea of freedom" (*RR* 187). Here, perhaps, theology and logology meet, as Burke states a central principle of his interest in Christian myth as symbolic narrative, as the ultimate project of the symbolic actor.

But Burke has still not exhausted the implications of the word "order." Later in this chapter he ponders the creation myth in the book of Genesis, pointing out that it is in the nature of all myth not only to "temporize" the "essence" that is at its heart but also to "personalize" it. This observation again takes us back to the notion of free agency contained in the very idea of an act. Burke takes the temporal aspect first. Instead of stating the principle of classification logically, explaining that there are "six primary classes" of creation, a myth will always insist on a narrative sequence, thought to have taken place in the beginning. It narrates "principles" as "principals": "Thus, instead of saying 'And this competes the first broad division, or classification, of our subject-matter,' we'd say: 'And the evening and the morning were the first day'.... And so on, through the six broad classes, ending 'last but not least,' on the category of man and his dominion" (*RR* 202). Turning now to the "personalization," he states: "This role is performed by the references to God's creative fiat, which from the very start infuses the sheerly natural order with the verbal principle (the makings of that 'reason' which we take to be so essential an aspect of human personality)" (*RR* 202). Burke offers his own logological translation of the biblical creation myth:

> The principle of personality implicit in the idea of the first creative fiats, whereby all things are approached in terms of the word, applies also to the feeling for symbol-systems on the part of the human animal, who would come to read nature as if it were a book. Insofar

as God's words infused the natural order with their genius, and insofar as God is represented as speaking words to the first man and woman, the principle of human personality (which is at the very start identified with *dominion*) has its analogue in the notion of God as a super-person, and of nature as the act of a super-agent. (That is, we take symbol-using to be a distinctive ingredient of "personality.") (*RR* 202–203)

Burke clearly indicates that the human investment in the whole story of creation, fall, and redemption may be analyzed in terms of symbolic action. But he has yet to explain fully the negative impetus behind it, in keeping with his insight that it is human language that introduces into the world the tension between order and disorder, obedience and disobedience, good and evil. Here he has to take the idea of "dominion," just introduced, and argue from it toward the idea of "mortification." He proposes that "the idea of Mortification is integral to the idea of Dominion" because "the scrupulous subject must seek to 'slay' within himself whatever impulses run counter to the authoritative demands of sovereignty." Thus we may expect that "all about a story of the 'first' dominion and the 'first' disobedience there should hover the theme of the 'first' mortification" (*RR* 206).

Burke now attempts to show "how the step from conscience-laden guiltiness to a regimen of mortification can be narratively translated into terms of the first step from 'sin' to death.' " Such a translation is important because "the principle of mortification is integral to the idea of redemptive sacrifice which we have associated with the idea of Order" (*RR* 208). The key point is that where animals seem to accept death as part of the natural order, human beings seem to regard it as a problem, finding it difficult to believe that it is the inevitable consequence of birth. Burke negotiates the theological meaning of this problem as follows:

[L]ike St. Paul, we may choose to interpret the Biblical account of the Creation and Fall as saying literally that, whereas other animals die naturally . . . all members of the human species die not as the result of a natural process but because the first members of the species "sinned." That is, death in man's case is primarily associated with the principle of personality (or "conscience"), such as the Bible explicitly relates to the verbal Covenant made by the first and foremost exponent of the creative verbal principle, in its relation to the idea of Order. Otherwise put: When death is viewed "personally," in moralistic terms colored by conditions of governance (the moral order), it is conceived not just as a natural process, but as a kind of "capital punishment." (*RR* 209)

While the word "death" is not quite synonymous with "mortification," but they are closely related. If we look up "mortification" in an etymological dictionary, we are referred back to the Latin *mortificare*, "to kill or subdue," and then even farther back to *mors*, "death." Burke does not give us this etymology, but he is clearly aware of it. His reasoning seems to be as follows. Human beings think that death must be a punishment for sin, so they associate sin with death. In order to deny the death within them, in accordance with the dictates of the guilt that is appropriate for sinners, they "kill or subdue"—that is, impose a state of death upon—their own fleshly appetites. They die strategically in order not to die forever at their natural deaths; they hope to be born again in the spirit. Mortification, then, is the direction inward of the same impulse that, directed outward, we call victimage. Instead of punishing another, or hoping to be saved by the sacrifice of another, we punish ourselves in a constant state of "self-sacrifice" (*RR* 206–207).

Burke's ingenuity threatens to obscure his argument, particularly as he does not draw any conclusions from his digression on mortification. At stake is the symbol-using animal's insistence on discovering the negative principle at every turn, whether inner or outer. It certainly makes sense of a phenomenon that is frequently encountered in reports of terrorist campaigns and massacres: the protagonists of these dramas, having punished all their victims, inevitably turn their weapons on themselves; or, as in the case of the perpetrators of the attacks on the United States on September 11, 2001, the very act of homicide is simultaneously an act of suicide.[12] However, Burke has yet to tie together the various strands of the cycle of terms that he claims to exist beneath the narrative form of the biblical myth. He attempts to do so in a section of this chapter titled "Dominion, Guilt, Sacrifice."

By way of a summary of his argument so far, he notes that "when we turn from the consideration of a terministic cycle in which the various terms mutually imply one another, to the consideration of the narrative terminology in these opening chapters of Genesis, we note that the narrative terms allow the idea of Order to be 'processed.'" He traces the linear sequence by which essence is temporized:

Here one can start with the creation of a natural order (though conceiving it as infused with a verbal principle); one can next proceed to an idea of innocence untroubled by thou-shalt-nots; one can next introduce a thou-shalt-not; one can next depict the thou-shalt-not as violated; one can next depict a new Covenant propounded on the basis of this violation, and with capital punishment; one can later introduce the principle of sacrifice, as would become wholly clear when we came to the Noachian Covenant where, after the great cleansing by water, God gave Noah the rainbow sign, "And Noah builded an altar unto the Lord; and took of every clean beast and of every clean fowl, and offered burnt-offerings on the altar." (8:20). Then gradually thereafter, more and more clearly, comes the emergence of the turn from mere sacrifice to the idea of outright redemption by victimage. (*RR* 216)

At first reading, Burke might seem to be attempting to demystify a sacred myth by translating it into secular terms. Or again, he might be taken to imply that the authors of the Bible were themselves consciously engaged in translating the essence of faith, already fully formed, into temporal sequence by way of making it more palatable. But on further reflection, we may see Burke's *Rhetoric of Religion* as testimony to the power of narrative, which he takes to be indispensable for the human mind, being inseparable from language. Certainly, those who have borrowed heavily from his work would interpret him that way. For example, the academic Marxist Fredric Jameson has written persuasively, guided by Burke more than by Marx, on "narrative as a socially symbolic act."[13]

The more specific inference to make is that logology, while always ready to translate the temporal, linear impetus of narrative into spatial, logical terms, respects the medium of myth, seeing it as a genuine element of theological meaning. As Burke explains in "Theology and Logology" (1979), a later reflection on some of the ideas espoused in *The Rhetoric of Religion*:

The Old Testament begins in its way quite as the N T Gospel of John begins in its, with pronouncements that overlap upon these two kinds of priority [i.e., logical and temporal]. Genesis "tells the story" of the divine word's [*sic*] informative power. John tells the story of the Logos, a Hellenistic stress upon the word that a "Judaizing" sect among the emergent Christian doctrinarians had unsuccessfully attempted to exclude from the canon.... Logologically, we confront the fact that, given the fluid relation between logical and temporal priority, the logical "firstness" of principles, when stated in the way of story (*mythos*), as with the opening chapters of Genesis, calls for translation into terms of *temporal* priority. (TL 166–167)

While Burke's business is to keep translating the mythic story into theological doctrine, and the terms of theological doctrine into the terms of terminology itself, he remains alert to the persuasive power of myth. Thus the polar relationship of order and disorder may be time-less from a supernatural perspective, but time is the dimension in which human beings engage imaginatively with its meaning: "Myth, story, narrative makes it possible to transform this timeless relation between polar terms into a temporal sequence. That is, myth can tell of a step *from* either one *to* the other" (TL 169). Moreover, myth involves not only an intriguing chain of events but also their charac-terization. As Burke notes, "Though terms can confront each other as antithetically as 'reward' and 'punishment,' nothing 'happens' until they are given functions in an irreversible, personalized *narrative*. Terms like 'disorder,' 'temptation,' 'disobedience' come to life when Adam is assigned the role of personally representing the principle of sin, and Satan is assigned the role of ultimate tempter. God has the role of setting up the Order and giving the critical negative order, so termin-istically necessary before a Fall can even be possible" (TL 170).

We may, then, say abstractly that Burke's logological account of biblical myth is designed to demonstrate its "entelechial" character, and thereby demonstrates how intrinsic "entelechy" is to human thought and language. What this demonstration involves is an exploration of not only the temporizing but also the personalizing of essence that myth achieves. Burke refers to this personalizing as a kind of "reduc-tion," but by "reduction" he means the advantage that myth has over the exposition of complex theological doctrines—namely, dramatic intensity. It should be clear, then, that Burke is full of admiration for what the Bible achieves:

[W]ith the principle of authority personalized as God, the principle of disobedience as Adam (the "old Adam in all of us"), the principle of temptation as an Aesopian serpent, Eve as mediator in the bad sense of the word, and the idea of temptation reduced imagistically to terms of eating (the perfect image of a "first" appetite, or essen-tial temptation, beginning as it does with the infantile, yet surviving in the adult), such reduction of the tautological cycle to a narrative linear progression makes possible the notion of an *outcome*. Thus when we read of one broken covenant after another, and see the sacrificial principle forever reaffirmed anew, narratively this succession may be interpreted as movement towards a fulfillment, though from the standpoint of the tautological cycle they "go on endlessly" implicating one another. (*RR* 217)

For Burke, the principles of personality and of purpose go together. In the Christian Bible the culminating figure is Christ, the focus of the New Testament. In "Theology and Logology" Burke writes of "the tactics of narrative personalizing (in effect a kind of substitution that represents a *principle* in terms of a *prince*)" (TL 167). Christ is the supreme person and the final purpose at once. This mode of understanding narrative—or, as Paul Ricoeur would say, "narrative understanding"—is called "typology."[14] Christ thereby becomes the culmination of all previous sacrificial victims in the Old Testament. Burke has already referred to "the Pauline logic whereby Adam's disobedience represents a guiltiness in Everyman with regard to Covenants," which demands that a "second Adam" can serve as "sacrificial substitute for mankind when the categorical guiltiness is being 'paid for' " (*RR* 175–176). Now he explains how his own approach would translate this temporal process while respecting its effectiveness as myth:

Logologically many forms of victimage are seen as variants of the sacrificial motive. Burnt offerings, Azazel, Isaac, Israel in exile and the various "remnants" who undergo tribulations in behalf of righteousness can be listed, along with Christ, as "reindividuation of the sacrificial principle." But a theological view of the narrative can lead to a more "promissory" kind of classification, whereby all sacrifices and sufferings preceding the Crucifixion can be classed as "types of Christ." When the devout admonish that "Christ's Crucifixion is repeated endlessly each time we sin," they are stating a theological equivalent of our logological point about the relation between the linear-temporal and the cyclical-tautological. Logologically, the "fall" and the "redemption" are but parts of the same cycle, with each implying the other. The order can be reversed, for the terms in which we conceive of redemption can help shape the terms in which we conceive of the guilt which it is thought to follow (quite as the quality of a "cure" can qualify our idea of the "disease" for which it is thought to be the cure—or as a mode of wish-fulfillment can paradoxically serve to reinforce the intensity of the wishes). But narratively, they stand at opposite ends of a long development, that makes one "Book" of the two Testaments taken together. (*RR* 218)

Thus one may opt either for narrative "typology" (Christ as the final and decisive sacrifice in a series, anticipated by all the others) or for cyclical "tautology" (Christ as an instance—albeit a major one—of the sacrificial principle). Either way, one has to confront the intractability of guilt, given the human fascination with the negative. Burke affirms without qualification that "guilt is intrinsic to the idea of Covenant" (*RR* 219).

Yet this position only raises a further question, the answer to which he provides: "Is victimage (redemption by vicarious atonement) equally intrinsic to the idea of guilt? The Bible, viewed either logologically or theologically, seems to be saying that it is" (*RR* 219). But that conclusion is by no means the end of the argument, or indeed of the analysis. For Burke, it is yet necessary to make a "Final Comparing of Cyclical and Rectilinear Styles," as indicated by the subsection that follows that last statement. This subsection affords insight into the name and nature of sin, which may be a matter of doctrine (theology) but which is usually articulated in terms of narrative (mythology). From this dual perspective our assumption about inherited guilt may need restating:

> "Original" sin is only the mythic way of talking about "essential" sin: "original" sin is that of the "old Adam" in us. It is sin "in principle." Hence it is the kind of guiltiness that, as translated into terms of temporal sequence, we "inherit" from our "first" ancestor in the male line, as the result of his "first" disobedience to the "first" thou-shalt-not imposed upon him by the first and foremost authority (to whom he was subject, but from whom he inherited dominion over all created things, including his woman). For that's the way to say "in principle" in narrative terms. (*RR* 222)

From this sin—the primal act of disobedience, the first "no" to the founding "thou-shalt-not"—there arises guilt, and the need to reaffirm the necessity of obedience: "Obedience says no to the self from within, 'conscientiously,' not merely through fear of policing from without" (*RR* 223). But the sin and the guilt are so great that more—either the subduing of the self or the sacrificing of other selves—is called for. "And here arise the modes of sacrifice that express themselves either 'suicidally,' as Mortification, or 'homicidally,' as the slaying of scapegoats more or less clearly identified with the traits of human personality. Hence, the idea of a primary transgression is rounded out by the idea of an ultimate redemption (both the first and last steps involving the principle of substitution, the 'old Adam' having sinned for us, and a corresponding Redeemer or Mediator of some sort being required to intercede for us)" (RR 223). The theology, expressed in the narrative project of typology, by which Christ completes or perfects the whole biblical story, "promises an ultimate linear progression to end all linear progressions."

But what of the sacrificial principle itself? Burke's logological answer is that "while the era of temporal dominion continues, the cycle of terms implicit in the idea of worldly order continues, forever circling back upon itself, thus forever 'guilty,' thus forever demanding 'redemption,' thus forever inciting anew to the search for a curative victim" (*RR* 223). But, then again, what of the promise held out by the biblical myth? Burke's response is pessimistic: "[I]t seems that, even if one believes in the idea of a perfect, supernatural, superpersonal victim, by identification with whose voluntary sacrifice one can be eternally saved, there is still the goad to look for victims here on earth as well, who should be punished for their part, real or imaginary, in blocking the believer's path to felicity, or perhaps in threatening to send him on his heavenly way too soon" (*RR* 223).

The crucial problem confronted here is not only the tautological cycle of terms, by which order inevitably implies guilt, guilt inevitably implies redemption, and redemption inevitably implies victimage. It is also the way that the social and celestial hierarchies reinforce each other. In short, "the idea of a 'Lord' (or Master) applies equally to supernatural and worldly governance" (*RR* 224). Burke, as we know, believes that social and cosmic "mysteries" will always imply each other because "mystery" is intrinsic to hierarchy and because hierarchy always culminates in the idea of the divine. But as we also know, he is always alert to the historical abuse of this permanent cultural feature. His earlier reflections on Hitler acquire new relevance here: "Thus, for a purely worldly order of motives, we should expect a correspondingly worldly kind of 'defilement,' with its call for a correspondingly worldly need of cleansing by sacrifice. Nazism provides the most drastically obvious instance of the ways in which such 'cleansing' operates, by an ideology depicting a 'perfect' victim in the guise of a 'total' enemy (a scheme involving redemption both by blood and by power)" (*RR* 224).

It would seem, then, that the "unification device" of the scapegoat, taken to an extreme in Hitler's Germany, is an inescapable fact of secular life, especially as it can always be substantiated by appeal to the sacred paradigm. (Burke, we recall, referred in his essay, especially in his essay to *Mein Kampf* to the "bastardization" of religious myth evident in Nazi ideology.) However, it would be wrong to leave off our consideration of Burke's principle of victimage by emphasizing only the gloomy conclusions to which it seems to lead. There is a hint of optimism in the later stages of Burke's chapter on Genesis in *The Rhetoric of Religion*, even though it may appear to be too cryptic in itself to take as a coherent statement of principle.

THE CULT OF COMEDY

Burke's chapter on Genesis demonstrates that his attitude to religious myth is consistently respectful, even if not always reverential. He is genuinely interested in what we may learn from it: "The Bible, with its profound and beautiful exemplifying of the sacrificial principle, teaches us that tragedy is ever in the offing. Let us, in the spirit of solemn comedy, listen to its lesson. Let us be on guard ever, as regards the subtleties of sacrifice, in their fundamental relationship to governance" (*RR* 235).

This vow to refuse the excesses of victimage, informed by respect for the most influential narration of the sacrificial motive—that of the Jewish and Christian Bibles—makes full sense only if we already know Burke's previous thinking. If we have to confront a tragic situation, then our best device is the comic frame or perspective. The epithet "solemn" reminds us that comedy is not the same as mere humor: it comprehends the full range of human emotions, while committing itself to an outcome favorable to human well-being. It is tolerant, eager not "to *waste* the world's rich store of error" (*ATH* 172). As such, of course, it has much in common with the message of the New Testament: it is a secular equivalent of the symbolic act of redemption.

But if the comic vision is the promise held out by Burke, it is a perspective that permits few illusions. In the later volume *Language as Symbolic Action* (1966), he offers a sobering "Definition of Man" that sums up many of those aspects of humanity that he has been documenting. Indeed, four of these aspects are listed in the first chapter of *The Rhetoric of Religion*, though without elaboration (*RR* 40). Here each "clause" is expanded, a "final codicil" added, and the whole in his statement placed in italics to emphasize its importance for Burke:

Man is
the symbol-using (symbol-making, symbol-misusing) animal
inventor of the negative (or moralized by the negative)
separated from his natural condition by instruments of his own
  making
goaded by the spirit of hierarchy (or moved by the sense of order)
and rotten with perfection. (LSA 16)

The first four clauses confirm what we have understood from Burke's earlier speculations on dramatism and his more recent speculations on logology. What distinguishes the human being from the world of mere motion is symbolicity. Human symbols inevitably build up into more and more complex systems, predicated upon notions of order, dominion, obedience, and so forth—culminating in the idea of an absolute symbol, or "Word." Burke here justifies his addition of the last clause, or codicil, in two stages—one that endorses the word "perfection" and one that explains why he has had regretfully to include the word "rotten."

First, Burke affirms that the "principle of perfection" is "central to the nature of language as motive." For the very desire to "name something by its 'proper' name," or to state one's needs so that one in effect "defines" the situation one is in, is "intrinsically 'perfectionist.'" Here he invokes again the Aristotelian principle of "entelechy," the notion that "each being aims at the perfection natural to its kind (or, etymologically, is marked by a 'possession of telos within')." Burke's only divergence from Aristotle is his confining of the term to the realm of "action" (the human tendency toward perfection by virtue of the nature of symbolicity) rather than "motion" (the tendency of nonhuman entities, such as trees, to grow and so fulfill their potential) (*LSA* 16–17).

Second—with regard to the word "rotten"—Burke refers to the danger implicit in the very idea of perfection, derived as it is from the culminative nature of symbol making:

Thus, the principle of drama is implicit in the idea of action, and the principle of victimage is implicit in the nature of drama. The negative helps radically to define the elements to be victimized. And inasmuch as substitution is a prime resource of symbol systems, the conditions are set for catharsis by scapegoat (including the "natural" invitation to "project" upon the enemy any troublesome traits of our own that we would negate). And the unresolved problems of "pride" that are intrinsic to privilege also bring the motive of hierarchy to bear here; for many kinds of guilt, resentment, and fear tend to cluster about the hierarchical psychosis, with its corresponding search for a sacrificial principle such as can become embodied in a political scapegoat. (*LSA* 18–19)

Given that the cultural perils of perfectionism would seem to outweigh the natural pleasures of fulfillment, it is imperative that the symbol-making animal learns how to prevent symbolic thoroughness manifesting itself in social persecution. The scapegoat ritual must be acknowledged as a process implicit in language, but it must also be watched, checked, and corrected. Once again, the choice of paradigm comes down to a literary genre: should one live life as a tragedy or as a comedy? In a footnote included almost casually at the end of the essay, Burke gives his answer. His reflections on victimage have led him to think of global catastrophes such as the Nazi attempt at genocide and also of the growth of weapons of mass destruction. These would seem to confirm a tragic view of human existence, but Burke declares his own choice of paradigm. As so often in his writings, it is the parenthetical remark that carries the weight of his thought:

> In his *Parts of Animals*, Chapter X, Aristotle mentions the definition of man as the "laughing animal," but he does not consider it adequate. Though I would hasten to agree, I obviously have a big investment in it, owing to my conviction that mankind's only hope is a cult of comedy. (The cult of tragedy is too eager to help out with the holocaust. And in the last analysis, it is too pretentious to allow for the proper recognition of our animality.) Also, I'd file "risibility" under "symbolicity." Insofar as man's laughter is to be distinguished from that of the Hyena [sic], the difference derives from ideas of *incongruity* that are in turn derived from principles of *congruity* necessarily implicit in any given symbol system. (*LSA* 20)

We are back once again to the need for perspective by incongruity, by which we are saved from the excesses of our own piety. But now it is clear that the overriding direction is that of the "comic corrective." A cult of tragedy may have the advantage of having victimage as its focus, but the danger is that the expectation of tragic violence may turn into the encouragement of tragic violence. In perpetrating the scapegoat ritual, one would, after all, simply be confirming one's own worst suspicions. Hence the gloomy self-importance of those who act on the dubious imperatives of the "final solution." By contrast, a cult of comedy, while shrewdly realistic, would prevent such excesses by being more humane in acknowledging one's own folly and in forgiving that of others. The comic vision is, in short, integral, where the tragic vision is divisive. Ideally, the one contains and corrects the other.

CATHARSIS AND BEYOND

We may have noted the phrase "catharsis by scapegoat," used above by Burke in his elaboration upon the final codicil of his "Definition of Man." Again, it would seem to be Aristotle whom he has in mind, for it was he who famously defended tragic drama because of its beneficial effects: "Tragedy is the representation of an action that is worthy of serious attention ... portraying incidents which arouse pity and fear, so that such emotions are purged by the performance."[15] Burke is fascinated by this "contract" of catharsis, by which the audience of tragedy agrees to acknowledge its hidden instincts, only to have them purified. Elsewhere in *Language as Symbolic Action* he uses the Aristotelian principle of purgation in his account of Aeschylus' trilogy, the *Oresteia*. He is concerned with how the three plays work on the level of formal entelechy by drawing on religious rites in order to resolve civic tensions. Here Burke's work follows, wittingly or unwittingly, that of the "Cambridge Ritualists" on myth and ritual. True, his insights are less historically specific, but they are also less burdened by the influence of Frazer.

To appreciate Burke's analysis of Aeschylus' trilogy, we will need to remind ourselves of the plot. The first play, *Agamemnon*, shows us Agamemnon returning victoriously to Argos after the Trojan War, only to be murdered by his wife, Clytemnestra. The second play, *The Libation Bearers*, centers on the act of revenge carried out by his son and daughter, Orestes and Elektra: they murder Clytemnestra and her lover, Aegisthus. In the third play, the *Eumenides*, we see the Furies in pursuit of Orestes, who is eventually put on trial. He is freed when Athena, goddess of wisdom, casts her vote in his favor. Moreover, he is no longer pursued, once Athena has reconciled the Furies to a new era of forgiveness and reconciliation. They assume a new identity, that of the Kindly Ones, who bless the land and its inhabitants.[16]

Burke's "Form and Persecution in the *Oresteia*" is a piece of work written in rather odd, strained language, consisting mainly of a report upon what he wrote on the *Oresteia* in a now abandoned book. Nevertheless, the essay seems to make sufficient sense as an independent speculation. Regarding the use of myth, Burke writes: "We were here generally concerned with stylistic resources whereby the important social relations involving superiority and inferiority could be translated into a set of 'mythic' equivalents. Disorders within the *polis* could automatically attain tragic scope and dignity by translation into a corresponding 'supernatural' terminology of motives. Hence, any civic issue could be reflected in a mythic idiom that transcended the political or social order, even if it did not have reference to the political or social order (and to the corresponding disorders)" (*LSA* 126).

This is an insight that very much anticipates the "structural" reading of Greek mythology developed by Jean-Pierre Vernant, for whom the "cunning intelligence" of the myth is seen at work on certain contradictions within Greek society. But what precisely is it that is being resolved? Burke next explains the form of the trilogy as being "persecutional" in direction, "a network of expectancies and fulfillments" that "can be summed up *dramatically* in such terms as Law, Right, Fate, Justice, Necessity" (*LSA* 127). These "Great Persecutional Words" provide the clue to the formal resolution. The process is analogous to that of the use of myth:

> Whatever the social origins of such motives may be, once they are converted into the fullness of tragedy they have become *cosmologized*. Whereupon an almost terrifying *thoroughness* of human honesty is demanded of us, as audience. For now we are in our very essence *persecuted*, and there can be no comfort until we have disclosed and appropriately transfigured every important motive still unresolved within us. That is, once the irresolutions of the body, of personal relations, and of social relations have been heroically transmogrified by identification with the Great Persecutional Words, which are in turn identified with the vastness of Nature and the mystery of Super-Nature, no pleasantly pluralistic dissipation of outlook is any longer tolerable. (*LSA* 127)

The formal and the mythic aspects are brought together in the conclusion to the essay, where we read: "Incidentally, we have elsewhere in our text observed how well the use of the traditional 'myth' in tragedy contributed to simplicity of design. For whatever the complexities of a unique situation may be, the myth reduces these to a few basic relationships. In this sense, the tragic playwright's use of myth enabled him to get, in his medium, the kind of functional simplifications that we have learnt to associate with Greek sculpture at its best" (*LSA* 137).

All told, the perfection of form, derived from myth, effects a catharsis of the sacrificial motive. The audience feels that the correct ritual has been enacted, that the gods have been given their due, and that humanity has been purged of its violent tendencies. Burke approves, as is evident from the epigraph to his *Grammar of Motives* (1945): "*Ad bellum purificandum*" ("toward the purification of war"). Aeschylus' tragedy manages, as it were, the scapegoating impulse: it purifies it by giving it complete dramatic expression. As Burke explains toward the end of that substantial volume, the need for war might be purged by encouraging "tolerance by speculation" or "Neo-Stoic resignation," which is by no means akin to a "cult of tragedy." Avoiding fatality and fanaticism alike, human beings would learn to acknowledge victimage as a first step to coming to terms with it: "To an extent, perhaps, it will be like an attitude of hypochondriasis: the attitude of a patient who makes peace with his symptoms by becoming interested in them" (*GM* 442–443). The desire to sacrifice others will not go away, but the fact that it will not go away makes it worthy of interest, if confined to the sphere of symbolicity. As William Rueckert puts it: "Purification by victimage is ... best effected ... in symbolic action generally, and poetic symbolic action specifically, for there actual victims can be replaced by symbolic ones, and actual physical violence can be replaced by verbal violence. This idea is the basis of Burke's theory of art as catharsis."[17]

But the tragic form, no matter how effective, still does not take us beyond the "persecutional" logic mentioned. Hence Burke concludes his essay on Aeschylus by reminding us what normally follows a tragic trilogy—namely, the "satyr" play:

The satyr play that rounded out this particular trilogy is missing. From our point of view, the loss to those who would systematically lurk, and would piously spy on great texts, is perhaps the greatest in all human history. For though we do know that the satyr plays were *burlesques* of the very characters who were treated solemnly in the tragedies, we would like to think that, in the great days, the *same* characters were *finally* burlesqued who had been treated heroically in the tragic trilogy. Such an arrangement would be very civilized. It would complete the completing. (*LSA* 137–138)

For no matter what benefits may be derived from the catharsis of tragedy, Burke remains convinced that "mankind's only hope is a cult of comedy." Such a cult is surely implicit in his advocacy of "tolerance by speculation" in the *Grammar*.

We might let C. Allen Carter sum up the Burkean case for comedy as the preferred paradigm:

> Comedy, according to Burke, encourages us to reassess our notions of infallibility. Given the dialectical permutations of language, culture, and personality, Burke recommends that we hold our beliefs tentatively and that we consider those who hold other views, not as irredeemably evil or malicious, but as misguided souls who are actually our partners in the building of knowledge.... He finds the most dangerous temptation of language to be a temptation towards victimage. The comic approach deflects overly passionate linguistic dynamics, specifically the tendency to deify allies and demonize opponents.... Specializing in incongruity is offered by Burke as an antidote to the desire to adopt a final attitude towards self and society.[18]

Timothy Crusius would seem to agree, but for him Burke goes as far as to identify tragedy with victimage and to see comedy as the cure for both. While this privileging of comedy might seem to contradict Burke's own praise for the catharsis effected by the *Oresteia*, it is no doubt correct to see the comic frame as intrinsic to the art of living that Burke espouses:

> Burke advocates comedy because he believes he has good reason to fear that history has a tragic denouement, a "repetition compulsion" requiring an endless line of victims that, short of eliminating the symbol-using animal entirely, can never absolve or cleanse. We begin to understand why comedy was necessary for Burke's *praxis*, why he insists that "criticism had best be comic." His valuing of comedy over tragedy, which inverts the traditional genre hierarchy, is neither perverse nor quixotic: Rather the comic perspective and much of Burke's *praxis* as a whole is designed to do one thing primarily, break the spell tragedy has over human motivation and create a comic persuasion as powerfully appealing as the mimesis of sacrifice itself.[19]

There is, of course, a biblical case for seeing the comic perspective as the resolution of tragic contradictions. True, the Greek tragedians managed to find the perfect form—derived from myth and presented as ritual—by which to achieve the necessary catharsis. Moreover, the culture was sophisticated enough to see the necessity for the tragic trilogy to be rounded out by the satyr play. But in the biblical—specifically Christian—tradition, comedy is more than humor: it is the divine answer to the riddle of history. The tragedy of sin and suffering culminates in a comic vision of the "good news" of the Messiah and of "a new heaven and a new earth" issued in with the apocalypse. To be more precise, two tragedies are contained by a comedy. The fall of Adam and Eve, which we may see as a *tragedy*, necessitates the crucifixion of God's son, Jesus, which is yet another *tragedy*. But this terrible event in turn allows for the resurrection of the one true Christ and the salvation of all humanity, which we may see, strictly speaking, as a *comedy*. Of course, the inference need not be drawn that Burke's comedy is Christian in character. However, his repeated declarations of respect for religious myth and ritual should remind us that his whole philosophy of logology is founded on the theological dialectic of words and Word. Certainly, his fascination with Christ the *Logos* is a constant trait in his later work.

When *Permanence and Change* was reprinted in 1954, Burke used the occasion to write an appendix that was largely devoted to distinguishing between the sacred and the secular aspects of victimage. Quoting from Samuel Taylor Coleridge's *Aids to Reflexion*—"The two great moments of the Christian Religion are, Original Sin and Redemption; that the ground, this the superstructure of our faith"— Burke elaborates: "Basically, the pattern proclaims a principle of *absolute* 'guilt,' matched by a principle that is designed for the corresponding absolute cancellation of such guilt. And this cancellation is contrived by *victimage*, by the choice of a sacrificial offering that is correspondingly absolute in the perfection of its fitness. We assume that, insofar as the 'guilt' were but 'fragmentary,' a victim correspondingly 'fragmentary' would be adequate for the redeeming of such a debt, except insofar as 'fragmentation' itself becomes an 'absolute' condition" (*PC* 284).

The problem of modern secular society is that it actually favors fragmentation. This condition can itself become so pervasive as to demand purgation: "Fragmentation makes for triviality. And though there are curative aspects in triviality ... they can add up to a kind of organized inanity that is socially morbid." Burke reflects that "if people were truly devout in the full religious sense of the term, there would be no difficulty here. For in the pious contemplation of a perfect sacrificial *universal* god, there might be elements of wholeness needed to correct the morbidities of fragmentation" (*PC* 287). Hence the advantage of Christianity, where the scapegoat is the son of an all-encompassing deity.

Burke's position here is pragmatic: he is concerned with what works. Religion has the advantage in this respect. Yet, as we read on, we realize that there is something about the Christian myth that he finds deeply inspiring. Typically, he makes this admission indirectly, in parentheses, in the course of declaring that he is not "pleading for religion." He makes a distinction between the kind of victimage appropriate to the century in which he writes, where hostility has become global and where two world wars have been witnessed, and the sacrificial motive that is symbolically perfected in the realm of Christian myth: "In referring to the curative totality of the perfect sacrifice, as modified by the predominantly secular nature of modern civilization, we would suggest that the kind of victimage most 'natural' to such a situation would be some variant of the Hitlerite emphasis (which puts the stress upon the idea of a total cathartic *enemy* rather than upon the idea of a total cathartic *friend*)" (*PC* 288). One who lays down one's life for others represents a more complete scale of values than the nation that seeks out a people to blame and persecute as an enemy. The motive of the Christian myth transcends the divisions that fuel the continuation of victimage. Moreover, the healing, inclusive power of the story remains as an inspiration to resist the material manifestations of the scapegoat mechanism, such as Nazi genocide.[20]

Burke's approach to Christianity, to myth, and to sacrifice in many ways anticipates that of the French theorist René Girard. In *Violence and the Sacred* (1972) Girard argues that religion arises from the repression of violence. Its chief impulse is the sacrifice of a human scapegoat, which allows the community to achieve unity by attributing the violence to the victim. Violence is thus at once denied and affirmed in a ritual act. Violence originates in "mimetic desire," the drive to imitate the model that one both admires and fears. It is the basis of a dilemma. The model seemingly exists to be imitated, but to imitate, the model completely would be to have and be what the model has and is, and so to displace one's rival entirely. Mimetic desire would, if fulfilled, result in the collapse of the social order, with chronic aggression the norm. Again, that is where the scapegoat figure serves its central purpose: the sacrifice of the scapegoat restores order and unity. The "impure" violence of resentment is purged by the "pure" violence of ritual. Myth is the narrative arising from the ritual, its function being to camouflage what is really going on, to lie about the violent basis of society.[21]

In *Things Hidden since the Foundation of the World* (1978) and in *The Scapegoat* (1982) Girard refines this argument that "Mimetic violence is at the heart of the system."[22] Myths are disguised texts of persecution. What in the ritual is the arbitrary persecution of a victim becomes in the myth the just punishment of a crime. This pattern of crime and punishment is the basis for social order. As for religion, the victim, having been chosen at random and slain, is deified and is thought to have been resurrected. In worshiping the god, one is worshiping the power, or rationalized violence, of the establishment. However, there is a scapegoat narrative that does not function in this way: that of Christianity, for what Christ represents is the repudiation of violent myth. As the willing victim who sacrifices himself for all humanity, Christ puts an end to the scapegoat mechanism. The Gospels proclaim love and demonstrate the futility of hatred. Christianity is a "revelation" rather than a religion, given that religion is tainted by violence: it opens our eyes to the "foolish genesis of bloodstained idols and the false gods of religion."[23] That is, it raises awareness rather than encouraging blind hatred.

The continuities between Burke and Girard should be obvious, but it is worth comparing them in order to make sure we have understood Burke correctly. We may grant that both seek to explain the connection between religion and violence; both refer myth back to ritual; both see the scapegoat ritual as the most important; and both are interested in how Jesus Christ's crucifixion illuminates the nature of sacrificial suffering. But note the following:

1. Burke starts from the "symbol-using animal"; Girard starts from "mimetic desire."
2. Burke sees guilt as arising from order; Girard sees "mimetic violence," the result of mimetic desire, as leading to social disturbance.
3. Burke understands the law—the "thou-shalt-not"—to be primary; Girard sees the scapegoat as primary.
4. Burke stresses the power of language to affect our attitudes to others and ourselves; Girard stresses the power of imitative behavior to affect language.
5. Burke sees victimage as inescapable, given the capacity of human language for negation; Girard sees language as a mere medium through which violence is expressed.

6. Burke sees Christianity as mythic but gives it a special place as a symbolic narrative that demonstrates how the impulse toward victimage might be contained or corrected; Girard sees Christianity as signifying the end of myth and of the scapegoating mechanism alike.

7. Burke advocates the restricting of victimage to the realm of symbolic action rather than letting it spill over into society; Girard sees persecution as pervasive, but trusts that it may be overcome by means of religious faith.

The contrast may outweigh the comparison, but the influence is indubitable. Indeed, Girard has explicitly acknowledged his debt in an interview included at the end of his volume of essays, *To Double Business Bound* (1978):

> Kenneth Burke acknowledges a "principle of victimage" that is at work in human culture and, to me at least, this is an extraordinary achievement.... [But] Burke sees victimage as a product of language rather than language as a product of victimage (indirectly at least, through the medium of ritual and prohibitions). He shares to some extent in what I would call the linguistic idealism of much recent French theory, but he does not push this idealism to some heights of absurdity.[24]

This is qualified praise, but it is obviously given by someone who knows that his own work would not have developed without such an ambitious theoretical example. This is clear when Girard concludes his acknowledgment by regretting that Burke has never been translated into French and that he remains so marginal in Europe, then looks forward to the day when "Kenneth Burke will be acknowledged as the great man he really is."[25]

Perhaps the charge of "linguistic idealism" will be seen to be less illuminating than Girard's statement of indebtedness. We have already quoted Robert Wess, who writes of Burke's "rhetorical realism," radically opposed to the "rhetorical idealism" of the deconstructionists. And it is this notion that language refers to something outside itself that will prove important, as we come to consider Burke's views on nature, and to consider how he relates myth to ecology.

5

MYTH AND ECOLOGY

Chapter 4 ended with René Girard's characterization of Kenneth Burke's work as a variant on the "linguistic idealism" that pervaded philosophy and literary theory over the second half of the twentieth century. We already know how Robert Wess would reply to that characterization. Now it is necessary to state as clearly as possible what Burke's view of the relationship between the word and the world is.

But before returning to Burke's own writings, let us consider what some other of his commentators have said. Samuel Southwell, for instance, is quite emphatic. Though his concern is with relating Burke's philosophy to that of Martin Heidegger, who is famous for his dictum "Language is the house of Being," Southwell argues that both philosophers affirm the existence of a reality beyond its human, linguistic construction. For Heidegger, this reality is "Being"; for Burke, it is "nature." Describing Burke's position, Southwell writes: "For Burke's part, he is always ready to refer to a distinction between the realm of experience created by language and 'reality' (though 'reality' is always in quotation marks). For Burke there *is* a material world and we are partly biological and partly cultural (linguistic) beings."[1] Timothy Crusius is even more insistent: "Burke is no idealist. There is much more to existence than mind. Nor, in Burke's view, can phenomena be reduced to linguistic constructions. Language is not all there is."[2] Moreover, Crusius sharply differentiates, *pace* Southwell, Burke's reverence for nature from Heidegger's "mystification" of "Being."[3] In this differentiation, he is not relying on intuition alone: Burke includes some quizzical asides on Heidegger in his "Dramatistic View of the Origins of Language" (*LSA* 419–479). But the larger burden of

Crusius' argument is that Burke's philosophy is very much a form of "praxis." That is, if we consider the phrase "symbolic action," we must give equal weight to both sides of the equation: not only symbol but also action, not only discourse but also deed. Crusius maintains that Burke means what he says when Burke describes his own philosophy as "an attitude embodied in a method" (*GM* 441). For Crusius, Burke's "method" is one "with definite aims or ends in view." More particularly, "The aim is *ecological balance.*"[4]

Here we might briefly take stock of William Rueckert's more recent reflections, which provide a useful coda to his substantial full-length study of Burke. In an essay included in his *Encounters with Kenneth Burke*, Rueckert explains the link between the terms "logology" and "ecology":

Rhetoric is grounded in logology (or logologic); logology is grounded in the speechless human body, which in turn has its grounding in the pre- and nonverbal realm of nature. Humans add language, and with it, the negative, to nature, and thus provide themselves with the means by which they can alter, manipulate, transform, and transcend (or attempt to transcend) their origins. One of the most fundamental of all logological principles is that, given words, humans will always drive and strive toward the generation of the WORD; or, put a little differently, beginning with nature and words (humans are the symbol-using *animals*), humans will always strive to ascend, via language, and driven by the entelechial, "beyonding" motive intrinsic to language, toward some form of supernature that is always beyond both nature and language. This is the movement from words to the WORD, or from the empirical to the meta-empirical realm. Once having arrived at the WORD, the human tendency is to descend with the WORD and infuse it into nature; or, one might say, to persuade nature with it. The counterpart to rhetoric in our material, empirical dealings with nature is technology, which, Burke says, is made possible by symbolicity. It is by means of technology that we coerce, manipulate, persuade, transform, and try to "improve" nature.[5]

In replying to his own rhetorical question, "What does all this have to do with ecology?" Rueckert declares: "Ecology is the study of the relationships between organisms and their environments, and humans, because of their capacity for symbolic actions, have a unique ability to alter radically their natural environment and in fact add a whole other human environment to the natural one. Humans can quite literally invent and add "unnatural" elements to the natural environment, which is something no other species can do. This capacity, according to Burke, derives from man's logocentricity."[6]

It is, then, the duty of the "symbol-using animal" to devise means of observing, checking, and preventing its own entelechial urge, its own push to perfection; for if we are the species that can alter nature through the power afforded by language, we are also the species that can prevent our rhetoric of "technological psychosis" (*PC* 296) resulting in the destruction of the planet. This is where the "comic frame," or "corrective," comes in, helping to maintain our humanity; and we maintain our humanity, according to Burke, by learning the lesson of humility.

Enough has been said to indicate that no study of Burke can over-look his concern for the fate of nature, which he began articulating early in his career and which grew ever more central to his work. Increasingly, he is being recognized as one of the most important environmental thinkers of the twentieth century.[7] Our task here, of course, is to relate Burke's ecology and logology to his interest in mythology. In this chapter I want, then, to bring out the "green" aspects of Burke's theory of myth. Once again, a certain amount of theory must be explained before we get to myth.

A QUESTION OF BALANCE

Burke's three critical books of the 1930s might be seen as containing the seeds of his ecological thinking, the full implications of which he pursues in the later volumes. In particular, he initiates the idea of nature as a "critical" concept—the standard by reference to which he can offer a "critique" of Western industrial society.[8] We may recall that *Counter-Statement* (1931) begins with the word "perhaps" and ends with the word "norm." In that work and in Burke's subsequent two books, the norm is identified more closely with what he calls "ecological balance."

In *Counter-Statement* itself Burke sets outs a "Program," stated in the central essay, justifying art in the context of myth. On the one hand, Burke tells us, art is "eternal" in so far as it deals with "the constants of humanity": "the recurrent emotions, the fundamental attitudes, the typical experiences." On the other hand it is also "histor-ical": "a particular mode of adjustment to a particular cluster of conditions." This cluster fluctuates "from age to age, from class to class, from person to person," thus calling for appropriate "changes of emphasis." Burke writes:

> The present Program speculates as to which emotions and attitudes should be stressed, and which slighted, in the aesthetic adjustment to the particular conditions of today. In contemporary America the distinguishing emergent factor is obviously mechanization, industrialism, as if affects political institutions, as it alters our way of living, as it makes earlier emphases *malapros* or even dangerous (*"malapros* or even dangerous"—consider for instance the many social difficulties arising from the doctrine of *laissez-faire*, though the counterpart of this doctrine, self-dependence and individualism, was an adequate adjustment to the conditions of pioneering). (*CS* 107–108)

Thus the aesthetic Program cannot be yet another excuse for self-centeredness, transposed from economic to literary activity. Rather, the writer or artist envisaged by Burke will be deeply conscious of a responsibility toward society. Of course, given his title, *Counter-Statement*, Burke believes that that responsibility may well manifest itself in a challenge to its assumptions. Here Burke draws attention, on the first of many occasions throughout his writing career, to the dangers of "industrialism," by which he means not so much the process of industrialization as the ideology of technological advance, which disregards any costs other than financial. He implies that the government itself colludes with this belief, and facilitates the profiteering of industrialists.

The best contemporary literature will "work corrosively upon those expansionistic certainties preparing the way for our social cataclysms" (*CS* 105). For an important function of writing is corrective, as Burke indicates in a provocative statement that anticipates his later case for "perspective by incongruity": "An art may be of value purely through preventing a society from being too assertively, too hopelessly, itself" (*CS* 105). The method is critical, but the connections are much wider than literary, for art is always implicitly political. The poet "may sing of pastoral moments on the shores of the Mississippi, nothing more; but if the things he extols there are to be found to be endangered by the growth of chain stores, his purely pastoral concerns involve by implication the backing of an anti–chain store candidate for President" (*CS* 113). Aesthetic concerns thus overlap with political concerns. The writer cannot ignore "social cataclysms." Pondering conditions in

Europe, and showing remarkable prophetic power (the book was, after all, written throughout the late 1920s and published in 1931), Burke warns his readers about the rise of fascism, which he sees as complementary to the industrialism that is prevalent in the United States: "The fascists, the hopeful, the propounders of business culture, believe that the future lies in perfecting the means of control." Against such a "practical" logic, the writer would seek "to throw into confusion the code which underlies commercial enterprise, industrial competition, the heroism' of economic warfare; would seek to endanger the basic props of industry" (*CS* 115).

The context of this declaration makes clear that Burke is not seriously suggesting that the industrializing project be totally abandoned and that the populace return en masse to the land. Rather, he is offering a "counter-statement" to the ideology of industrialism, the rationale for the exploitation of the earth. Typically, his position depends on paradox: "[I]t is among the farmers, the only surviving American conservatives, that a radical anti-industrialist movement must be fostered." He embellishes this declaration with an intriguing footnote: "That is, there is a likelihood of 'rebellion' in America only if there is some conservative group whose interests make it the equivalent of a radical group. Ideologically conservative—functionally radical" (*CS* 118). The paradox deepens when Burke points out that artists themselves may politically align themselves with the agrarians, even though they stand morally for a way of living beyond the "cluster of values ... which are now shared by agrarian and industrialist elements alike" (*CS* 117–118). For the function of art in the given climate is to be antipractical and Bohemian; it is to affirm democracy in the sense of the right to "leisure." Its motto is "When in Rome, do as the Greeks" (*CS* 119).

From where, however, does art draw its critical strength? The answer is: myth. We have already seen how in *Counter-Statement* Burke appeals to certain "universal forms" or "psychological universals" that always seek temporal realization. We need not rehearse his argument presented in Chapter 3, but the point is that the appeal to myth is part of Burke's attempt to move toward that final word of the book—namely, "norm." The choice is either to submit to the destructive dictates of industrialism, expressive of the present moment of history, or to find a perspective beyond that moment, a state of equilibrium that would survive the "hurly-burly" of modernity.

This attempt is implicit in the very title of *Permanence and Change* (1935). As in Heidegger's *Being and Time*, so here we discern a desire for a transhistorical truth, even if the very conjunction of terms draws attention to the inextricable link between the realms: there can be no "Being" that is not manifest in "time," no "permanence" that is not visible within "change." Both Heidegger and Burke resist the lure of metaphysical certainty; yet both resist as well the temptation to lapse into a facile relativism. Burke, who always regarded himself as equally a philosopher and a literary critic, goes as far as to propose an alternative to metaphysics, which he calls "metabiology."

The premise of this mode of understanding would be the reciprocal relationship between organism and environment; it would allow for an equipoise between them. Suspicious of those thinkers who claim to stand on the "rock of certainty," it would ask whether they were quite as thorough as they pretend to be. Burke points out, for instance, that Friedrich Nietzsche's philosophy of the "superman," while it may seem consistent as far as it goes, is inadequate as an account of humanity's place on the planet. For the "will to power" overemphasizes conflict and the goal of supremacy. It illustrates the "trained incapacity" of competitive capitalism; its "insight" is overwhelmed by its "blindness." In short, if we were to choose the Nietzschean option, that "man is essentially a fighter," we should not be "sufficiently *methodical*" (*PC* 234–235). The same objection is made to Karl Marx, whose proposal that capitalism be politically revolutionized, without taking into account the wider context of industrial production, is not "sufficiently *methodical.*" "The Marxian perspective," notes Burke, "presents a point of view outside the accepted circle of contingencies. Or more accurately stated: the Marxian perspective is *partially* outside this circle. It is outside as regards the basic tenets of capitalistic enterprise. It is inside as regards the belief in the ultimate values of industrialism" (*PC* 224). Both communism and capitalism subscribe to the ideology of material improvement, regardless of the environmental cost. Quite simply, they ignore nature. Hence "dialectical materialism" may prove less "methodical" than the "dialectical biologism" outlined by Burke (*PC* 229).

The premise of this way of seeing is Burke's conviction that the human drama is played out in a context—namely, nature—that is more "rich and strange" (to adapt William Shakespeare) than human hubris is prepared to admit. (In terms of the dramatistic pentad discussed in Chapter 3, we should say that nature is the ultimate "scene" of any conceivable "act.") That hubris has now taken on a sinister turn, in the form of "technological psychosis." In the introduction to *Attitudes Toward History* (1937), Burke refers to "the invention of technical devices that would make the rapid obliteration of human life an easily available possibility." This crisis affects more than humanity. As Burke explains, though "human stupidity" has always involved "destructiveness," now "a truly New Situation is with us, making it all the more imperative that we learn to cherish the mildly charitable ways of the comic discount," for "by nothing less than such humanistic allowances can we hope to forestall (if it can be forestalled!) the most idiotic tragedy conceivable: the willful ultimate poisoning of this lovely planet, in conformity with a mistaken heroics of war—and each day, as the sun still rises anew upon the still surviving plenitude, let us piously give thanks to Something or Other not of man's making" (*ATH* v).

The allusion to an absolute that is conveniently vague may be humorous rather than comic, but the overall intention is highly serious. And later in the book, we see what principle it is that would inform this humility. Trusting that human beings will always have "transcendent" ideals, yet conceding that human beings also have legitimate "material" interests, Burke proposes that the "comic frame" involves an "ecological balance" between them (*ATH* 167). Had he simply said "balance" he could be taken to mean that any "bureaucratization of the imaginative" must be scrutinized carefully to ensure that the practical realization of ideals does not involve a fatal literalization of their original spirit. But the epithet "ecological" offers a significant emphasis. As Burke admits in the "Afterword" to *Attitudes Toward History*, written nearly five decades after the original book, there is some uncertainty in the original phrasing as to whether the appeal to ecology is figurative. But he does insist that the book is informed by a proper sense of what the implications of such an appeal are (see *ATH* 411). A few pages before the original mention of "ecological balance," he writes: "[Ecology] teaches us that the *total* economy of this planet cannot be guided by an efficient rationale of exploitation alone, but that the exploiting part must itself eventually suffer if it too greatly disturbs the *balance* of the whole." Thus, we must see the dangers of the "profit" motive when, as is already happening, the laws of ecology are "countering deforestation and deep plowing with floods, droughts, dust storms, and aggravated soil erosion" (*ATH* 150). In other words, Burke's conviction is that we need to know and accept our modest place within the hierarchy of existence—or, if we object to the vertical metaphor, in the "continuum" of existence.

With such catastrophes as those listed in mind, Burke considers that a more useful thinker than Marx or Nietzsche would be Charles Darwin, provided we understand him correctly. In *Permanence and Change* Burke offers his corrective to the dominant "evolutionism," which he sees as a corruption of Darwinist theory. Far from condoning competitive, aggressive, and destructive behavior, Darwin in fact vindicates a sense of community. Burke notes that "Darwin himself had specifically recognized that the struggle of life gives rise to cooperative attitudes, that tenderness, charity, good humor are as truly factors in the survival of man as was any primitive ability to track and slay animals in the jungle. But this aspect of his doctrine was generally ignored—and the struggle of life was usually interpreted in a bluntly militaristic sense. As a result, the world seemed to be composed simply of harsh antitheses, impossible choices, like the choice between *conquest* and *surrender*" (PC 174). Darwin is a better model, not only because of *method* but because of the intellectual import of what he says and because of the greater inclusiveness of his account of organism and environment. It offers more scope for both humanity and nature than does either Marx's or Nietzsche's.

Burke is anxious to stress that the "metabiology" he is proposing is a tentative "method" rather than a rational certainty. It is a matter of spiritual intuition, more likely to be discerned in myth and ritual than in pure theory:

> Our ways or methods vary in their details, and in the criteria by which we test them. In earlier thinking the Way was capitalized, but it was a literal translation of the Greek word, *hodos*. In modern thought we have disguised it by calling it *met-hodos*, which means the "way after." In any case we are and always have been methodical. Mr. Paul Radin wrote a book, *Primitive Man as Philosopher*, to prove that savages are as advanced in their thinking as we are; and Messrs. Ogden and Richards wrote a book, *The Meaning of Meaning*, to prove that we are as backward in our thinking as savages—and I have begun to wonder whether we must choose between them. (PC 234)

Because Burke's instinct is to seek permanence amidst change, he proposes that "the Way" represents a human constant, variously expressed throughout history. Hence modern humanity should not think itself radically different from its "primitive" ancestor: "Might we, noting the suspiciously close connection between the *hodical* and the *methodical*, be once more encouraged to look for a unitary technique, called in religious verbalizations the *way after*? Might we assume a constancy of message throughout history precisely to the extent that the biologic purpose of the human genus have remained a constant—and might we, attempting the sort of translation which Ogden and Richards advocate, suspect that it appears on the surface, where it manifests only the shifting symbolizations of history and status?" (*PC* 234).

Permanence amid change, unity amid diversity: without denying the need to be alert to "shifting symbolizations," Burke believes that we make sense of ourselves and our world by responding to constant, universal forms, such as he discerns in mythology. There is, he infers, a "Way" beyond particular ways.

"IN THE BEGINNING WAS THE TAO"

Though he is interested in the Greek etymology, Burke knows that "the Way" also means "the Tao," as in the ancient wisdom of Lao Tzu. Arising five centuries before Christ, the religion of Taoism taught attunement to the natural world. As for the Tao itself, definition is difficult: it is not nature itself, nor is it God in the Judaic or Christian sense. It is, rather, a spiritual force that manifests itself in the flow of natural phenomena. At its heart is paradox, that of the "coincidence of opposites." As John Mabry notes: "The symbol of the Tao looks like two tadpoles, one white, one black, chasing each other's tails. The white tadpole has a black dot, like an eye, and the black, a white eye.... The white one is called yin, the black one, yang. Separate them and you really have nothing but tadpoles, but together they make an image of eternity, a circle, a whole, the Tao. They represent the concept of opposites which are dependent upon each other for their being."[9]

Burke's interest in Taoism is evident from *Permanence and Change* onward. In that volume he asks, rhetorically: "Might the great plethora of symbolizations lead, through the science of symbolism itself, back to a concern with 'the Way,' the conviction that there is one fundamental source of human satisfaction, forever being glimpsed and lost again, and forever being restated in the changing terms of reference that correspond with the changes of historic texture?" (*PC* 183–184). He might have had in mind the following statement from the *Tao Te Ching*:

> Holding fast to the old Way,
> we can live in the present.
> Mindful of the ancient beginnings,
> we hold the thread of the Tao.[10]

For Burke, it is only by invoking such a principle—transcendent and permanent, even while it is apprehended as immanent and ever-changing—that we move beyond modernity, with its anxiety of "improvement." If the choice is between constant innovation and a sense of continuity, Burke would opt for continuity:

> If we choose to emphasize the shifting particularities, we approach human problems *historically*, as in the philosophies of *becoming* which seem to have reached their flowering in Nineteenth Century thought.... If we choose to emphasize the underlying similarities, we return through symbolism to a philosophy of *being*, the Spinozistic concern with man *sub specie aeternitas*. We replace the metaphor of progress (and its bitter corollary, decadence) with the metaphor of a *norm*, the notion that at bottom the aims and genus of man have remained fundamentally the same, that temporal events may cause him to stray far from his sources but that he repeatedly struggles to restore, under new particularities, the same basic patterns of the "good life." (*PC* 163)

Again, we should emphasize that Taoism itself is all about "the good life," made possible when humanity attunes itself to the "norm" of nature rather than asserts itself over it. One translation of the *Tao Te Ching* renders a famous passage as follows:

> When man interferes with the Tao,
> the sky becomes filthy,
> the earth becomes depleted,
> the equilibrium crumbles,
> creatures become extinct.[11]

This insight is congenial to someone like Burke, who advocates planetary humility as the best hope for humanity. In keeping with the Taoist principle of least interference, he commends observing and correcting the indiscriminate urge toward profit and progress.

Burke comes to make his case for a philosophy of "being," as opposed to one of "becoming." He uses language that must have surprised his contemporaries and that may well give today's readers pause for thought:

> In subscribing to a philosophy of being, as here conceived, one may hold that certain historically conditioned institutions interfere with the establishment of decent social or communicative relationships, and thereby affront the permanent biologic [*sic*] norms.... We in cities rightly grow shrewd at appraising man-made institutions— but beyond these tiny concentration points of rhetoric and traffic, there lies the eternally unresolvable Enigma, the preposterous fact that both existence and nothingness are quite unthinkable. Our speculations may run the whole qualitative gamut, from play, through reverence, even to an occasional shiver of cold metaphysical dread—for always the Eternal Enigma is there, right on the edge of our metropolitan bickerings, stretching outward to interstellar infinity and inward to the depth of the mind. And in this staggering disproportion between man and no-man, there is no place for purely human boasts of grandeur, or for forgetting that men build their cultures by huddling together, nervously loquacious, at the edge of an abyss. (*PC* 272)

We might want, given Burke's reputation as a protostructuralist, to read this audacious statement as an anticipation also of the *post*-structuralist destabilization of the human subject. True, it is profoundly unsettling. But it is, I suggest, saying something more than what became the academic consensus of the later twentieth century; for if the effect of thinkers such as Roland Barthes, Jacques Derrida, and Michel Foucault was to encourage the notion that the human subject is dispersed within the semiotic system of its given culture, Burke is proposing that the source and context of our existence, beyond both individual identity and cultural formation, are a primal emptiness, or "abyss."

One is reminded again of the *Tao Te Ching*, in which the ancient sage paradoxically affirms the primacy of nothingness: "Heaven and earth / begin in the unnamed." Again, of the Tao he says "never can it be named. It reverts, it returns / to unbeing."[12] Emptiness, implies Lao Tzu, is necessary for the everyday world to function, and vice versa:

Thirty spokes
meet in the hub.
Where the wheel isn't
is where it's useful....
Cut doors and windows
to make a room.
Where the room isn't
There's room for you....
So the profit in what is
is in the use of what isn't.[13]

We should not infer that Taoism encourages nihilism. Rather, it acknowledges "unbeing" as origin, in the sense that no human beings, any more than any other natural phenomena, are "substantial." As we have already gathered from Burke's dramatism, he sees individual lives as "consubstantial," existing only in relationship. In human terms, we all play a role in a collective drama. Nor is the model of drama confined to the human sphere. As Burke concludes in his chapter "The Poetry of Action," which concludes *Permanence and Change*, "the ultimate metaphor for discussing the universe and man's relations to it must be the poetic or dramatic metaphor" (*PC* 263). The idea that humanity is in an intersubjective relationship with the cosmos has obvious affinities with Taoism.

While Burke himself does not make the parallel explicit here, we are also reminded of certain aspects of Buddhist wisdom—in particular, the early Buddhist philosopher Nagarjuna's notion of "conditioned coproduction," which means that the existence of every entity is contingent and contextual, dependent on its correlation with other entities. Nagarjuna by no means denies the existence of creatures, human or nonhuman, any more than he denies the existence of trees, sky, and stars. But he denies their existence as essential entities. He espouses a "middle way" between "eternalism" (the view that the self, other persons, and things have a fixed value) and "nihilism" (the view that if everything is born and dies, then nothing is of value). This middle way treats supposedly distinct beings as functioning somewhere between the conventional idea of existence and the absolute idea of nonexistence. For a human being to realize this state of affairs is to attain "emptiness": "To be empty is no longer to be full of oneself."[14] Still, the word "emptiness" is a metaphor, drawn from the everyday experience of rooms, wheels, bells, and jars. Nagarjuna warns against reifying it, against making it into yet another substance. Burke seems alert to this kind of error—hence his own delight in giving new life to figures of speech, and in avoiding finality of definition. There is, then, much in common between Nagarjuna's "middle way" and Burke's lesson of humility made possible by the "comic frame."

This Taoist and Buddhist tendency is pervasive in Burke's thinking. For example, we referred in Chapter 3 to the invocation of the Tao in his exposition of the philosophy of dramatism. It may therefore seem odd that Burke decided to develop his own "logology," in the light of the Judaic and Christian mythologies. In *The Rhetoric of Religion* (1961) the referent is the Bible, from which Burke derives his idea of the primacy of the sacred "Word," implied by, and manifest in, all other words. The opening of the Gospel According to John, echoing and confirming the creation myth of Genesis, is well known: "In the beginning was the Word, and the Word was with God, and the Word was God" (John 1:1). However, a Taoist translation of that Gospel begins: "In the beginning was the Tao, and the Tao was with God, and the Tao was God." The late Christian thinker Bede Griffiths remarked on this: "In thus substituting the Chinese Tao for the Greek Logos, which we translate [as] the 'Word,' [the Taoist translator] has placed Chinese philosophy in the same relation to the Gospel as Greek philosophy was placed originally by St. John's use of the word 'Logos.'"[15] In the context of Burke's reading of the Bible, this may remind us that Taoism has its myth, just as does Christianity. We know Burke to be fascinated by Christianity, with due reservations about extending the principle of victimage beyond the narrative of Jesus' passion to social and political life. But perhaps we might infer from Burke's own "metabiology" a myth not dissimilar to that which relates to the Tao, which in turn has Biblical parallels.

John Mabry's exposition of the Taoist "mythos of the fall" may prove helpful here: he notes: "Long ago, in the Edenic period of the ancients, the Universe and humankind were in harmony. But then humans began to "tamper" with nature and now we, their descendants, are faced with the responsibility of discovering how to live healthy lives of compassion and reverence for the Tao and all it contains. If we continue to go contrary to the Tao, we will experience one frustrating obstacle after another until our deaths."[16] We might substantiate this narrative by reference to passages such as this from the Taoist sage Chuang Tzu, which describes the period before the "fall": "In the age when life on earth was full, no one paid any special attention to worthy men ... they were honest and righteous without realizing that they were 'doing their duty.' They loved each other and did not know that this was 'love of neighbor.' . . . They lived freely together giving and taking, and did not know that they were generous. For this reason their deeds have not been narrated. They made no history."[17]

While there is no concept of sin in the Taoist myth of the fall from paradise, there is the clear idea that to live out of harmony with nature is a lapse from the norm of the Tao. Mabry is reminded of "Jesus' two great commandments regarding our love of God, and for our neighbor as ourselves (Mark 21:30–1). And since [according to Taoism] the Earth and all that is in her is not only our neighbor but a part of us, Christians can agree with the Taoist that us not to behave in a reverential way is also sin."[18] Of course, while the human dimension of the story might parallel the biblical structure of fall and redemption, there is a significant difference in the concept of divinity behind each. In the creation myth told in the first chapter of Genesis, God is identified with order and light, as opposed to chaos and darkness:

> And the earth was without form, and void; and darkness was upon the face of the deep. And the Spirit of God moved upon the face of the waters. And God said: "Let there be light": and there was light. (Genesis 1:2–3)

The chaos and the darkness are here aspects of the creation itself. But in previous mythologies, we often find that they are understood to be preexistent. In his essay "Myth, Poetry, and Philosophy," as we have seen, Burke takes the "combat myth" to be rooted in an early cosmogonic narrative. In the Babylonian creation myth, the primordial, watery abyss is represented by Tiamat, who is overcome by her son, Marduk. Scholarship suggests that the Israelites produced their creation myth after returning from exile in Babylon. They wanted to vindicate their own god, Yahweh, as the one and only God, but could not circumvent the problem of there being a preexistent force, a chaos that had to be in some sense conquered. Indeed, the Hebrew word for "the deep," *tehom*, may well derive from the Babylonian *Tiamat*.[19] With Taoist myth, by contrast, there is no such confusion: the Tao is calmly identified as a founding void, nothingness, or emptiness, though without any sinister implications. In Buddhism, as in Taoism, emptiness is the very state that we all need to regain: for a human being to become "empty" is to be freed of the illusion of a substantial self.

We might, then, wonder how Burke would situate himself in relation to biblical and Taoist myths. Fortunately, he has given us a clue in his *Book of Moments: Poems 1915–1954*. "Creation Myth" begins:

> In the beginning there was universal Nothing.
> Then Nothing said No to itself and thereby begat Something,
> Which called itself Yes. (*CP* 5)

Then, with "No" and "Yes" having cohabited and begot "Maybe," all three beget "Guilt," which is also known as "Order." In turn, "Guilt" (or "Order") begets "History." The "myth" concludes: "Finally, History fell a-dreaming / And dreamed about Language ..." (*CP* 5).

Here Burke the myth theorist overlaps with Burke the mythmaker, albeit of an ironic or whimsical character. Still, we may find a brief consideration of his myth illuminating, particularly as its focus is the nature of the negative, so crucial to so much of his theory. In "Creation Myth" Burke explicitly states that nothingness is primary. However, as we know, Burke's "Definition of Man" includes the clause "inventor of the negative." Is there not a contradiction? In the poem there is a "Nothing" before humanity begins to speak. In the essay it is human language that is said to introduce the idea of negation. The apparent confusion is resolved if we remind ourselves that what comes into existence with words is the "hortatory," or "moralistic," negative: the "thou-shalt-not." The ontological negative—nonbeing as opposed to being—may yet be thought to precede the hortatory negative, especially if we accept the Taoist notion of nonbeing as a mysterious yet immensely productive emptiness. Thus "Creation Myth" presents language as the dreaming that accompanies the fall into history. After all, when Burke defines the human being as the "symbol-using animal," he is not referring to a supposed superiority over other animals. Indeed, on every occasion thereafter, when revisiting his "Definition," he stresses that we are "Bodies that Learn Language," as in his 1984 "Afterword" to *Attitudes Toward History* (*ATH* 390). He is interested as much in our animality as in our symbolicity. Yet in keeping with his constant attention to Christian theology, the fall occasioned by language is a "fortunate" one. Just as words separate us out from the world, so words have the capacity to forge a new relationship to the world—that of responsible stewardship—in accordance with the redemptive power of the Word. Language marks the break from nature, but language, especially poetic or mythic language, has the power to restore us to nature, newly understood as the manifestation of the Tao or *Logos*. Logology is complemented by ecology.

Burke is especially interested in how language functions by revealing differences. We have already considered his theory that, in order for human beings to make initial sense of the world they must subscribe to an orientation, a way of seeing, a version of piety. We know, too, that for Burke, any way of seeing is simultaneously a way of *not* seeing, that every insight relies on a certain amount of blindness. In his more critical moods he favors the phrase "trained incapacity." But when putting the matter as neutrally as possible, he writes of "terministic screens." This phrase suggests that words, as well as being beginnings, are also endings: our understanding terminates with the kind of terminology we choose to describe the world. In "Terministic Screens," an essay included in *Language as Symbolic Action* (1966), Burke states emphatically: "Even if any given terminology is a *reflection* of reality, by its very nature as a terminology it must be a *selection* of reality; and to this extent it must function also as a *deflection* of reality" (*LSA* 45).

Burke is well aware of the implications of this discovery. If different persons see reality through different "terministic screens," then the idea of an integral, transhistorical vision is potentially threatened. All we may end up with are competing "realities," each justified by its own kind of language. How, Burke asks, can we "avoid mere relativism?" His answer lies in a "collective revelation of long standing." He here refers explicitly to the Tao—though, to be exact, he also mentions the Hindu-Buddhist principle of *karma*, among others, as well as the Greek *hodos*. Each indicates the "Way," the notion of an "action" underlying the universe (see *LSA* 53–54). For human beings, the "Way" is only understood by virtue of their possessing the capacity for "symbolic action." This capacity carries with it disadvantages and advantages, but, above all, responsibilities. These responsibilities, for Burke, are focused on the imperative of the Word, now understood to be coextensive with the Way. In treating the *Logos* as akin to the Tao, Burke may have in mind the cosmology of the pre-Socratic philosopher Heraclitus. According to Fritjof Capra, Heraclitus taught that "all changes in the world arise from the dynamic and cyclic interplay of opposites and he saw any pair of opposites as a unity. This unity, which contains and transcends all opposing forces, he called the Logos." In appealing to this unity, Capra says, Heraclitus came close to the "organic view" of ancient Indian and Chinese philosophy.[20]

Burke's essay on "Terministic Screens" culminates in "Dialectician's Hymn," which significantly begins:

> Hail to thee, Logos,
> Thou Vast Almighty Title,
> In whose name we conjure—
> Our acts the partial representatives
> Of thy whole act. (*LSA* 55)

It goes on to address those responsibilities just mentioned:

> May we give true voice
> To the statements of thy creatures.....
> Thus may we help Thine objects
> To say their say—
> Not suppressing by dictatorial lie,
> Not giving false reports
> That misrepresent their saying.
> If the soil is carried off by flood,
> May we help the soil to say so. (*LSA* 55–56)

In using words on behalf of the world, we honor the Word; in making our symbolic acts serve nature, we echo the founding act that we call "the Way." As Burke puts it: "Let the Word be dialectic with the Way— / Whichever the print / The other the imprint" (*LSA* 56). Thus we attain permanence in the very process of change, maintaining the life of the planet:

> And may we have neither the mania of the One
> Nor the delirium of the Many—
> But both the Union and the Diversity—
> The Title and the manifold details that arise
> As that Title is restated
> In the narrative of History. (*LSA* 56)

We may recall here Burke's appeal to the "metaphor of a norm" in *Permanence and Change*, where he writes of the necessary "struggle to restore, under new peculiarities, the same basic pattern of the 'good life' " (*PC* 163). For Timothy Crusius, Burke's norm "clearly has affinities with an ecosystem, dynamic in that species are always mutating and the environment always changing, sometimes gradually, sometimes suddenly, catastrophically, but 'struggling' nevertheless to maintain, 'under new peculiarities,' the integrity and equilibrium of the whole."[21] Yet it is not enough for us to reaffirm Burke's ecological concerns here. We need to purse their relation to his theory of myth, already implicit in his reflections on the Tao as well as in his own poetic exercises in mythmaking.

"NATURE," "SUPERNATURE," "COUNTER-NATURE"

Any attempt to assess Burke's theory of the relationship among myth, language, and ecology must address the underlying question of how Burke regards the middle term. His most direct statement on our linguistic capacity, apart from his "Definition of Man," is the "Appendix: On Human Behavior," which he added to the 1954 edition of *Permanence and Change*. Typically, an important point is made in a footnote: "Though other animals may manifest the rudiments of language or of tool-using, man's distinctive genius is in his capacity for doing things at one remove, as when he uses words about words and makes tools for making tools" (*PC* 276). In other words, the human animal may be defined in terms either of logology or of technology, for both illustrate Aristotle's principle of "entelechy," whether it be terms (logology) or tools (technology) that are pushed toward perfection.

Burke's theory of language, then, culminating as it does in the philosophy of logology, celebrates the capacity of human beings to do far more than refer directly to objects and other persons. Words are not isolated units of information but rather elements in a whole way of seeing. Burke's starting point is humanity's capacity for symbolic action. Language is as much a "doing" as a "saying"; it is a means of giving shape and significance to reality. Problems arise, of course, when we ask to what extent this reality is created by the language that brings it into the human scope. If reality is linguistic at the point of reception, then could not the word be said to bring the world into being? We noted at the end of Chapter 4 that René Girard, while admitting his indebtedness to Burke, regretted Burke's proximity to the fashionable "linguistic idealism" of current literary theory. While it is to be hoped that the study so far has demonstrated that Burke stands well apart from this position, his attention to language might be misconstrued.

To prevent this misconstrual, we need to digress briefly to consider Burke's theory of "entitlement," presented in the essay "What Are the

Signs of What?" Here he declares that "instead of starting with the relation between words and the things of which the words are signs, we start with verbal expressions (even whole sentences) that are to be treated as ways of entitling, or of summing up, nonverbal situations" (*LSA* 370). That is, language is always contextual and serves as the human being's attempt to negotiate—we might say, in suitably Burkean manner, "come to terms with"—an environment.

For Burke, talk of *logos* inevitably leads to talk of *mythos*, so that the essay also reminds us that, if words and sentences situate us in relation to the world we are in the act of encountering, then myths would be a more articulate, rich, and resourceful mode of "entitlement." Indeed, the mythic process that Burke calls the "temporizing of essence" might be regarded as a large-scale tactic for making a community feel at home in the world. He cites the creation myths analyzed by Bronislaw Malinowski—myths that legitimize the tribe by seeing it as being descended from "supernatural ancestors." Because those ancestors "had a social order identical with the social order which currently prevail[s]," the order is effectively justified, "having been inherited from the tribe's mythic progenitors" (*LSA* 364). The repetition in the present of one short myth about the past is not only a means of "translating logical terms into their narrative or temporal counterparts" but also a device for "entitling" a whole situation—that of the tribe's relationship to itself, to other tribes, to nature, to history and to the universe. It is like a "theme song," a few bars of which can "serve as an appropriate abbreviation" for the whole "context of situation" (*LSA* 370, 373).

These speculations lead Burke to propose, tentatively and humorously, that we may be permitted to think of "things" as "the signs of words." Just as much in casual, everyday utterance as in the formal reiteration of a revered narrative, "the thing would obviously be a visible, tangible sign of the essence or spirit contained in the word itself" (*LSA* 373). Trees exist, but they do not know themselves as "trees"; and when we refer to them by name, they are being subsumed under a terministic order of our making. Burke proposes that we conceive of four such orders: the "natural," the "verbal," the "sociopolitical," and the "supernatural." The natural order is the "less-than-verbal" realm of "visible tangible things and operations." The verbal order is the realm of words itself, studied under the categories of "grammar, rhetoric, poetics, logic, dialectic, philology, etymology, semantics, symbolism, etc." The sociopolitical order covers "personal and social relations," addressed by "terms like 'justice,' 'right,' and 'obligation.'" And the "supernatural order" covers everything that lies beyond the other three (*LSA* 373–374). Burke proceeds to elaborate on his fourfold model, offering a simple illustration:

> These four should cover the ground, though they are not mutually exclusive. For instance, a word such as "person" belongs in the sheerly *natural* insofar as a person must have a living body subject to the laws of motion; it is in the *verbal* order inasmuch as the rationality of a person is involved in kinds of mental maturity that require a high degree of aptitude at symbol-using; it is in the *sociopolitical* order because of the sociopolitical relationships and roles involved in personality; and it is in the *supernatural* order at the very least to the extent that it involves attitudes towards words for this order and towards the institutions representing this order, while furthermore the person is often said to be derived from some transcendent principle of pure personality that is designated by whatever term may be the Title of Titles for this fourth realm. (*LSA* 374)

It is with the supernatural order, then, that the idea of a word containing a "spirit" or "essence" is given its full entelechial expression. This is the order which contains those terms in which all others culminate.

However, of the four orders, it is the second, verbal one that merits the most attention for Burke here: "[T]hough all four . . . are orders of words, this one is an order of words about words" (*LSA* 375). This order should be the central concern of the symbol-using animal. But that does not mean the other orders are subordinate to it. True, the sociopolitical order is the most obviously linguistic of the remaining three. Burke draws our attention to how words such as "democracy," "rights," or "obligations" have no clear existence in a nonverbal realm, but are institutional "fictions," necessary to the functioning of a human community (*LSA* 375–376). But what of the first and the fourth orders? "[A]t least as far as the technicalities of the case are concerned, the natural and supernatural orders could have wholly extra-verbal referents" (*LSA* 376), and so have some claim to independence. But we would be naive to want to separate out either realm—natural or supernatural—from the activity of language.

Referring to the second of these, Burke reminds us that "even if there is a supernatural realm, the 'science' of this realm is sheerly verbal; namely, 'theology,' or 'words about God' " (*LSA* 376). Moreover, "No matter how firm may be one's conviction that his terminology for the supernatural refers somehow to a real order of existence, there is the obvious fact that he necessarily borrows his terms from the terms prevailing in the three wordly orders" (*LSA* 376). That is, God may be spoken of as having an arm, hand, or voice (natural order), may be identified as Word (verbal order), and may be looked up to as Father or Lord (sociopolitical order). But if the supernatural realm can be understood only by metaphor and analogy, is the natural the one realm that stands apart from the "terministic" imperative? Burke's answer is suitably circumspect. If, he writes, we acknowledge that language is "the bonc between man and the natural," then it might well follow that

> [N]ature, as perceived by the word-using animal, would be thought of as not just the less-than-verbal thing that we usually take it to be. Rather, as so conceived and perceived, it would be infused with the spirit of words, and of the social orders that are implicit in any given complex verbal structure. Nature, as the early Greek metaphysical physicist put it, would thus be full of gods, gods in essence linguistic and sociopolitical. . . . [So] if the things of nature are, for man, the visible signs of their verbal entitlements, then nature gleams secretly with a most fantastic shimmer of words and social relationships. And quite as men's views of the supernatural embody the forms of language and society in recognized ways, so their views of the natural would embody these same forms, however furtively. In this sense, things would be the signs of words. (*LSA* 378–379)

One can see how such statements could be used to support a view of Burke as the patron of "linguistic idealism," but we should not misunderstand what he is proposing here. He is *not* proposing that reality is a linguistic creation. He *is* proposing that human beings cannot help but perceive and conceive the natural and supernatural realms in terms of a way of seeing that is also a way of saying. The inference we may draw is that if we are acting upon the world when we speak about the world, then we have to be careful to observe ourselves in the course of our actions, to ensure that we behave responsibly.

As we know, Burke is anxious that nature not be demeaned, dismissed, or destroyed because of human arrogance. But he is always careful not to deny the supernatural dimension of existence, much as he is aware of how far it is terministic in meaning. In the very essay just quoted, Burke warns against a "debunking" attitude toward the fourth order. For example, the skeptic might seek to explain away religion in merely ideological terms, pointing out the analogy between divine rule and the outdated social system known as feudalism: "Our debunker points out that, insofar as the eternal supernatural pattern is but the ideal duplication of a more or less obsolete temporal social pattern, the here-and-now on earth can be made to seem like the dim analogue of its ideal otherwordly perfection" (*LSA* 377). Burke's riposte is that "the thought of an ideal perfect order might make men all the more exacting when they considered the respects in which the actual worldly order fell short of this ideal" (*LSA* 377–378). It is the otherwordly perspective of religion that enables it to challenge rather than to confirm the worldly status quo. This utopian possibility is conceivable only if we allow for the supernatural dimension as something more than a linguistic construction.

Burke's willingness to respect not only the natural but also the supernatural order may prove inconvenient to commentators of a materialist persuasion.[22] But if we are to take him on his own terms, then we need to recognize that he consistently argues for the need to transcend the given cultural or historical consensus, while acknowledging the constraints it inevitably places on his own "terministic screen." Indeed, in considering his views on myth throughout this book, and in considering his own mythmaking, we have had access to a vision that borders on the religious. This is the Burke who approves of the revelation offered by Platonic myth. It would seem that it is from Plato, and from the Neo-Platonism espoused by Plotinus, that Burke gets his sense of hierarchy as a necessary order, by which this world of multiplicity implies an ultimate unity beyond it. The Many are understood to be emanations from the One. True, this insight may be gleaned from a study of the way in which words relate to the Word, but perhaps this linguistic relationship only makes sense because of our disposition toward integration. As Burke reminds us in *A Grammar of Motives*: "Plato equated the divine with the abstract, apparently because both transcend the realm of the senses. Hence, nearly everything that this greatest of dialecticians says of 'heaven' can be profitably read as a statement about *language*. And that man cheats himself who avoids Plato because of a preference for purely secular thought" (*GM* 253). Burke obviously wishes to avoid that preference, as is clear from his avowed determination to follow "the dialectic of the upward way" (*GM* 293–294).

Burke does not find this impulse contradicted by Plato's disciple either. He refers approvingly to Aristotle's "chain of being" (as it came to be known by his "scholastic" admirers in the Middle Ages), which stretches from rocks, stones, and trees all the way up through humanity and the angelic order to God. In this light Burke's fascination with the very notion of hierarchy makes sense: the word "hierarchy," after all, comes from a Greek phrase meaning "sacred rule." Burke seeks to reconcile the Platonic with the Aristotelian hierarchies in his own tentative defense of mysticism—that is, the apprehension of sacred unity within natural diversity. Made at some length in his *Grammar of Motives* (1945), the point is made most succinctly and persuasively at the close of his *Rhetoric of Motives* (1950). Here is how Burke ends that volume:

> [S]ince, for better or worse, the mystery of the hierarchic is forever with us, let us, as students of rhetoric, scrutinize its range of entrancements, both with dismay and with delight. And finally let us observe, all about us, forever goading us, though it be in fragments, the motive that attains its ultimate identification in the thought, not of the universal holocaust, but of the universal order—as with the rhetorical and dialectic symmetry of the Aristotelian metaphysics, whereby all classes of beings are hierarchically arranged in a chain or ladder or pyramid of mounting worth, each kind striving towards the *perfection* of its kind, and so towards the kind next above it, while the strivings of the entire series head in God as the beloved cynosure and sinecure, the end of all desire. (*RM* 333)

Mysticism for Burke is rooted in the apprehension of nature. This notion explains his enthusiasm for the founder of the American transcendentalist movement, Ralph Waldo Emerson, to whom he devotes a substantial essay in *Language as Symbolic Action* (1966). Burke affirms that an important symbolic function in any culture is "pontification," "the building of a *terministic bridge* whereby one realm is *transcended* by being viewed *in terms of* a realm 'beyond' it" (*LSA* 187). As Burke summarizes Emerson's philosophy: "The everyday world, all about us here and now, is to be interpreted as a *diversity of means* for carrying out a *unitary purpose* (or, if you will, the *principle* of purpose) that is situated in an ultimate realm *beyond* the here and now. The world's variety of things is to be interpreted *in terms of* a transcendent unifier (that infuses them with a single spirit)" (*LSA* 190–191) To put the matter most simply: "Nature is to be treated in terms of Supernature" (*LSA* 192). Emerson's writing is alert to the possibility of "revelation." For "whatever the world is, in its sheer brute nature as physical vibrations or motions it *reveals itself* to us *in terms of* sights, sounds, tastes, scents, touch, summed up as pleasure or pain. Thus you already have the terministic conditions whereby even the most material of sensations can be called 'apocalyptic' (since the word but means 'revealing')—and Emerson does apply precisely that word." (*LSA* 192)

Burke observes that a recurrent symbol is that of the stars: "If a man would be alone, let him look at the stars," writes Emerson (quoted *LSA* 193). Burke notes his debt to the closing imagery of Dante's great, emphatically hierarchical poem, the *Divine Comedy*. More broadly, Dante's "pontificating" technique of writing draws on the mythic model of the incarnated deity: "The simplest instance of such a bridging device is to be seen in the dialectic of the Christian creed. If you make a distinction between 'God' and 'Man,' you set up the terministic conditions for an intermediate term (for bridging the gap between the two orders): namely, 'God-Man' " (*LSA* 192–193).

The end of Burke's essay on Emerson is especially important, as he chooses to apply the model of transcendence outlined there to James Joyce's story "The Dead" (from his volume *Dubliners*). In concentrating on the symbol in which that story culminates, Burke also has something to say about the nature of myth. All we need to know to appreciate his point is, first, that the story has the motif of snow running through it, thus providing a suitably wintry setting, and, second, that in the final paragraph the snow acquires fuller significance, placing both the physically dead and the spiritually dead in a larger, cosmic context. Burke comments:

> The final twist, what Joyce would call an "epiphany," is contrived by the transforming of "snow" from a *sensory* image to a *mythic* image. That is, in the first part of the story, the references to snow are wholly realistic ("lexical" snow, snow as defined in a dictionary). But at the end, snow has become a *mythic* image, manifesting itself in the world of conditions, but standing for transcendence above the conditioned. It is a snow that bridges two realms—but, as befits the behavior of snow, this Upward Way is figured in terms of a Downward Way, as the last paragraph features the present participle, "falling." (*LSA* 199)

Lest we miss the point, Burke reminds us of an earlier "mythic image":

> In the early part of his trip to the Underworld, Virgil encountered those of the dead who could not cross Cocytus and the Stygian swamps. Charon would not ferry them to their final abode because they had not been buried. Then comes the famous line:

Tendebantque manus ripae ulterioris amore
(And they stretched forth their hands, through love of the
farther shore).

That is the pattern. Whether there is or is not an ultimate shore
towards which we, the unburied, would cross, transcendence involves
dialectical processes whereby something HERE is interpreted *in
terms of* something THERE, something *beyond* itself. (*LSA* 200)

Thus, we have noted three *natural* symbols—stars, snow, and
shore—that acquire *supernatural* significance through becoming
mythic images. But is it legitimate to view the phenomena of the
natural world as images of a "higher" world rather than to celebrate
their immediate reality? Perhaps one ought to differentiate between
the actual world of flora and fauna on the one hand, and the idea of
a transcendent essence that that world has traditionally been taken to
embody on the other. In short, "nature" is not the same as "Nature,"
and we should be cautious in the use of the latter term.[23] After all, the
notion of a permanent, transcendent Nature has been used over the
centuries to justify the social status quo and some dubious cultural
assumptions. Burke himself is especially aware of the possibility of
"social mystification" by appeal to "cosmic mystery." But he is also
right, I suggest, in pointing out that this use—or abuse—in no way
discredits mysticism: "Mysticism is no rare thing. True, the attaining of
it in its pure state is rare. And its secular analogues, in grand or
gracious symbolism, are rare. But the need for it, the itch, is everywhere. And by hierarchy it is intensified" (*RM* 332). Transcendence is
natural to humanity. Every word implies the Word; the many imply the
One; every action implies the Way.[24]

Does an emphasis on the supernatural involve a negligence of the
natural, allowing for its degradation and pollution in the name of a
"higher" realm? Not according to Burke. In his 1984 "Afterword" to
Attitudes Toward History, he elaborates on his phrase "bureaucratization of the imaginative," emphasizing the tension between the two ways
of looking at the world that are conjoined in it. "The human animal's
specific prowess in the ways of symbolicity makes for two kinds of
perspective," he writes. "One encompasses the vast complex of social
relationships, properties, authorities that centers in the principle of
personality. The other starts from the kinds of transformations in the
conditions of living (departures from a primitive state of nature) due to
the technological development of *instruments*. The two perspectives

(one *doctrinally* culminating in myths of the Supernatural, the other driving toward fulfillment in a *technologically* ever-'emergent' realm of Counter-Nature) are variously at odds" (*ATH* 378–379).

It is Burke's contention that the traditional invocation of "Supernature" is a better guarantor of the flourishing of "Nature" than the modern ambition to create an exclusive realm of "Counter-Nature." To honor the natural world as the manifestation of the divine is to grant it more security and status than to assess its merit as grist for technological exploitation. Granted that human beings have intervened in the function of the biosphere at least since the invention of agriculture in the Neolithic era, it is still possible to distinguish between a responsible and an irresponsible attitude to the planet. Burke believes that we are more likely to avoid destroying the earth if we maintain our mythic roots. For in "myths of the Supernatural," which emphasize "personality" (the figures of the gods), we maintain the possibility of relationship, whereas if our horizon is dominated by technology, we are resigned to mere "instrumentality."

A DEMONIC APOCALYPSE

The capacity to narrate myths is, for Burke, an ambiguous one, like the capacity for language itself. "Man" is the "symbol-using (symbol-making, symbol-misusing) animal," Burke tells us in his famous "Definition" (*LSA* 16). When human beings bring stories into the world, along with symbols, they bring the danger that our differentiation from other animals and from the planet may turn to dissociation.

Let us first note what Burke says about the evolutionary impact of human "story" on the environment—of *mythos* on *oikos*. He sums up his views in his essay, "Dramatism and Logology" (1985). When humanity moved from "sensations" to "words for sensations," the notion of "story" was introduced:

> Surrounding us wordy animals there is the infinite wordless universe out of which we have been gradually carving our universes of discourse since the time when our primordial ancestors added to their sensations *words* for sensations. When they could duplicate the taste of an orange by *saying* "the taste of an orange," that's when STORY was born, since words *tell about* sensations. Whereas Nature can do no wrong (whatever it does is Nature) when STORY comes into the world there enters the realm of the true, false, honest, mistaken, the downright lie, the imaginative, the visionary, the

sublime, the ridiculous, the eschatological (as with Hell, Purgatory, Heaven, the transmigration of souls, foretellings of an inevitable wind-up in a classless society), the satirical, every single detail of every single science of speculation, even every bit of gossip—for although all animals in their way communicate, only our kind of animal can gossip. There was no story before we came, and when we're gone the universe will go on sans story. (DL 90)

Burke is so taken with the idea that what human culture adds to the realm of nature is the ambiguous gift of narrative that he returns to it two years later, in a short article contributed to the *Journal of Mental Imagery*. This concerns the contribution to North American psychology of the Pakistani-born Akhter Ahsen, notable for his attempt to treat "image" in terms of "story," and for his insistence that symbolism makes sense only in the narrative context of myth.[25] Specifically, Burke's is a response to an article by Ahsen on "Image Psychology and the Empirical Method," contributed earlier to the same journal. Typically, Burke uses the opportunity to make his own ambitious speculations:

As I see it, when our primeval ancestors went from sensation and feelings to *words* for sensations and feelings, the duplication process produced the kind of departure from the state of nature that flowered in the *personal* principle as originally developed in myth (and the "supernatural"). The other departure was the *instrumental* (the state of "Counter-Nature" resulting from the symbol-guided interventions of technology, the step from myth to ideology). Freud is to mythology (the personal principle) as Marx is to ideology (the instrumental principle). My line-up thus culminates in the step *from* psychology to logology, with considerable stress upon the *economic* factor, which is more implicit than explicit in myth. (AIPEM 44)

Those seeking further elucidation of this distinction between kinds of "departure from the state of nature" will look in vain. Burke is here at his most cryptic. He is glancing back over his earlier writings and trying to find an underlying thread that is relevant to his reflections on Ahsen's own interest in "story." Fortunately, we have already come across the distinction between myth and ideology, so that the analogous distinction between personality and instrumentality should make sense. Less familiar is the attribution of Sigmund Freud to the mythic dimension and of Karl Marx to the ideological. However, we do know that

Burke sees psychoanalysis as based on a myth and as involving a ritual. What is added now is the notion that, as such, psychoanalysis is implicitly congenial to nature and human nature alike. Marxism, by contrast, is now seen, by contrast to the viewpoint of Burke's "Revolutionary Symbolism," as irredeemably hostile to the dignity of both. As is explicitly stated, a "personalistic myth of the Supernatural" is necessary if we are not to descend into a "mechanistic universe," whereas Marxism, which claims to expose ideology, actually constitutes a dangerous ideology in its own right, that of "Counter-Nature" (AIPEM 45).

Burke's broader point in both of the articles just quoted is that the evolutionary step signified by "story" is the source of both mythology and ideology, of both personality and instrumentality, of both "Supernature" and "Counter-Nature." That is why we have to be so careful in the cultivation of its skill. For not only do we have to maintain the "collective revelation" that Burke refers to when affirming the Tao, but we also have to be careful that modern myths do not take a technological turn. This turn is quite possible, given the tendency for narrative to endorse the scapegoat ritual. For "victimage" may come to comprehend not only society but also the planet.

In his essay on "Poetics and Communication" (1970) Burke reflects on ecology and rhetorical "identification." He is thinking in particular of the way in which a leader may achieve "charisma" by identification with the ideals of the group. The leader is pleased to represent the supposed essence of the group; its members are pleased to belong to an exclusive order. Both are identified by the exclusion of a common enemy, victim, or scapegoat through the rhetorical trope of antithesis (the collective "yes" made possible only by the attendant "no"), which implies similarly hostile attitudes to nature. Burke pursues this theme, remarking on its ecological implications. He first expands the semantic range of "identification":

> Nor should our troubled thought on the subject of identification be confined to the specifically socio-political realm. Our spontaneous identification with the powers of our technology can lead to quite a range of bluntnesses. Thus, a person with no greater technological aptitude than the ability to buy something if you give him the money to buy it with, can consider himself intrinsically superior to the members of a primitive tribe which, by its exceptional skills and sensitivities, can eke a livelihood out of a wilderness. There is much of this tendency in our typical view of things. Almost without thinking, we incline to be like the fellow who had delusions of

grandeur because, each time he approached the door of a super-market, it of itself opened to let him pass. (PAC 413)

He can now expose and counter the violence latent in the current attitude of humanity to the earth:

Dramatistic admonitions suggest: It would be much better for us, in the long run, if we "identified ourselves" rather with the natural things that we are progressively *destroying*—our trees, our rivers, our land, even our air, all of which we are a lowly ecological part of. For here, in the long run, a pious "loyalty to the sources of our being" (Santayana) would pay off best, even in the grossly material-istic sense. For it would better help preserve the kinds of natural balance on which, in the last analysis, mankind's prosperity, and even our mere existence, depend. But too often, in such matters, our attitudes are wholly *segregational*, as we rip up things that we are not—and thus can congratulate ourselves upon having evolved a way of life able to exhaust in decades a treasure of natural wealth that had been here for thousands of years. (PAC 413–414)

These reflections are echoed by the comment in *Dramatism and Devel-opment* (1972) that if we are to espouse "Humanism," it had better be an "anti-technological Humanism" that "would be 'animalistic' in the sense that, far from boasting of some privileged human status, it would never disregard our humble, and maybe even humiliating, place in the totality of the natural order" (*DD* 54).

Burke is more explicit still in another essay of the same period, which takes the form of reflections on his own career. He explains that he has always been interested in ritual, and in the choice between tragedy and comedy. Of his recent work, he remarks:

[I]n studying the nature of order, I became more and more involved in the conviction that order places strong demands upon a sacrificial principle (involving related motives of victimage and catharsis). Thus, while still opting for comedy, I became fascinated by the symbolism of ritual pollution in tragedy. But during the last couple of years my engrossment has shifted to the evidence of material pragmatic pollution in technology. I loathe the subject, even as I persist in wondering what can possibly be done about it. Men victimize nature, and in so doing they victimize themselves. This, I fear, is the ultimate impasse. (AIWS 26)

One thing Burke did do about that impasse was to initiate the symbolic action of a satire on pollution that drew on the rich reserve of myth. In the first of his summations of the evolutionary significance of "story," he refers to different kinds of narrative, such as "the visionary," "the eschatological (as with Hell, Purgatory, Heaven ...)," and "the satirical." In the early 1970s Burke drafted a kind of demonic apocalypse, a dystopia, a vision of ultimate planetary degradation that he called "Helhaven." The completed work was to be categorizable as a satire, in that satire takes existing trends, exaggerates them, and sees where they lead. The symbol-using animal cannot help but work toward completion, consummation, perfection. Satire is the appropriate form when the perfecting process goes sour. Unlike tragedy and comedy, satire rejects rather than accepts the world; but in the energy of its rejection, it may alert its readers to what is being done to the world. Burke speculates on such matters in his essay "Why Satire, with a Plan for Writing One" (1974), which also contains the basic idea of "Helhaven."[26]

Burke suggests early on in the essay that the source of both the logic of technological pollution and the satire that might parody it is the human impulse to "go to the end of the line." That is, he invokes again the Aristotelian principle of "entelechy," as previously adapted by Burke to describe the process by which human language aspires to completion:

Each specialized nomenclature, for instance, suggests further possibilities in that direction—and the person who glimpses them is "called," thus being under a kind of compulsion to track down the implications of his terministically goaded vision. Utopias are obvious examples of this goad. And in this purely formal, or logical sense. Marxism would be an example of such thoroughness, regardless of the distinction that some partisans might want to introduce here between an outright Utopia and the socialist future that Marx held to be implicit in the nature of capitalism's birth, growth, and decay. (WS 314)

Again, we see that Marxism, whether viewed as myth or ideology, has by now become for Burke all too close in its aggressively perfectionist impulse to the capitalist myth of industrial "progress." More broadly, Burke is concerned with the perilous ambiguity of the human capacity of symbolicity. Words may bring human order to the world, but the ideas suggested by words may attain a dangerous power, imposing themselves on the world. "At the very start, one's terms jump to conclusions," Burke tells us (*CP* 299); and the "termination" implicit in certain kinds of terminology, notably that of technology, may yet prove fatal. Satire is the appropriate response to the destructive ambition implicit in language because its very premise is that one should "go to the end of the line." Satire parodies perfectionism.

Burke mentions Marxism in passing here, but the particular cultural context he has in mind is what is usually referred to as the "pioneer" or "frontier" myth. This narrative has informed North American experience and expectations from the landing of the Pilgrim fathers to the war in Vietnam: it justifies constant expansionism, appropriation, domination; it is the story of "manifest destiny."[27] One of the premises of Burke's blueprint for his Helhaven vision is that this myth lies behind the current cult of industrial progress, which he sees as despoiling the "promised land" of America. Eden, the paradisal garden, becomes Babylon, the demonic metropolis:

> Think of the situation thus: Technology is in its very essence rational. Yet the accumulation of its instruments, with their unwanted by-products, has in effect transformed the fruits of our rationality into a prodigious problem, thereby giving rise to many compensatory cults of irrationality. On the other hand, as I shall try to show, the satirizing of technology can be as rational as technology itself. And thereby, once again, we glimpse the possibility of a compromise. For the satire can be as rational as the "technological psychosis" out of which it arises; yet at the same time in its way it can manifest great sympathy with the trends embodied in the irrationality of current anti-technologic trends. And even though conditions that once seemed absurd (the implicit and even explicit equating of "culture" with a cult of commodities) now seem ominous, the task of the satirist is to set up a fiction whereby our difficulties can be treated in the accents of the promissory. (WS 315)

In a self-avowedly opportunistic manner, Burke attributes the blame for the transition from "pioneer myth" to "technological psychosis" to one of North America's most revered poets:

Whitman, in his accents of gladness, had given us the clue:

> I know not where they go,
> But I know that they go toward the best—toward
>   something great.

The satirist's quasi-solution should track that down, not just leaving it *en route* as with Whitman's words, but to the end of the line. The turn involves certain implications in such poems of Whitman's as "The Song of Occupations," "The Song of the Open Road," "The Song of the Broad-Axe," and "O Pioneers." But they are to be seen satirically in the light of subsequent developments. Considered thus, they are reducible to a proposition of this sort. Since they were celebrating almost an orgy of construction, and since there is no construction without destruction, it is now clear that those poems were joyously ushering in the very era of care-free destruction now nearing its care-worn culmination in environmentalist problems due to technologically caused pollution. (WS 315–316)

Burke knows that he is being unfair to Whitman when he takes Whitman's poems to be "in effect (or at least for purposes of satire they could be viewed as) utterances by a great prophetic bard of real estate promotion. Of course there was much more to Whitman than that, and I am among those who have said so" (WS 316). But Whitman is an entirely appropriate choice for Burke, given that Burke sees Whitman's brand of utopian optimism as leading, at "the end of the line," to the dystopian horrors that threaten us now (WS 317).

Having justified his choice of the genre of satire, and having co-opted the American "bard" into the Helhaven project, Burke turns to the more traditionally mythic dimension of his blueprint. Looking back on the years before he had decided to take technological pollution as his subject, he reflects on his interest in both comedy and tragedy:

> For years I had worked valiantly to uphold what I thought of as a "Comic Perspective." And I still won't quite relinquish it. Then, on working with socio-psychological problems to do with the nature of human congregation, I became convinced that the establishing of an Order in human affairs involves a *sacrificial* principle. With such thoughts in mind, I studied the modes of victimage in tragedy, and in highly developed theological structures. I am not here being inconsistent. For though the principle of victimage is obviously central to

tragedy, it itself is not exclusively tragic. Tragedy enters with the principle of sympathetic resignation, but Hitlerism is evidence enough that the principle of victimage can be viciously polemical. For instance, consider Hitler's use of it as a rhetorical and adminis- trative device for unifying his party. It was an example of what I would call "congregation by segregation," unifying a people by antithesis, in terms of a common enemy. Though tragedy would well befit an account of Hitler's victims as such, the situation with which we are concerned would be of a different sort, with a relation to technology that ultimately involved us all. (WS 313)

It was in this context, Burke tells us, that he came to see how far the principle of "victimage" extends. "Thoughts on Greek tragedy and its implied theology had got me particularly interested in ideas and images of *ritual* pollution," he explains. "But later, I found myself taking notes on pollution in the most pragmatic, literal, scientific sense; namely: pollution as the 'unwanted by-products,' or 'side effects,' of advances in modern industry" (WS 313).

The subject of Burke's projected satire is not only the scapegoat ritual, as understood traditionally, but also the victimization of nature by humanity, which is a recent and horrific variant on the ancient pattern. In projecting it, Burke takes the opportunity to update his observations on Hitler's abuse of myth. For now he needs to extend the principle of "congregation by segregation," so that the term "holo- caust" comprehends not only the extermination of a race of people but also the destruction of the biosphere itself. People victimize one another, and people victimize the planet. "Victimage" is the logic of the "technological psychosis," or "Hyper-Technologism" (WS 317, 318)

But what is Helhaven? It represents a world in which only the owners of technology, who have profited from its indiscriminate expan- sion, are rich enough to escape from the consequences, to inhabit "a scientifically designed culture-bubble on the moon": "HELHAVEN, the expertly planned and guided enterprise of Lunar Paradisiacs, Incorpo- rated. A womb-heaven, thus in the most basic sense Edenic, yet made possible only by the highest flights of technologic progress—hence, Eden and the Tower [of Babel] in one. A true eschatology, bringing first and last things together—the union of Alpha and Omega" (WS 316). In accordance with the logic of perfectionism, and in accordance with the rules of satire, Helhaven takes the current situation "to the end of the line." In the West, those with the wealth live as far away as possible from the pollution they create, in exclusive country mansions. In global terms, the prosperous countries consume most of the world's resources, exploiting and polluting the rest (see WS 319). Either way, the poor suffer the consequences of the process from which the rich benefit. Burke imagines that it might come to pass that those with sufficient capital will decide to vacate an ailing planet, living in a lunar "haven" or "heaven," far beyond the terrestrial "hell" that they have created. He sees them as cocooned in a "culture-bubble," safe from the ravages of nature which they perpetrated. One is reminded of Burke's interest in the ritual of rebirth, by which individuals are socialized by first returning to a preforensic, womb-like state. The irony now, of course, is that rebirth is no longer possible—for the individual, for society, or for the earth—and that the retreat into the womb has become a deeply irresponsible mode of conduct on behalf of the privileged few.

Helhaven might also remind us that, many years ago, Burke proposed his ideal myth for the age. In the post World War II context in which he wrote "Ideology and Myth," it was still possible to look forward to a world that might enjoy the fruits of the "purification of war." With the rise of "Hyper-Technologism," the future has become a nightmare. The myth has to take the form of a demonic apocalypse. But we may still look to it for those formal characteristics that Burke associated, in "Myth, Poetry, and Philosophy," with a myth that works well. For example, we get much amplification of the scene:

> Thus, I can envision such ideal future circumstances as when Helhaven, our transcendent culture-bubble, has a Luna-Hilton Hotel, in every way indistinguishable from its uniform counterparts in the hotel-chains you find now all over the world. The main difference between the Luna-Hilton and its opposite numbers on the terrestrial globe is that the guest will have a simulated outlook from each imitation window. For but a small fee, he can, as it were, gaze upon a beautiful lake, or upon a distant, snow-capped mountain, or a tropical beach—or if he gets home-sick for urban things back here, by but pressing a different button, he can watch, squirming beneath him, a typical tangle of traffic, simulated even with the same noises, plus the stench (yet though the smell will be like on Earth, it will be scientifically free of all the poisons that actually accompany such conditions here). (WS 320)

This enrichment of the scene is more than merely stylistic. Mythic amplification allows Burke scope to enforce his insight that the demonic future has already begun. We are therefore in the last days:

The lay-out of the place would be in general simply things here over again, except that technological artificiality would be complete. This is an important point to keep in mind. For underneath the satire must be the fact that *in principle* the Helhaven situation is "morally" here already. For instance, you're already in Helhaven insofar as you are, directly or indirectly (and who is not?) deriving a profit from some enterprise that is responsible for the polluting of some area, but your share in such revenues enables you to live in an area not thus beplagued. Or think of the many places in our country where the local drinking water is on the swill side, distastefully chlorinated, with traces of various industrial contaminants. If, instead of putting up with that, you invest in bottled spring-water, to that extent and by the same token you are already infused with the spirit of Helhaven. Even now, the kingdom of Helhaven is within You. (WS 320)

Because the future is already here, with our fate therefore sealed, that other formal requirement of myth—namely, "peripety," or reversal of plot—is not possible. Burke's vision offers little hope of heroic escape from the forces of death. His intention is to force his readers to confront the possibility that their worst nightmare has already happened.

Still, there is much imaginative interest in his mythopoetic sketch, hinted at by the ironic allusion to the Bible at the close of the last passage quoted. In summing up the ramifications of his vision of Helhaven, Burke uses ironically pompous language: "When we are confronting so fundamental a problem of sociology, precisely then, in keeping with the methodology of logology the first principle of axiology advises us to look for some analogy of morphology in the realm of theology" (WS 323). As to that analogy, he finds it "as though made to order, in the last book of the New Testament, the Apocalypse." That book "is a summing up if there ever was one, hence manifesting to perfection the kind of drive I would call entelechial, despite its divergence from the technological variety we have been considering" (WS 323).

Here we need a brief definition of terms. We recall that in his list of kinds of "story," Burke included the "eschatological." "Eschatology" (from the Greek *eschaton*, or "end") is "the doctrine of the last things, such as the end of the world, the establishment of the Kingdom of God." Eschatological writing does not specify *when* the end will come. "Apocalyptic" writing is no more precise, but assumes the end to be close at hand—that is, an apocalypse is an "imminent" eschatology. We may say, then, that Helhaven is an apocalyptic vision, which reveals the imminent "end" that the "technological psychosis" has in store for us. Helhaven takes the form of Burke's "notes toward" an ironic version of the last book of the Christian Bible, Revelation, in that the world order that it sees as ushered in is, far from being a messianic kingdom, a state of legalized madness. Moreover, it mimics the apocalypse by blurring the distinction between the "not yet" and the "already." When Burke declares that "The kingdom of Helhaven is already within you," he is ironically alluding to Jesus' pronouncement to his followers that "the kingdom of God is within you." This declaration belongs to the specifically Christian category of "realized eschatology": that is, the realm that was hitherto thought to belong in the future, whether distant or imminent, has now been made present by the incarnation of Christ.

As early as *A Grammar of Motives* (1945), Burke states his preference for "religious futurism" over "secular futurism," which exemplifies the "philosophy of Becoming": it constantly demeans the present in the name of a financially secure future. For example, "industrial capitalism requires the expenditure of tremendous effort on work that is intrinsically worthless, and hence would be totally irrational except as tested futuristically, by the promissory nature of pay-day" (*GM* 333–334). Again, the "reduction of the present to the future" may be seen in "the aggressive futurism of National-Socialist expansion and (or) the balked futurism of would-be business enterprisers who, deprived of an outlet for their ambitions, and with no other conception of effort to replace these, turn in their disgruntlement to a hatred of Jews, foreigners, Negroes, 'isms,' etc., as a ritualistic outlet" (*GM* 335–336). By contrast, religion fosters a "philosophy of Being": so, for example, in the Gospels, "the potential, the ideal future ... [is] proclaimed to be *the very substance of the present* (the Kingdom of Heaven *is* within you)" (*GM* 332). "Christ was not making a purely directive statement: 'Let us have peace,' but was proclaiming that Peace was identical with Being, and that Being now *is,* and that only insofar as people were peaceful did they actually partake of Being, and the promissory must be *now, implicit,* 'within you' " (*GM* 336). We may take this statement to be Burke's endorsement of the "elevation of the future to the present," if we may coin the complementary phrase suggested by his own "reduction of the present to the future."

For we know that Burke's abiding interest in myth is twofold. On the one hand, he sees it as existing within the dialectic of eternity and time: it is both transcendent and temporal, both universal and historically specific. On the other hand, he insists that its form and function belong to the present, even while it speaks of the past. Either way, it is best explained by a "philosophy of Being." This explanation remains valid for Burke even if the myth is apocalyptic: the apocalypse is no more confined to history, and no more subject to a "philosophy of Becoming," than any other myth. As he puts it in "Doing and Saying" (1971), "the culminative connotations of the entelechial can become translated into terms of the mythic past, though thoughts of a culmination in the apocalyptic future can also be a narrative way of temporizing essence" (DS 116). Burke's interest, we may say, is more in "temporizing essence" than in "essentializing time," more in "Being" than in "Becoming."

It will be clear, then, that "realized eschatology" is a principle in which Burke has a great deal of imaginative investment. The vision of Helhaven becomes especially resonant, for the rich are seen to corrupt the notion of the presence of the messianic Kingdom in the name of Mammon, whose business is future oriented—specifically, profit making. Moreover, the logic of their triumph is the "congregation by segregation" that Burke identifies with the ruthlessness of capitalism and the political program of Nazism, both of which rely on the scapegoating ritual. Helhaven is what one might call an infernal or demonic version of realized eschatology. It may be seen as a parody of "secular futurism" from the perspective of "religious futurism," provided we understand that the religious future is really about the present. In other words, this is Burke's *Apocalypse Now*.[28]

Let us trace some further apocalyptic dimensions of Burke's myth. The Book of Revelation culminates in the victory over the Beast and over the Whore of Babylon, along with "the dragon, that old serpent, which is the Devil, and Satan," by the Messiah and his angels (Rev. 20:2). The Messiah establishes "a new heaven and a new earth: for the first heaven and the first earth were passed away: and there was no more sea" (Rev. 21:1).

Thus, the creation myth narrated in the first chapter of Genesis is retold with an "apocalyptic" turn. Where Adam and Eve fell from the garden, their descendants—or at least those who have remained faithful to God and have recognized his Son, the "second Adam"—are raised up to the heavenly city of Jerusalem. We have progressed from creation to re-creation, from old to new Adam, from Eden to Jerusalem, from sin to salvation. Still, as has been implied, the salvation is selective. John of Patmos, the putative author of Revelation, sees an angel bring "the seal of the living God" to bestow upon "an hundred and forty and four thousand of all the tribes of the children of Israel," who are thus marked out as worthy to stand in white robes around the throne of God (Rev. 7:2–15). Of these chosen ones, we read: "They shall hunger no more, neither thirst no more; neither shall the sun light on them, nor any heat. For the Lamb which is in the midst of the throne shall feed them, and shall lead them unto living fountains of waters; and God shall wipe away all tears from their eyes" (Rev. 7:16–17).

The chosen ones of Helhaven are also sealed off from suffering in their lunar "culture-bubble." Meanwhile, those in the outer darkness—on the polluted earth—are denied living waters because they are, quite simply, undrinkable:

> As in [the Book of] Revelation ... all should come to a focus in a crucial distinction between The Chosen and the Reprobates, except that in the fictive technological fulfillment, the counterpart of those not among The Chosen would not be sinners, but simply out of luck. It became clear that the design called for the ironic version of an exalted promissory attitude, such as would befit the "Vision" of an ultimate peaceful existence in a perfectly air-conditioned culture-bubble on the Moon, a transcendent step beyond the radical polluting of the Earth. And "perfection," as thus perversely defined, would in turn be perfected if, by the conditions of the fiction, things were so set up that those among The Chosen had been largely responsible for the very conditions on Earth they were escaping. (WS 324)

In short, by drawing on the apocalyptic tradition, Burke is able to confirm and update the "Vision of Division" (332).

The irony takes on a dual significance. On the one hand, the original biblical vision of the salvation of the righteous has been corrupted, so that it now concerns the salvation of the rich. On the other hand, Burke knows that there is much in the supposedly idyllic aspects of the apocalypse of John, which we can now see (thanks to our experience of the long history of ecological catastrophe) to be implicitly demonic. There is a hint of this aspect in the heavily symbolic declaration in Revelation that "there was no more sea." This is understandable in a mythological context in which the primordial waters were traditionally associated with the threat of chaos—as in both the Babylonian and the Israelite creation narratives, along with their complementary flood stories concerning Utnapishtim and Noah.[29] But in an era where the seas are being polluted by garbage and sewage, and need vigorously protecting, the words ring hollow. Again, Jerusalem is described as follows: "the street of the city was pure gold, as it were transparent glass," or again, "the city had no need of the sun, neither of the moon, to shine in it; for the glory of God did lighten it, and the Lamb thereof" (Rev. 21:21–23). This celebration of divine artifice, this denial of nature, may now offend those concerned with the preservation of "this lovely planet." The twist to the apocalyptic promise compounds Burke's dual irony.

One other aspect of his apocalyptic vision merits a mention, and that is the substitution of the figure of the Messiah with that of "The Master." It is he who rules Helhaven. But unlike the savior who speaks with the authority of the Israelite prophets behind him, "The Master" is a managerial functionary who has acquired sufficient charisma by virtue of claiming continuity with the bardic, pioneering tradition of Walt Whitman—for the poet's naive desire to become a free spirit is all too easily translated into terms of free enterprise. The image of the unimpeded journey along the open road is all too convenient for the promotion of industrial expansion. The "Apocalyptic Vision of Division" reveals that "Whitman's promises are as good as ever [before]": "The *ills* of technology could be left to soil the Earth, the *virtues* of technology could rise transcendently elsewhere" (WS 327).

Lest Burke's focus on the Whitmanesque "Master," arch-apologist for capitalist industrialism, suggest that his animosity is directed at his native economy, he reminds his reader in parenthesis at this point of a famous Marxist theorist's position: "I think of an equally neat but less radical variant in [Georg] Lukács's discovery that everything wrong with technology is to be identified with capitalism, and everything right with it is to be identified with socialism" (WS 327). Also relevant here are the remarks on the "Marxist eschatology" in the "Afterword" to *Attitudes Toward History*: "Even if you granted, for the sake of the argument, that ('come the Revolution') the utopia of a classless society becomes transformed from an ideality to a reality, there would remain the ever-mounting purely *instrumental* problems intrinsic to the realm of Counter-Nature as 'progressively' developed by the symbol-guided 'creativity' of technological prowess itself" (*ATH* 424–425). The main point to register here, then, is that the object of Burke's satire is the "technological psychosis" itself, regardless of whether the justification for it comes from capitalism or communism. But, given his own inwardness with the national identity, given his years of struggling for ecological principles against North American economic policy, and given his fondness for reading revered poets against the grain, Burke has opted to place Helhaven in a recognizably capitalist context.

Burke is now ready to sum up his draft for a myth. In doing so he again draws on its biblical background. Not only is Helhaven a supposedly "heavenly city" that turns out to be thoroughly demonic, exaggerating even the worst excesses of the Babylon of the Book of Revelation, but it also has obvious affinities with that symbol of human arrogance, the Tower of Babel. The ironic turn that Burke gives to this biblical perspective is, that in his proposed variant upon the paradigm of apocalypse, it will be Babylon/Babel that triumphs:

> The stress is thus stylistically placed upon an inverted quasi-idealistic, futuristic, alchemical device for transforming the base metals of pollution into the Vision of a New Jerusalem satirically golden. Behind it all, inspiriting it all, lies the Master's firm, devout conviction that, the greater and more thorough the progress of technological pollution (as enshrined in the cult of ever-mounting energy-production and energy-consumption), the more urgent will be the yearnings and efforts of the Chosen to build the womb-heaven of the Paradisiac Lunar Culture-Bubble, an Edenic realm made possible only by the ultimate inventions and corresponding butcheries of the Technologic Tower. (WS 327)

In Christian myth, the vision culminates in the absolute victory over the forces of evil, with the Messiah riding aloft and the Devil confined to his pit, and with eternal life emerging out of death and destruction. In Burke's myth, the vision culminates in the promise of never-ending technological rebirth, with profit emerging out of pollution: "Having attained an Apocalyptic understanding of dialectical principles in their role as The Chosen who are to transcend conditions here on Earth, the Lunar Paradisiacs can smile (not maliciously, but hopefully) at the evidences that, if but technology continues to proliferate as it is now doing, things can end, not in a reactionary rejection of technology (which is the essence of human rationality), but in a super-technology that can rise out of the very decay it is producing" (WS 330). Again, we recall Burke's early interest in rebirth ritual as a mode of socialization, but, of course, the treatment is now ironic, and it is the demonic forces that are reborn.

Though Burke categorizes his Helhaven as a satire, with the implication that one satirizes only a condition that is capable of being changed, it may occur to the reader who reaches the end of "Why Satire" that there should be a question mark attached to its title. Why should Burke bother to use satire when the world to which he is responding seems to be beyond all hope? Indeed, we get the sense from some other of his later articles, quoted earlier, that at the end of his career Burke had reached a state of despair about the ecology of the planet—for example, his conviction that the "ultimate impasse" is that humanity victimizes nature and itself simultaneously. This despair is ably delineated by William Rueckert:

> What we have in Helhaven is not the vision of moral tragedy Burke developed in his catharsis-centered poetics, in which individuals and society are polluted, purged, and redeemed; this is a biospheric vision in which man pollutes the whole planet *beyond* purgation and redemption. In following out the logic or entelechy of his own genius (a genius Burke regards as marvelously inventive and resourceful), man literally rots his own home with perfection and unbalances this world beyond where the dialectic of creation and destruction (the dialectic of counter-statements) can maintain it. In Burke's satiric projection, man becomes a burlesque, a caricature, a grotesque of himself and finally a monster of pollution. He passes the point beyond which the natural world can be purged and redeemed. The redemptive action of tragedy is no longer possible. The corrective actions of comedy and satire are no longer possible. . . . Nothing is left but counter-nature. *No context or scene is left in which to make counter-statements.* The fullness of reality has been reduced to hypertechnologism.[30]

If this state of affairs is "terminal" as well as "terminological," the apocalyptic myth of Helhaven would signify the end of myth itself, in the sense that myth for Burke offers the possibility of attaining transcendence and integration. If technology is now our absolute, then the capacity of myth to make a "bridge" across the natural, social, and cosmic dimensions seems futile. However, the lesson we might draw from the body of Burke's theory of myth is that, so long as humanity has the capacity for symbol and story, it has the capacity to correct their disastrous tendencies. "Logology," after all, is based on the premise that the human species uses not only words but "words about words." All in all, we might take the following statement by Burke as more in keeping with his lifelong enterprise than the moods of hopelessness that intermittently plagued him toward the end:

> [T]he proper study of mankind is man's tendency to misjudge reality as inspirited by the troublesome genius of symbolism. But if we were trained, for generation after generation, from our first emergence out of infancy, and in ways ranging from the simplest to the most complex, depending upon our stage of development, to collaborate in spying upon ourselves with pious yet sportive fearfulness, and thus helping to free one another from the false ambitions that symbolism so readily encourages, we might yet contrive to keep from wholly ruining this handsome planet and its plenitude. (PM 162)

In the light of this, we might concur with Richard Thames that "Burke the metabiologist would be a physician too," continually engaged in the diagnosis of humanity and planet alike. His conviction in the healing power of inclusive, charitable, and "comic" knowledge still stands: "A modern Hippocrates, Burke practices a sacred craft: he seeks to comprehend our nature so that a balance lost can be refound and health can be restored, both ours and earth's."[31]

CONCLUSION

The introduction to this book ended with a tentative version of a Burkean definition of myth, offered as an alternative to the more narrowly ideological kind. Here again is that definition: "A narrative that effects identification within the community that takes it seriously, endorsing shared interests and confirming the given notion of order, while at the same time gesturing toward a more comprehensive identification—that among humanity, the earth, and the universe." Recall that this definition was not meant to be final, any more than Burke's own statements on myth, quoted and discussed throughout this study, were ever meant to be final.

No theory of myth is exhaustive, of course. But Burke is a theorist especially aware of the vulnerability of any theoretical perspective. We need, he tells us, to recognize that a "way of seeing" is simultaneously a "way of not seeing." More, perhaps, than any other theorist of myth, Burke is circumspect to the point of obsession. But then, we could hardly take seriously his particular insights on the nature of mythology if he were not true to his own commendation of the "comic" frame, which not only is "charitable" to other theorists but also dictates that he become an "observer of himself," while theorizing. We might prefer words of finality; what we get "notes toward" the final Word.

Yet there is one clear inference that may be drawn from my Burkean definition of myth. This is the idea that Burke wishes to put humanity in its place. I would like to emphasize this point because the casual reader of his work might infer that Burke is unapologetically anthropocentric, proudly asserting the distinctiveness of the human species. "Man," we recall, "is the symbol-using animal"—from which we might want to deduce that humanity is privileged by virtue of language. But I hope that we have demonstrated in this study that Burke is by no means attempting to glorify our species over all others. If the human need for the idea of perfection may be illustrated benignly by the tendency of words to imply the one, inclusive Word, it is also evident malignly in the remorseless drive of technology to construct a totalitarian "Counter-Nature." That is why Burke wants to question perfectionism in its modern form, particularly insofar as it appropriates everything nonhuman under the sign of humanity. True, the Bible itself may be said to do this. In Chapters 2 and 3 of the Book of Genesis we read that Adam and Eve were granted dominion over the rest of creation. But for Burke, the paradisal myth, like the apocalyptic myth, is no match for the "Helhaven" that he sees being produced before our eyes by unrestrained technological perfectionism.[1]

One way that Burke manages to question this drive is by invoking "Supernature": the idea of a realm that transcends human scope, even if it is inevitably figured in human terms, provides a necessary check on human arrogance. "Nature" is similarly effective: the idea of a realm that is the dwelling place of humanity, but which humanity tampers with at its peril, should also prove chastening. Indeed, for Burke it is the duty of "Man" to look not only inside himself but also toward others of his kind; and not only toward others of his kind but also outside of both self and group. This looking outside would involve both looking *up*, to the heavens and beyond (the supernatural order), and looking *around*, at his habitat and beyond (the natural order). That is why I stressed the need, in my Burkean definition of myth, not just for cultural identification but also for environmental and cosmic identification.

"Identification," of course, is a word that Burke uses with particular care. It is his preferred term for what is effected through rhetoric— the word "persuasion" being inadequate to convey the power of words to act as bonds. As we have seen, Burke knows all too well that this process has its sinister aspect, which he calls "victimage" or the "scapegoat mechanism." Yet, typically with Burke, it is the tension in terminology that attracts the attention. Human beings must live in harmony with things outside of themselves, and a society is a legitimate means of finding connection. But the point is to observe what we are about when using words to build up our social world, and to be especially aware of those who are thereby excluded, demonized, and victimized. Ultimately, if identification becomes fanatical, it results in wholesale destruction—not just of other races, as in the Nazi program of racial purification, but of the planet itself, as in globalizing, technological capitalism. Thus, we need a corrective sense of identification, benignant rather than malignant, inclusive rather than exclusive, integral rather than divisive. Burke's "Nature" and "Supernature" provide these correctives. Hence his dedication to the cause of ecology and his fascination with mysticism. Ecology is about a natural arrangement of living beings, based on biodiversity. "Man" is put in his place by the interrelatedness of human and nonhuman life. Mysticism, while it may be rooted in nature, puts "Man" in his place by revealing the human need for a "beyond."

One term that I have conspicuously excluded from my definition is "hierarchy." The idea of "Nature" may be said to be hierarchical in that each and every living thing may be viewed in the context of an ascending order of complexity: for example, atom, molecule, cell, organism, ecosystem, biosphere. The idea of "Supernature" may be said to be hierarchical in that it involves the notion of a "chain of being" which culminates in some form of divinity. However, I thought it best to avoid the term "hierarchy" because of its peculiar complexity in Burke's philosophy. There again, that should not prevent our reflecting briefly on its significance. The word "hierarchy," as noted, means "sacred rule." This is the sense that Burke wishes to preserve in the light of modern antagonism toward the very idea of *order*, even while he wishes to resist its more sinister manifestations. The problem is that, on the whole, Burke uses the word "hierarchy" to cover both the negative sense of social oppression and the positive sense of spiritual transcendence.

We can resolve the ambiguity by briefly comparing Burke with the contemporary philosopher Ken Wilber, who explicitly delineates two contradictory processes. Taking the word "hierarchy" itself to be neutral, Wilber yet makes a clear distinction between one kind and another. On the one hand there is a pathological kind of hierarchy, which expresses itself in a desire for dominion over other people and the planet. On the other hand there is a healthy, normative kind of hierarchy, which he calls "holarchy." This is the principle by which every whole spontaneously forms part of a larger whole, in ascending order of complexity. We have already cited one such case: the progression from atom to biosphere. Given Burke's fascination with "symbol using," we might also cite the levels of complexity involved in written language: word, sentence, paragraph, book. Or again, thinking "socio-anagogically," we have: individual, society, world, cosmos. According to Wilber, "holarchy" is the necessary means by which every phenomenon is to be apprehended and understood contextually and integrally.[2]

Yet I must not leave the impression that Burke is unaware of the difficulties involved in using one term to cover both the positive and negative aspects of order. In Chapter 1, I quoted from his reflection on the term, given in the 1959 appendix to the second edition of *Attitudes Toward History*. Here we will need to quote at slightly greater length, to be especially sure of his meaning. He is writing about the social manifestations of the hierarchical impulse:

> [O]rder is impossible without *hierarchy* (a ladder of authority that extends from "lower" to "higher," while its *official functions* tend towards a corresponding set of *social ratings*). Call this design "hierarchy" when you are feeling friendly towards it. When you are feeling unfriendly, call it the "hierarchical psychosis"—or, more simply, the Rat Race, which is what the conditions of empire add up to, in their drearier manifestations. (*ATH* 374)

The specific context here may be social, but the very attempt to differentiate meanings within the one term is more widely significant, for it reflects Burke's fascination with the very ambiguity of the term "hierarchy." It might have been better had he tried to maintain and expand that useful distinction between the "hierarchical psychosis" and hierarchy proper, which promised to be as illuminating as Wilber's: on the one hand social "hierarchy" is necessary but potentially oppressive; on the other hand cosmic "holarchy" is desirable and potentially liberating.

In many ways Burke prepared the way for the "integral philosophy" that Wilber now espouses, so that comparison is legitimate—despite the fact that Wilber has rarely cited Burke.[3] Wilber's aim is the integration of scientific knowledge with religious wisdom, while maintaining an evolutionary impetus. His assumption is that humanity starts from the "prerational" stage of archaic culture, and his conviction is that it will move through and beyond the "rational" stage of modernity toward a "transrational" stage that comprehends and exceeds the previous two stages. The "postmodern spirituality" that Wilber endorses, and that he believes to be slowly taking shape among a small percentage of the world's population, is one that is able to attune itself with fresh conviction and responsibility to the insights of mysticism.[4] Though the hierarchical implications of this scheme might well have interested Burke, we can surely see Burke questioning the implicit assumption that in order to achieve the transrational level we must first show ourselves to be thoroughly rational.

Recall in particular Burke's challenge to J. G. Frazer's arrogant dismissal of magic as a botched attempt by the "savage" to control natural phenomena—that is, magic as an abortive kind of applied science. Burke regards the claim to have gone beyond the "magical" orientation as an example of evolutionary arrogance and argues that it misleads us into thinking that it is possible simply to replace one "order of rationalization" with another. But from Wilber's perspective, we might want to say that, in reacting against the triumphalism of modernity, Burke could be accused of glorifying archaic culture, and of implying that its piety is far superior to our own. Moreover, while he nowhere declares that science itself is the enemy, and while he usually makes it clear that he is opposed instead to "scientism," or the cult of science, his reaction against the "philosophy of becoming" aligns him with the enemies of modernity, such as Martin Heidegger. Wilber's perspective is, we might say, more integral insofar as it is more progressive and comprehensive, and so belongs with those who would embrace modernity as a necessary stage of development toward complete understanding, such as G. W. F. Hegel.

Burke in many ways, then, anticipates the premises of Wilber's "integral philosophy" but lacks Wilber's willingness to encompass science within it. Or rather, he will integrate it only on his own terms. Moreover, he would question the whole notion of progress. In these respects, he may appear parochial by comparison with Wilber's global sense. There again, his model of integration appears to me to be richer in other respects. In particular, Burke shows far more understanding of the workings of mythology, which tend to get overlooked by Wilber, who wishes to subordinate the mythic level of understanding (prerational) to the mystical level of understanding (transrational).[5] Burke's contribution to the theory of myth is rather fuller while being less schematic. After reading him carefully, we will find it difficult to characterize mythology dismissively as an inferior or inadequate mode of understanding. He shows us how far and how deeply we need myths, and how intrinsic they are to the cultural imagination.

Yet it is precisely Burke's insistence on elucidating and assessing the origin and function of myth that might distract readers from his own interest in the transrational. Readers might register the cultural perspective *on* myth while overlooking the cosmic perspective that for him is opened up *by* myth. It is this perspective that allows us to detect partial continuity between Burke's thought and Wilber's. But it is this same perspective that sets Burke apart from many exponents of cultural studies. Thus at the end of the introduction, in setting out my Burkean definition of myth, I sought to distinguish Burke from Roland Barthes. While both agree that "mythology" and "ideology" are related terms, and that myth may be instrumental in the consolidation of the dominant culture, it is Burke who is the genuine mythographer. Not only does he propose that mythology may transcend ideology but he also sees mythology itself as a key to the very idea of transcendence. Without being a mystical thinker himself, Burke is interested in seeing how far myth takes us toward a level of understanding that we associate with mysticism. He wants to read particular, historically situated narratives in terms of a transcendent, integral vision.[6]

The final question to address is whether this dual interest constitutes an intractable problem or a creative paradox at the heart of Burke's myth theory. On the one hand Burke is remorseless in his exposure of the "error of interpretation" that underlies myths of sacrificial redemption, of congregation by segregation, and of new life bought by others' deaths. On the other hand he never loses faith in the revelatory power of myth, in its potential to afford a glimpse of the "beyond." But can he maintain both? This dilemma resonates with another problem we posed, regarding the possibility of integrating the scientific with the mystical. If Burke is saying that the true content of myth is "victimage," then perhaps myth is something that we ought to leave behind as "prerational." If Burke is saying that myth is all about the "dialectic of the upward way," then its revelatory significance will survive the demise of its cultural expression, no matter how rooted that culture may be in a cycle of guilt and punishment, and so myth will help us to apprehend the realm of the transrational. Burke wants to say both: he wants to acknowledge the violence while allowing for the vision; he wants to maintain both the cultural and the cosmic perspectives.

Perhaps, however, the problem is not so intractable as it might appear, if it is restated as an attempt to be genuinely integrative. For Burke is surely correct to make allowances for—to "discount"—"the world's rich store of error." Were he to claim that myth might serenely be identified with full-blown transrational wisdom, he would rightly be accused of idealism. Were he to restrict myth to articulating the "prerational" impulse to violent segregation, he would rightly be dismissed as yet another exponent of the "hermeneutics of suspicion." Either way, he would show himself "insufficiently *methodical*," as he himself would put it.

If we can learn to think with and through Burke's method, we may find that apparent dilemmas are not so intractable after all. To deny ourselves the benefits of Burkean dialectic because we find Burke himself to be sometimes elusive would be regrettable indeed. Insofar as reading Burke makes readers question their own positions, and forces them to consider the possibility that "everything is more complicated than it seems," his contribution to myth theory is substantial. But I would wager also that, if readers are prepared to entertain the coexistence of the two aspects of myth that we have just indicated— that of violence and that of vision—they will find that they never look at other people, the earth, or the heavens in quite the same way again. We might think of this coexistence as a kind of "perspective by incongruity." And we might remind ourselves of how fitting that viewpoint is for a myth theorist who espouses a comic attitude to human endeavor even while he allows for its tragic planetary consequences.

It might, then, be appropriate to end with the suitably playful invocation of an unnamed higher force with which Burke concludes his enigmatic poem "Introduction to What." Here we have a glimpse of the comedy—at once human and divine, natural and supernatural— that contains all tragedies. It is this comic vision to which his theory of myth continually aspires without ever stating:

Yours for the Light, the Doctrine, the Rebirth, the Promise, the Great Praiseworthy, the Over-Flowing Through Sheer Abundance, the Beginning-and-End-in-One, the Unfolding, the Homecoming, the Perfect Turn From Estrangement, the Revelation, the Moment Within the Moment (drawn out forever), the Ultimate, the Crossing, the Looking Back Into the Future and Forward into Pastness....

The Welling-Forth of Absolute Springtime, the Flowering in Winter, the Motionless Revolving, the Doctrine Without Dogma, the Law Without Lawyers, the Word Sans Syllables, the Grant Without Strings Attached....

The sunrise at sundown, the New Forever Now. (*CP* 109)

NOTES

Introduction

1. Dan Nimmo and James E. Combs, *Subliminal Politics: Myths and Mythmakers in America* (Englewood Cliffs, NJ: Prentice-Hall, 1980), 16.
2. Roland Barthes, *Mythologies*, trans. Annette Lavers (London: Paladin, 1973), 111, 139–43.

1. Myth and Society

1. William Rueckert, *Kenneth Burke and the Drama of Human Relations* (2nd ed. Berkeley and Los Angeles: University of California Press, 1982), 267. Rueckert is alluding in particular to the repeated pronouncement made by Burke's character, "The Lord," in his dialogue with his second-in-command, "Satan," which forms the concluding section of *The Rhetoric of Religion* (1961): "It's more complicated than that."
2. In the *Rhetoric* Burke omits the hyphen, but restores it in subsequent uses of this epithet.
3. See Ovid, *Metamorphoses*, trans. Mary Innes (London: Penguin, 1955), 29–31, 78–80.
4. See, for example, Stephen Greenblatt, *Shakespearean Negotiations: The Circulation of Social Energy in Renaissance England* (Berkeley and Los Angeles: University of California Press, 1991).
5. Stephen Bygrave, *Kenneth Burke: Rhetoric and Ideology* (London: Routledge, 1993), 51.
6. James L. Kasteley, "Kenneth Burke's Comic Rejoinder to the Cult of Empire," *College English*, 58 (1996): 308.
7. Ibid.

2. Myth and Literary Criticism

1. Burke, unusually, always wrote his own forewords. This one, written in 1967, was incorporated in the third edition of 1972—the text used here.
2. See "The Babylonian Creation," in *Poems of Heaven and Hell from Ancient Mesopotamia*, trans. N. K. Sandars (London: Penguin, 1971), 73–111.
3. David Blakesley, *The Elements of Dramatism* (New York: Longman, 2002), 138–39, 196.
4. Samuel Taylor Coleridge, *Biographia Literaria*, ed. George Watson (London: Dent, 1967), 167.

5. See Robert A. Segal, "Introduction," *Jung on Mythology* (London: Routledge, 1998), 16–17, 39–43.
6. There is a parallel with Paul Ricoeur's "hermeneutics of suspicion," which he sees as a necessary condition for a "hermeneutics of affirmation." See Paul Ricoeur, *Freud and Philosophy*, trans. Denis Savage (New Haven: Yale University Press, 1970), 28, 36.
7. See, for example, Mircea Eliade, *The Sacred and the Profane: The Nature of Religion*, trans. Willard R. Trask (New York: Harcourt, 1959).
8. Samuel B. Southwell, *Kenneth Burke and Martin Heidegger: With a Note against Deconstruction* (Gainesville: University of Florida Press, 1987), 18.
9. C. Allen Carter, *Kenneth Burke and the Scapegoat Process* (Norman: University of Oklahoma Press, 1996), 30.
10. Frank Lentricchia, *Criticism and Social Change* (Chicago: University of Chicago Press, 1983), 68–69.
11. Timothy W. Crusius, *Kenneth Burke and the Conversation after Philosophy* (Carbondale: Southern Illinois University Press, 1999), 79.
12. Jean-Pierre Vernant, *Myth and Society in Ancient Greece*, trans. Janet Lloyd (London: Methuen, 1982), 259.
13. There is one notable occasion on which Lévi-Strauss adopts a detailed ethnographic approach—in his 1964 essay on the American Indian myth of Asdiwal. Yet even this is the exception that proves the rule, as is made clear by Roland A. Champagne in *The Structuralists on Myth: An Introduction* (New York: Garland, 1992), 33–56.
14. Robert Wess, *Kenneth Burke: Rhetoric, Subjectivity, Postmodernism* (Cambridge: Cambridge University Press, 1996), 12.

3. Myth and "Ritual Drama"

1. See Sir James George Frazer, *The Golden Bough: A Study in Magic and Religion*, Robert A. Segal, ed. (abr. ed., London: Macmillan, 1922).
2. Robert A. Segal, "Introduction," *The Myth and Ritual Theory: An Anthology* (Malden, MA: Blackwell, 1998), 4–5.
3. Frazer, *The Golden Bough*, 11.
4. Ibid., 51.
5. Ibid., 53.
6. Ibid., 56.
7. Ibid., 325.
8. Jane E. Harrison, *Themis* (Cambridge: Cambridge University Press, 1912), 328.
9. Jane E. Harrison, *Ancient Art and Ritual* (1913; repr., London: Oxford University Press, 1951), 9–10.
10. Harrison, *Ancient Art and Ritual*, 135.
11. Rueckert, *Kenneth Burke and the Drama of Human Relations*, 31.
12. This contention would in future years be made also by Mircea Eliade. As discussed in chapter 2, in his later essay "Doing and Saying" Burke questioned Eliade's theory of myth. However, as we have seen, it was not this aspect of Eliade's thought—the survival of myth in secularized form—that Burke addressed; rather, it was the obsession with origins.
13. See Ford Russell, *Northrop Frye on Myth: An Introduction* (New York: Routledge, 1998).
14. The pairing of these terms has proved influential. See, in particular, Paul de Man, *Blindness and Insight: Essays in the Rhetoric of Contemporary Criticism* (New York: Oxford University Press, 1971). However, de Man's usage is much more rarefied than Burke's, confined as it is to the realm of pure aesthetics.
15. M. H. Abrams, *The Mirror and the Lamp: Romantic Theory and the Critical Tradition* (New York: Oxford University Press, 1953), 3–29.
16. Rueckert, *Kenneth Burke and the Drama of Human Relations*, 128.
17. Ibid., 128–29.
18. Carter, *Kenneth Burke and the Scapegoat Process*, 62.

4. Myth and "Victimage"

1. David Blakesley, *The Elements of Dramatism* (New York: Longman Press), 198.
2. See Max Weber, *The Theory of Social and Economic Organization*, trans. A. M. Henderson and Talcott Parsons (New York: Free Press, 1947), 357–62.
3. Victor Turner, *The Ritual Process* (Harmondsworth, England: Penguin, 1974), 166.
4. Ibid., 100.
5. Ibid., 265.
6. Ibid., 125.
7. Frazer, *The Golden Bough*, 562ff.
8. Interestingly, Eliade was to come to a similar conclusion. See Mircea Eliade, *Myths, Dreams and Mysteries: The Encounter between Contemporary Faiths and Archaic Reality*, trans. Philip Mairet (London: Fontana, 1968), 25ff. Compare also C. G. Jung, "Wotan," in Segal (ed.), *Jung on Mythology*, 181–194. It is interesting to see three very different thinkers independently coming to similar conclusions.
9. Carter, *Kenneth Burke and the Scapegoat Process* (Norman: University of Oklahoma Press, 1996), 18.
10. Ibid., 21.
11. The term "demythologization" is often used rather loosely to refer to the attempt to disregard the mythic medium of the Bible in order to locate its doctrinal truth. However, it should be noted that this was not quite how it was used by its originator, Rudolf Bultmann, whose aim was to counter the literal interpretation of biblical myth as having a referential meaning with a symbolic interpretation of biblical myth as having an existential meaning. In doing so, Bultmann sought to make it acceptable to the modern, scientific mind. The more accurate term for the kind of interpretation which Bultmann was *not* advocating, but all too often is dubbed "demythologization," is "demythicizing." See Robert A. Segal, "The Existentialist Reinterpretation of Myth," in *Myth and the Making of Modernity*, ed. Michael Bell and Peter Poeliner (Amsterdam: Rodopi, 1998), 115–24.
12. In this case, of course, the Islamic extremists who engineered these attacks could be said to be treating the United States as a scapegoat for the ongoing troubles of the Middle East. But Burke, I am sure, would be just as interested in the rhetoric of the U.S. President in the aftermath of the disaster: George W. Bush, significantly reviving the phrase used by the allies in the Second World War to describe the triple enemy of Germany, Italy, and Japan, referred to three apparently unrelated nations—Iraq, Iran, and North Korea—as constituting "an axis of evil." Demonization and the desire for a scapegoat could not be more explicit.
13. Note, for example, I am quoting the subtitle of Fredric Jameson's *The Political Unconscious: Narrative as a Socially Symbolic Act* (London: Methuen, 1981).
14. For Ricoeur on narrative understanding, see Paul Ricoeur, "Northrop Frye's *Anatomy of Criticism*, or the Order of Paradigms" in *A Ricoeur Reader: Reflection and Imagination*, ed. Mario J. Valdes (Hemel Hempstead, England: Harvester, 1991), 242–55. For a fuller account of typology, see A. C. Charity, *Events and Their Afterlife: The Dialectics of Christian Typology in the Bible and Dante* (Cambridge: Cambridge University Press, 1987); and Laurence Coupe, *Myth* (London: Routledge, 1997), 106–15.
15. Aristotle, *Poetics*, 1449b, ll.24–28.
16. See Aeschylus, *The Oresteia*, trans. Ted Hughes (London: Faber, 1999).
17. Rueckert, *Kenneth Burke and the Drama of Human Relations*, 152.
18. Carter, *Kenneth Burke and the Scapegoat Process*, 125.
19. Crusius, *Kenneth Burke and the Conversation after Philosophy*, 205–6.
20. An irony not contemplated by Burke in this context is that the Christian myth of sacrificial redemption has itself been used through the ages as an excuse for anti-Semitism. The Jews, not the Romans, have been blamed for the crucifixion of Christ. The fact that the New Testament itself encourages this misunderstanding simply compounds the irony. See Hyam Macoby, *The Mythmaker: Paul and the Invention of Christianity* (London: Weidenfeld, 1985). These insights do not, however, invalidate Burke's response to what he takes to be the essence of Christianity—namely, its ideal of forgiveness, its "comic" endorsement of the "charitable attitude."

21. See René Girard, *Violence and the Sacred*, trans. Patrick Gregory (Baltimore: Johns Hopkins University Press, 1977).
22. René Girard, *Things Hidden since the Foundation of the World*, trans. Stephen Bann and Michael Metteer (Stanford, CA: Stanford University Press, 1987), 18.
23. René Girard, *The Scapegoat*, trans. Yvonne Fraccero (Baltimore: Johns Hopkins University Press, 1986), 212.
24. René Girard, *"To Double Business Bound": Essays on Literature, Mimesis, and Anthropology* (Baltimore: Johns Hopkins University Press, 1978), 220.
25. Ibid., 221.

5. Myth and Ecology

1. Southwell, *Kenneth Burke and Martin Heidegger*, 43.
2. Crusius, *Kenneth Burke and the Conversation after Philosophy*, 88.
3. Ibid., 93ff.
4. Ibid., 199.
5. William H. Rueckert, *Encounters with Kenneth Burke* (Urbana: University of Illinois Press, 1994), 173–74.
6. Ibid., 174.
7. See Laurence Coupe, "Kenneth Burke: Pioneer of Ecocriticism," *Journal of American Studies* 35 (2001): 413–31.
8. See Cary Wolfe, "Nature as Critical Concept: Kenneth Burke, the Frankfurt School, and 'Metabiology,' " *Cultural Critique* 18 (1991): 65–96.
9. John R. Mabry, *God as Nature Sees God: A Christian Reading of the Tao Te Ching* (Rockport, MA: Element, 1994), 115–16.
10. Lao Tzu, *Tao Te Ching*, trans. Ursula K. Le Guin (Boston: Shambala, 1997), 18.
11. Stephen Mitchell, *The Tao Te Ching: A New English Version* (New York: Harper and Row, 1988), 39.
12. Lao Tzu, *Tao Te Ching*, 3, 14.
13. Ibid., 14.
14. Stephen Batchelor, *Verses from the Center: A Buddhist Vision of the Sublime* (New York: Riverhead, 2000), 43. This volume is an accessible and elegant translation of Nagarjuna's most important work, the Mulamadhyamakakarika. See also David J. Kalupahana, *Nagarjuna* (Albany: State University of New York Press, 1986).
15. Bede Griffiths, *The Golden String* (London: Harvill, 1954), 173.
16. Mabry, *God as Nature Sees God*, 171.
17. Thomas Merton, *The Way of Chuang Tzu* (New York: New Directions, 1965), 76.
18. Mabry, *God as Nature Sees God*, 171.
19. See S. H. Hooke, *Middle Eastern Mythology* (London: Penguin, 1991), 106.
20. Fritjof Capra, *The Tao of Physics* (London: Flamingo, 1982), 25.
21. Crusius, *Kenneth Burke and the Conversation after Philosophy*, 223.
22. Burke's reputation in the academy is as an advocate of either Marxist or Freudian materialism. For example, one summary of his work identifies him with "the conviction that the proper basis of aesthetics is no longer metaphysics but a firmly naturalistic psychology." See Elmer Borklund, "Kenneth Burke," in Burklund, *Contemporary Literary Critics* (London: St. James, 1977), 100.
23. See Laurence Coupe, "General Introduction," *The Green Studies Reader: From Romanticism to Ecocriticism*, ed. Laurence Coupe (London: Routledge, 2000), 3.
24. Burke reiterates this theme, albeit in more technical terms, in "Mysticism as a Solution to the Poet's Dilemma," in *Spiritual Problems in Contemporary Literature*, ed. Stanley Romaine Hopper (Gloucester, MA: Peter Smith, 1969), 95–115.
25. See Akhter Ahsen, *Manhunt in the Desert: The Epic Dimensions of Man* (New York: Brandon House, 1979).
26. A large part of this essay is reprinted in Coupe, ed., *The Green Studies Reader*, 96–103.
27. See, for example, John Hellmann, *American Myth and the Legacy of Vietnam* (New York: Columbia University Press, 1986); and David H. Murdoch, *The American West: The Invention of a Myth* (Reno: University of Nevada Press, 2001).

28. I refer to Francis Ford Coppola's horrific vision of the Vietnam War, rendered with appropriately mythic structure and symbolism, in his film of that title, released in 1979. See Coupe, *Myth*, 17–21, 29–30, 81–88.
29. For the Noah narrative, see Genesis 6–9. The account of Utnapishtim and the flood forms part of the Babylonian story featuring the hero, Gilgamesh, who undertakes a quest for immortality. See *The Epic of Gilgamesh*, trans. Benjamin R. Foster (New York: Norton, 2001), 84–95.
30. Rueckert, *Encounters with Kenneth Burke*, 282.
31. Richard H. Thames, "Nature's Physician: The Metabiology of Kenneth Burke," in *Kenneth Burke and the Twenty-first Century*, ed. Bernard L. Brock (New York: State University of New York Press, 1999), 28–29.

Conclusion

1. See Coupe, "Kenneth Burke: Pioneer of Ecocriticism."
2. Ken Wilber, *Eye to Eye: The Quest for the New Paradigm* (Boston: Shambala, 2001), 143–48.
3. The only allusion to Burke by Wilber that I have found is in Wilber's *Up from Eden: A Transpersonal View of Human Evolution* (Wheaton, IL: Quest, 1996), 164–66, where he endorses Burke's theory of victimage.
4. See Ken Wilber, *The Marriage of Sense and Soul: Integrating Science and Religion* (New York: Broadway, 1999); and *Eye to Eye*, 1–34, 180–221.
5. To be fair to Wilber, he does give an interesting defense of the argument that "the mythic" is a stage that we had better go beyond, even while allowing for its residual power. See Wilber, *Up from Eden*, 93ff.
6. On Burke's ambivalence toward mysticism, see his "Mysticism as a Solution to the Poet's Dilemma," *Spiritual Problems in Contemporary Literature*, ed. Hopper, 95–115.

BIBLIOGRAPHY

Primary Sources

Burke, Kenneth. "Ahsen's 'Image Psychology and the Empirical Method.' " *Journal of Mental Imagery* 11 (1987): 42–47.
———. "As I Was Saying." *Michigan Quarterly Review* 11 (1972): 9–27.
———. *Attitudes Toward History.* New York: New Republic Press. 1937. 2nd ed. Los Altos, CA: Hermes Publications, 1959. 3rd ed. Berkeley: University of California Press, 1984.
———. *Collected Poems, 1915–1967.* Berkeley and Los Angeles: University of California Press, 1968.
———. *The Complete White Oxen: Collected Short Fiction of Kenneth Burke.* Berkeley and Los Angeles: University of California Press, 1966.
———. *Counter-Statement.* 1931. New York: Harcourt Brace, 1931. 2nd ed. Los Altos, CA: Hermes Publications, 1954. Reprint, Berkeley: University of California Press, 1968.
———. "Doing and Saying: Thoughts on Myth, Cult, and Archetypes." *Salmagundi* 7 (1971): 100–119.
———. "Dramatism." In *Communication: Concepts and Perspectives*, ed. Lee Thayer, 327–60. Washington, DC: Macmillan, 1967.
———. *Dramatism and Development.* Heinz Warner Series, vol. 6. Worcester, MA: Clark University Press, 1972.
———. "Dramatism and Logology." *Communication Quarterly* 33 (1985): 89–93.
———. "Dramatism as Ontology or Epistemology: A Symposium." *Communication Quarterly* 33 (1985): 17–33.
———. *A Grammar of Motives.* New York: Prentice-Hall, 1945. 2nd ed. New York: George Braziller, 1955. Reprint, Berkeley: University of California Press, 1969.
———. "Ideology and Myth." *Accent* 7 (1947): 195–205.
———. "In Haste." *Pre/Text* 6 (1985): 329–77.
———. *Language as Symbolic Action: Essays on Life, Literature, and Method.* Berkeley and Los Angeles: University of California Press, 1966.
———. "Mysticism as a Solution to the Poet's Dilemma." In *Spiritual Problems in Contemporary Literature*, ed. Stanley Romaine Hopper, 95–115. Gloucester, MA: Peter Smith, 1969.
———. *On Human Nature: On Gathering While Everything Flows, 1967–1984.* ed. William H. Rueckert and Angelo Bonadonna. Berkeley: University of California, 2003.
———. *On Symbols and Society*, ed. Joseph R. Gusfield. Chicago: University of Chicago Press, 1989.
———. "Order, Action, and Victimage." In *The Concept of Order*, ed. Paul G. Kuntz, 167–90. Seattle: University of Washington Press, 1968.

———. *Permanence and Change: An Anatomy of Purpose.* New York: New Republic Press, 1935. 2nd ed. Los Altos, CA: Hermes Publications, 1954. 3rd rev. ed. Berkeley: University of California Press, 1984.

———. *Perspectives by Incongruity*, ed. Stanley Edgar Hyman. Bloomington: Indiana University Press, 1964.

———. *The Philosophy of Literary Form: Studies in Symbolic Action.* Baton Rouge: Louisiana State University Press, 1941. 2nd ed. 1967. 3rd ed. Berkeley: University of California Press, 1973.

———. "The Poetic Motive." *Hudson Review* 40 (1958): 59–60.

———. "Poetics and Communication." *Perspectives in Education, Religion and the Arts*, ed. Howard E. Kiefer and Milton K. Munitz, 401–18. New York: State University of New York Press, 1970.

———. "Revolutionary Symbolism in America." Unpublished paper, 1935. In *The Legacy of Kenneth Burke*, ed. Herbert W. Simons and Trevor Melia, 267–80. Madison: University of Wisconsin Press, 1989.

———. *A Rhetoric of Motives.* New York: Prentice-Hall, 1950. 2nd ed. New York: George Braziller, 1955. Reprint, Berkeley: University of California Press, 1969.

———. *The Rhetoric of Religion: Studies in Logology.* Boston: Beacon Press, 1961. Reprint, Berkeley: University of California Press, 1970.

———. *Terms for Order*, ed. Stanley Edgar Hyman. Bloomington: Indiana University Press, 1964.

———. "Theology and Logology." *Kenyon Review*, n.s., 1 (1979): 151–85.

———. *Towards a Better Life: A Novel; Being a Series of Epistles, or Declamations.* 1932. 2nd ed. Berkeley: University of California Press, 1966.

———. "Towards Helhaven: Three Stages of a Vision." *Sewanee Review* 79 (1971): 11–25.

———. "Why Satire, With a Plan for Writing One." *Michigan Quarterly Review* 13 (1974): 307–37.

Secondary Sources

Appel, Edward C. "Implications and Importance of the Negative in Burke's Dramatistic Philosophy of Language." *Communication Quarterly* 41 (1993): 51–65.

Blakesley, David. *The Elements of Dramatism.* New York: Longman, 2002.

Borklund, Elmer. "Kenneth Burke." In his *Contemporary Literary Critics*, 98–105. London: St. James, 1977.

Brock, Bernard L., ed. *Kenneth Burke and Contemporary European Thought: Rhetoric in Transition.* Tuscaloosa: University of Alabama Press, 1995.

———. *Kenneth Burke and the Twenty-first Century.* New York: State University of New York Press, 1999.

Brummett, Barry, ed. *Landmark Essays on Kenneth Burke.* Davis, CA: Hermagoras, 1993.

Bygrave, Stephen. *Kenneth Burke: Rhetoric and Ideology.* London: Routledge, 1993.

Carter, C. Allen. *Kenneth Burke and the Scapegoat Process.* Norman: University of Oklahoma Press, 1996.

———. "Logology and Religion: Kenneth Burke on the Metalinguistic Dimension of Language." *Journal of Religion* 72 (1992): 1–18.

Chesebro, James W. *Extensions of the Burkean System.* Tuscaloosa: University of Alabama Press, 1993.

Coupe, Laurence. "Kenneth Burke: Pioneer of Ecocriticism." *Journal of American Studies* 35 (2001): 413–31.

———. *Myth.* London and New York: Routledge, 1997.

———. "Words and the Word: Burke's Logology and Elliot's Mythology." In *The Ways of Creative Mythologies*, ed. Maria Kuteeva, 39–44. Telford: Tolkien Society Press, 2000.

Crusius, Timothy W. *Kenneth Burke and the Conversation after Philosophy.* Carbondale: Southern Illinois University Press, 1999.

Donoghue, Denis. "Kenneth Burke." In *Ferocious Alphabets*, 112–19. London: Faber and Faber, 1981.

Eddy, Beth. *The Religious Naturalism and Cultural Criticism of Kenneth Burk and Ralph Ellison.* Princeton, NJ: Princeton University Press, 2003.

Frank, Armin Paul. *Kenneth Burke.* New York: Twayne, 1969.

Hartman, Geoffrey H. "The Sacred Jungle 3: Frye, Burke, and Some Conclusions." In Hartman, *Criticism in the Wilderness: The Study of Literature Today,* 87–114. New Haven, CT: Yale University Press, 1980.

Heath, Robert L. *Realism and Relativism: A Perspective on Kenneth Burke.* Macon, GA: Mercer University Press, 1986.

Henderson, Greig E. *Kenneth Burke: Literature and Language as Symbolic Action.* Athens, GA: University of Georgia Press, 1988.

Henderson, Greig E., and David Cratis Williams, eds. *Unending Conversation: New Writing by and about Kenneth Burke.* Carbondale: Southern Illinois University Press, 2001.

Hyman, Stanley Edgar. "Kenneth Burke at Seventy." In *The Critic's Credentials,* ed. Phoebe Pettingell, 69–73. New York: Atheneum, 1978.

Jameson, Fredric. *The Political Unconscious: Narrative as a Socially Symbolic Act.* London: Methuen, 1981.

———. "The Symbolic Inference; or, Kenneth Burke and Ideological Analysis." In his *The Ideologies of Theory: Essays 1971–1986,* vol. 1: *Situations of Theory,* 137–52. London: Routledge, 1988.

Kasteley, James L. "Kenneth Burke's Comic Rejoinder to the Cult of Empire." *College English* 58 (1996): 307–26.

Kimberling, C. Ronald. *Kenneth Burke's Dramatism and Popular Arts.* Bowling Green, OH: Popular Press, 1982.

Knox, George. *Critical Moments: Kenneth Burke's Categories and Critiques.* Seattle: University of Washington Press, 1957.

Lentricchia, Frank. *Criticism and Social Change.* Chicago: University of Chicago Press, 1983.

McMahon, Robert. "Kenneth Burke's Divine Comedy: The Literary Form of *The Rhetoric of Religion.*" *PMLA* 104 (1989): 53–63.

Nimmo, Dan, and James E. Combs. *Subliminal Politics: Myths and Mythmakers in America.* Englewood Cliffs, NJ: Prentice-Hall, 1980.

Rod, David K. "Kenneth Burke and Suzanne Langer on Drama and Its Audiences." *Quarterly Journal of Speech* 72 (1986): 306–17.

Roorda, Randall. "KB in Green: Ecology, Critical Theory, and Kenneth Burke." *ISLE: Interdisciplinary Studies in Literature and Environment* 4 (1997): 39–52.

Rueckert, William H. *Encounters with Kenneth Burke.* Urbana: University of Illinois Press, 1994.

———. *Kenneth Burke and the Drama of Human Relations.* Minneapolis: University of Minnesota Press, 1963. 2nd rev. ed., Berkeley: University of California Press, 1982.

———, ed. *Critical Responses to Kenneth Burke: 1924–1966.* Minneapolis: University of Minnesota Press, 1969.

Selzer, Jack. *Kenneth Burke in Greenwich Village: Conversing with the Moderns, 1915–1931.* Madison: University of Wisconsin Press, 1996.

Sheard, Cynthia Miecznikowski. "*Kairos* and Kenneth Burke's Psychology of Political and Social Communication." *College English* 55 (1993): 291–310.

Simons, Herbert W., and Trevor Melia, eds. *The Legacy of Kenneth Burke.* Madison: University of Wisconsin Press, 1989.

Southwell, Samuel B. *Kenneth Burke and Martin Heidegger: With a Note against Deconstruction.* Gainesville: University of Florida Press, 1987.

Tompkins, Philip K. "On Hegemony—'He Gave it No Name'—and Critical Structuralism in the Work of Kenneth Burke." *Quarterly Journal of Speech* 71 (1985): 119–31.

Warnock, Tilly. "Reading Kenneth Burke: Ways In, Ways Out, Ways Roundabout." *College English* 48 (1986): 62–75.

Wess, Robert. *Kenneth Burke: Rhetoric, Subjectivity, Postmodernism.* Cambridge: Cambridge University Press, 1996.

White, Hayden, and Margaret Brose, eds. *Representing Kenneth Burke: Selected Papers from the English Institute.* Baltimore: Johns Hopkins University Press, 1982.

Wolfe, Cary, "Nature as Critical Concept: Kenneth Burke, the Frankfurt School, and 'Metabiology.'" *Cultural Critique* 18 (1991): 65–96.

INDEX

A

Abrams, M. H., 76
absolute guilt, 135
action
  human, 119
  motion and, 86
  symbolic, 89, 91, 140
Adam and Eve, fall of, 135
aesthetic approach to literature, 29
aesthetic truth, 62
aesthetics, 42
alienation, 103
ancient collective revelation, 6
ancient Greece, great tragedians of, 72
anti-technological humanism, 167
apocalypse, 173
archetype(s), 45, 46, 47, 51
  cult of, 49
  imaginative dimension of, 16
  Plato's, 63
argumentative conversation, 15
Aristotle, 72, 156
  chain of being, 160
  dramatic value of plots, 33
  principle of entelechy, 156
authority symbols, 71
avant-garde literary journal, 2

B

Barthes, Roland, 6, 186
beauty, comfort in, 77
Bergson, Henri, 60
Bible, dramatistic nature, 88
biblical myth, 51, 118, 119

bourgeois nationalism, 9
Buddhism, 151, 152
bureaucratization of the imaginative, 101,
  102, 105, 145, 163
Burke
  aestheticism, 29
  definition of human being, 153
  life and times, 1–3
  myth and, 3–6
Burkology, 8
burnt offerings, 125

C

Cambridge Ritualists, 59, 72, 131
capitalism, 87
  German, 109
  Marxist case against, 13
  ruthlessness of, 175
capitalist
  materialism, 107
  myth, 168
Carter, C. Allen, 52, 111
catharsis
  -centered poetics, 179
  by scapegoat, 131
chain of being, 160
changes of emphasis, 142
chart, 75, 76
Christ's crucifixion, 125, 135, 137
Christian myth, 120
Christian rationalizations, 98
Christianity, 101, 112, 137, 151
class
  morality, 100, 102
  overemphasis on, 10